WALKING THE FOREST WITH CHICO MENDES

Venezuela

Colombia

Guyana

Suriname

French Guiana

RORAIMA

AMAPÁ

Amazon

Amazon

AMAZONAS

PARÁ

MARANHÃO

CEARÁ

1. RIO GRANDE DO NORTE
2. PARAÍBA
3. PERNAMBUCO
4. ALAGOAS
5. SERGIPE

1.
2.
3.
5.

PIAUÍ

ACRE

RONDÔNIA

MATO
GROSSO

TOCANTINS

BAHIA

Salvador

Peru

Bolivia

Brasilia

GOIÁS

MINAS
GERAIS

ESPÍRITO
SANTO

MATO GROSSO
DO SUL

SÃO
PAULO

Paraguay

PARANÁ

Rio de Janeiro

São
Paulo

Chile

SANTA
CATARINA

RIO GRANDE
DO SUL

Argentina

Uruguay

Brazil

0   200 400 kilometers

0   200   400 miles

WALKING THE FOREST WITH CHICO MENDES

Struggle for Justice in the Amazon

GOMERCINDO RODRIGUES

Edited and translated by Linda Rabben

Introduction by Biorn Maybury-Lewis

University of Texas Press
Austin

Previously published in Brazil as *Caminhando na Floresta* by Gomercindo Rodrigues, 2003.

Requests for permission to reproduce material from this work should be sent to:
    Permissions
    University of Texas Press
    P.O. Box 7819
    Austin, TX 78713-7819
    www.utexas.edu/utpress/about/bpermission.html

∞ The paper used in this book meets the minimum requirements of ANSI/NISO Z39.48-1992 (R1997) (Permanence of Paper).

LIBRARY OF CONGRESS CATALOGING-IN-PUBLICATION DATA
Rodrigues, Gomercindo.
[Caminhando na floresta. English]
Walking the forest with Chico Mendes : struggle for justice in the Amazon / Gomercindo Rodrigues ; edited and translated by Linda Rabben.—1st ed.
    p. cm.
    Includes bibliographical references and index.
    ISBN 978-0-292-71705-3 (cloth : alk. paper)—ISBN 978-0-292-71706-0 (pbk. : alk. paper)
    1. Mendes, Chico, d. 1988. 2. Conservationists—Brazil—Biography. 3. Rubber tappers—Brazil—Biography. 4. Rain forest conservation—Amazon River Region. 5. Deforestation—Control—Amazon River Region. I. Rabben, Linda, 1947– II. Title.
SD411.52.M46R63 2007
333.75'16092—dc22
[B]

                                                        2007005148

To my wife, Sanderléia,
and my sons, Clovis Gabriel and Eduardo Augusto,
with much love and affection

CONTENTS

ABBREVIATIONS

ALBRAS	Brazilian Aluminum, Inc.
ARENA	National Renovation Alliance
CEB	Grassroots Religious Community
CNS	National Rubber Tappers' Council
CONTAG	National Agricultural Workers' Confederation
CPT	Pastoral Land Commission
CTA	Amazon Workers' Center
CUT	Central Workers' Federation
CVRD	Rio Doce Valley Corporation
DF	Federal District (Brasília)
Eletrobrás	Brazilian Electricity Authority
IBAMA	Brazilian Environmental Institute
IBASE	Brazilian Institute for Socioeconomic Analysis
IBDF	Brazilian Forest Protection Institute
IDB	Inter-American Development Bank
INCRA	National Institute for Colonization and Agrarian Reform
MDB	Brazilian Democratic Movement
PFL	Liberal Front Party
Planafloro	Natural Resource Management Project
PMACI	Program for Protection of the Environment and Indigenous Peoples
Polamazônia	Amazon Development Pole
Polonoroeste	Northwestern Development Pole
PSDB	Brazilian Social Democratic Party
PT	Workers' Party
PV	Green Party
RJ	Rio de Janeiro
SIVAM	Amazon Vigilance System
SP	São Paulo
STR	Rural Workers' Union
SUCAM	Superintendency for Public Health Campaigns
SUDAM	Superintendency for Amazon Development
SUDECO	Central-West Development Institute
SUDHEVEA	Superintendency for the Development of Rubber

UDR	Democratic Ruralists' Union
UFAC	Federal University of Acre
UNI	Union of Indigenous Nations
Unicamp	São Paulo State University at Campinas

IN THE STEPS OF THE RUBBER TAPPER

BY MARINA SILVA

I N PORTUGUESE, *saudade* means longing, yearning, home-
sickness, nostalgia. That's what I feel as I wander through the story
Gomercindo Rodrigues tells, as I remember the moments I shared with so
many other wanderers. Among them was my unforgettable comrade, Chico
Mendes. Fifteen years later, we—all of us who shared his life—still find ourselves affected by his loving friendship, his simple ways, his indisputable leadership. Perhaps his greatest legacy, which we try to cultivate, is his special way
of sounding out his comrades before making decisions, his tireless devotion
to making alliances.

Today the historic accomplishment of Chico Mendes, with his tactful
style and democratic behavior, is obvious. He organized a resistance movement that established pioneering links between environmentalists and
unionists, Indians and extractivists, political parties and civic organizations,
Amazonian people and the world. Most important, he put together environmental and social justice issues in practice, not just in theory. The violent way
his work was interrupted seems to have acted as a call to conscience for leaders and authorities.

The history of Acre's rubber tappers has since been recorded in countless
articles, books, theses, films, songs, verse, and prose. These come from different viewpoints and diverse places, almost always motivated by the repercussions of the crime, in contrast to the virtues of the social movement, and the
vision of the extractive reserves and the unprecedented alliance of the peoples of the forest.

Gomercindo's perspective is different. Walking the forest and the rubber
estates of Xapuri, he describes scenes and moments of this history from a

militant's point of view. This is no remote or abstract account. Guma—as his friends call him—is part of the history he recounts. He testifies, denounces, doubts, investigates, complains, and advocates, almost always in the hope of changing the state of affairs. It is as if he occupied stretches and territories of his story to show, at least, his indignation.

I'm very familiar with this militant anxiety to change things. I'm also part of this movement. In our activism in Acre, we are comrades. We always debate issues, and sometimes we disagree. But I recognize that it would be hard to recount such a difficult moment of our lives in any other way. Chico's death was the dramatic conclusion of a long chapter of exploitation and violence, marked by the crimes that took from us Wilson Pinheiro, Ivair Higino, and so many others.[1]

Living with the communities of the Acre River valley, Gomercindo is right on track with his history of the rubber tappers. He relates the birth of the Rural Workers' Union of Xapuri, the Rubber Tapper Project,[2] the *Poronga* bulletin,[3] the first cooperatives, and the *empates*[4] against the clear-cutting of Cachoeira[5] and other estates. In 1986, at a union meeting, Big Raimundo (Raimundo Barros, Chico's cousin) explained that the cooperatives were not working out. Guma had just arrived to help. Confronting the rubber tappers' distrust, the nighttime storms in the forest, crossing overflowing creeks, and running as fast as he could to keep up with Raimundo Tatá, a local rubber tapper, Guma had as his first task visiting estates with the Amazon Workers' Center questionnaire in hand.

With rapid steps, after recounting the rubber boom and bust and the first known act of biopiracy (70,000 rubber tree seeds smuggled to Kew Gardens in London in 1876), Guma tells Chico's saga during the last years of his life.

Looking back, I remember how the author's bold and impulsive style seemed to complement the moderate negotiator's style of Chico Mendes. How many times did Chico try to calm Guma by calling him to share his favorite leisure-time activity, a game of dominoes? But the author adds that Chico was afraid of jaguars. It's difficult not to laugh at the image of a frightened Chico, still a boy, protecting himself in the forest with his little dog, which fled in panic every time it smelled a jaguar.

Guma recalls the historic empate in the Bordon area.[6] I was there, with Mauro Almeida, Filomena, Maria Canção, and Nande's daughters. We succeeded in partially stopping that clear-cut. Another moving empate took place on the Cachoeira estate to stop the entry of Darli Alves, the rancher who would later order Chico's murder. It's good to remember that victory by more than one hundred rubber tappers, especially one detail: The forty state police posted to the area to ensure the clear-cut were forced to stand at attention when the teachers and children of the estate spontaneously sang the Brazilian national anthem. Despite the tense situation, the police commander agreed to delay the cutting.

Note the passages about an almost forgotten, underground history, such as how the "hillbillies," recently arrived from the Northeast, used to hunt the Indians, egged on by the rubber barons who saw the Kaxinawá and the Jaminawa as "beasts of the forest." These were the same Indians who gave latex, the raw material of the nineteenth-century Industrial Revolution, to the colonizers. This period also saw the enslavement of the rubber tapper, who was always in debt to the trading post. Whoever lived through it knows how it was. At home from my father I learned basic commercial arithmetic to prevent the boss from cheating us.

It's also good to recall the culture that grew up in the shade of the rubber trees, such as traditional marriage by "stealing" the daughter and the inevitable fury of her father, who probably had carried out the same ritual years before. The fear of Mapinguari, the monster with an eye in his forehead. The "Mother of the Rubber Tapper" and the agreement she made with bachelors for a plentiful harvest of latex. The "Little Country Boy of the Forest," considered a protector of animals. All this is part of a rich mythology that taught us to use the resources of the forest sustainably. It was primitive but effective because it was based less on technique than intuition.

Much of this imaginary was undone by another myth, this one pragmatic and opportunistic, of the "empty" Amazon. Thus the dictatorship starting in the 1960s promoted state subsidies for the irresponsible installation of hydroelectric projects, highways, and strip mining. In Acre we reacted to the invasion of the "southerners" by creating unions and grassroots church communities, with the support of Bishop Moacyr Grechi[7] and João Maia, who directed CONTAG in Acre.[8]

Throughout this saga, which is now part of our country's history, we have the presence of people who are historic figures, especially Chico Mendes. But beyond the history and the interpretations that sprang up to satisfy so many interests, those of us who lived through it all, who were there, have the duty to recall the human conviviality and Amazonian simplicity with which it all happened.

There are many stories contained in history. One cannot read or write them without one's heart opening up at every word. That's why I started this foreword with the same word I'll use to end it, evoking the days when we traveled the densely forested trails to which we return along the paths of memory, to find a dear comrade and once again learn to walk with him: saudade!

Marina Silva was appointed environment minister of Brazil in 2003. A rubber tapper and daughter of rubber tappers, she learned to read and write when she was sixteen, finished high school, and graduated from the Federal University of Acre. Later she became active in the Workers' Party and served as a senator from Acre in the Brazilian Congress. [LR]

ACKNOWLEDGMENTS

Author's Acknowledgments

To Marina Silva for the very lovely foreword.

To Nilo Diniz, Rosa Roldán, and Marcos Jorge for editing and suggestions.

To Júlia Feitoza for proposing the project to the Acre State Agency for Cultural Incentives and for production.

To Carlos Carvalho for the photos.

To Tião Mendes, rubber tapper, for his participation in the [original] cover photo.

To the state government of Acre for funding.

To the Araújo Supermarket for support.

To all those who encouraged me to write this book.

To the rubber tappers who taught me to be part of their history and almost everything I've learned in twenty years in Acre.

Translator's Acknowledgments

I wish to thank Mary Allegretti for introducing me to Chico Mendes and to Gomercindo Rodrigues, Mariazinha, and other rural unionists in Acre and other Brazilian states. I am also grateful to Amnesty International, Moyra Ashford, Sue Branford, the Brazil Network, the Cornell University Latin American Studies Program, Instituto Socioambiental, Jan Rocha, Steve Schwartzman, Miranda Smith, Alison Sutton, Terence Turner, and many others for their encouragement, assistance, and hospitality over the years.

Biorn Maybury-Lewis deserves special mention for his splendid introduction, informed by deep personal knowledge and experience of Acre and other parts of the Amazon over many years.

Thanks to Miranda Smith, Olga Becker, and *A GAZETA do Acre* for giving permission to reproduce their photographs.

Finally, Gomercindo Rodrigues was a notably patient, kind, and helpful partner in this effort: *Abraços, meu amigo.*

WALKING THE FOREST WITH CHICO MENDES

~~~~~~~~~~~~~~~~~~~~~~~~~~~~~~~~~~~~

INTRODUCTION TO THE ENGLISH EDITION

BY BIORN MAYBURY-LEWIS

GOMERCINDO RODRIGUES is one of thousands of agronomists, lawyers, priests, health workers, students, teachers, professors, small-business people, government functionaries, and others who invested precious time and energy while often risking their lives to help build Brazil's rural union movement. He conducted his early years of organizing work, in the 1980s, with the great slain rubber tapper leader, Chico Mendes. Hence the evocative title of Linda Rabben's excellent translation of Rodrigues's memoir: *Walking the Forest with Chico Mendes*. Guma walked the forest all right, for many thousands of kilometers, helping to organize the rubber tappers in the western Brazilian Amazon state of Acre. But he also walked side by side with Chico Mendes through a lethal struggle over land, resources, and the Amazon. Ultimately, like many ordinary people around the world, Chico Mendes and his comrades faced the critical practical and philosophical question of our time: how to wisely confront narrow-minded interests pursuing socially and environmentally catastrophic policies?

This struggle culminated in Mendes's cowardly assassination by gunmen in the employ of Amazonian rural elites on a fateful evening in late December 1988. The battle in which he found himself goes on in the Amazon and thousands of other places around the world wherever people are grappling with the problem of the appropriate attitude to take toward one another and the natural environment.

Gomercindo Rodrigues served as an adviser (*assessor*) to the rubber tappers and their Rural Workers' Union in Xapuri, Acre, a small town near the Bolivian-Brazilian frontier on the far western edge of the Brazilian Amazon. It is the seat of a municipality of the same name, comprising a large swath of Amazonian forest. Most of the rural workers in Xapuri were, and for the most part remain, rubber tappers—extractivists and sellers of natural latex from the rubber trees indigenous to the region. At the time of Chico Mendes's assassination on December 22, 1988, Gomercindo Rodrigues was a Brazilian agronomist, a man from outside the state of Acre and the region who was on his way to becoming a man of the Amazon. During the decade following Mendes's death, Rodrigues changed professions, first attending the law school in Rio Branco, Acre's capital, and then becoming a lawyer, defending to this day the workers in the rubber tappers' movement that Chico Mendes led until his untimely death.

Chico Mendes's assassination reverberates still in his beloved Amazon region and far beyond. Yet those uninitiated in Brazilian or Amazonian studies, much less the history of the rubber tappers' and the Brazilian rural workers' movement, might fairly pose a number of questions. Obviously Mendes's passing was tragic and premature. He died relatively young, at the age of forty-four, leaving a wife, three children, and many friends and comrades, as well as his life's work unfinished. But what is the broader significance of his death? What difference did the life of this man from a remote corner of the Amazon make to the rest of us—particularly those who are neither Brazilians nor familiar with the Amazon?

It turns out that an objective answer to these questions is far from straightforward. In the aftermath of Chico Mendes's assassination, a fascinating intellectual struggle occurred immediately and continues until the present regarding the meaning of his life and death. It has real practical implications for the region, Brazil, and the world in which we now live.[1] European, North American, and Brazilian environmentalists who had allied themselves to Mendes in their efforts to do something about the catastrophic pace of deforestation of the Amazonian environment—a process lamentably still unfolding at this writing in 2006—hailed him as a fellow environmentalist par excellence. Claiming him as one of their own, they remembered him as a man who paid with his life for his tenacious and creative defense of the rainforest.

Irritated by this interpretation, representatives of the Brazilian rural workers' union movement and their allies around the world maintain that people are killed in analogous circumstances in contemporary Brazil, not for their belief in protecting the environment, but for organizing the poor in trade unions, social movements, and political parties. For Brazilian unionists, Mendes's environmentalism—though clearly of great importance—was nowhere near as important as his role as a leader in the rural workers' movement of Brazil. They argue that no rural worker is killed for saving trees but for having the audacity to confront large interests on behalf of ordinary people. The unionists and their international socialist allies maintain by and large that we must remember Mendes as another victim of class warfare.[2]

What I propose to argue in this introduction to Gomercindo Rodrigues's important memoir is that although both of these broad interpretations of Chico Mendes's life work have significant elements of truth, neither of these ideal-types—"Mendes as environmentalist," "Mendes as radical unionist"— quite encapsulates the complexity and contradictions of the man and his work. The work embodied in this remarkable man's life reflects the central dilemmas of our times. He was more than the champion of one cause or another.

· · ·

One cannot understand the crisis Chico Mendes, Gomercindo Rodrigues, and the rubber tappers' movement of the Brazilian Amazon faced in the late 1980s without beginning with a brief description of the Brazilian rural workers' movement as it emerged in the 1970s, during the right-wing military dictatorship that took over Brazil from 1964 to 1985. The long dictatorship had as its centerpiece its desire to eradicate, or at least keep under control, Brazil's social movements. When the dictatorship finally ended, Brazil entered a five-year period (1985–1990) of extraordinary tension and violence in the countryside, as both sides—the various categories of rural workers versus the landlords and their allies—anticipated some form of agrarian reform.[3] They jockeyed for position either to promote or to defend against it. Chico Mendes and the rubber tappers' movement were directly caught up in this rising rural tension, culminating in Mendes's 1988 assassination.

The 1964–1985 military dictatorship ruled through what political scientists call a bureaucratic-authoritarian state. It was not a state that simply plundered the public treasury for the enrichment of the generals who ran it. Rather, it was a military-led, expanding bureaucracy whose agenda included the elimination of progressive, sometimes quite radical, leftist social movements and guerrilla organizations (in both the urban and rural areas) and the advance of Brazil's capitalist development trajectory. Moreover, it intended to foster this capitalist development while keeping tight control of unions and political parties, which, as the dictatorship grew more rigidly authoritarian after December 1968, were allowed only if they were state sanctioned and subject to close government regulation. This was an extraordinarily repressive time, a dark period in Brazilian history. Although the Brazilian state actors could be lethally violent—especially in their campaigns to eradicate urban and rural guerrilla movements in the 1960s and 1970s—the Brazilian regime was not as murderous as its fellow bureaucratic-authoritarian regimes of the time in neighboring countries, in particular those of Argentina and Chile.

The Argentine and Chilean police and military murdered many thousands. But the Brazilian version of this form of military state lasted by far the longest, twenty-one years.

The military regime began its tenure by eradicating three rural drives to organize the rural poor: the peasant league movement in Brazil's Northeast, centered in the state of Pernambuco; the incipient, Communist Party–led rural workers' movement in and around the then-capital city of Rio de Janeiro, in a rich, tropical-agriculture zone known as the Baixada Fluminense, as well as in parts of the interiors of the states of São Paulo and Bahia; and the small family farmer movement, known as MASTER, organized by President João Goulart's brother-in-law, Leonel Brizola, in the far southern state of Rio Grande do Sul. (Goulart was the civilian president the military unseated in its April 1, 1964, coup d'état.) The military killed, disappeared, or forced into exile many of the leaders and rank and file of these three movements because it feared some kind of revolutionary success inspired by Fidel Castro's recent and phenomenal victory in the Cuban Revolution.

As is now well known, peasants in Cuba's Sierra Maestre played an important role in keeping Castro and his closest followers alive when they were nearly annihilated following the disastrous battle at the beginning of their revolutionary struggle, in which the troops of the Cuban dictator, Fulgencio Batista, eliminated nearly all of Castro's small band of revolutionaries. The Brazilian generals were not going to allow a repeat, in their country, of the survival of any revolutionary movement in rural areas. Given that the generals embraced the Cold War mentality of the time,[4] the Brazilian military physically eliminated the peasant and rural worker movements that had sprung up in the countryside, especially in Rio de Janeiro, Pernambuco, and Rio Grande do Sul.

If one analyzes the character of the Brazilian military regime (right-wing, antipopular, developmentalist, closely allied with the U.S. Cold War effort, initially fearful of Castroism), one logically could have expected no rural organizing to take place in the countryside following this early campaign of rural repression. Indeed, nothing of significance did happen in the Brazilian countryside until the late 1960s, when a guerrilla campaign against the regime, led by the Communist Party of Brazil (Partido Comunista do Brasil, PC do B), began to operate in north central Brazil, in the Bico de Papagaio region of the southeastern Amazon. A major counterinsurgency campaign ensued, involving regular army units, secret police, and gross violations of the human rights of the area's peasant populations. The military wiped out the PC do B forces in the first years of the 1970s.

Meanwhile, defying the logic of these closely related historical events, a new form of unionism began to emerge once again in the northeastern state of Pernambuco.[5] This was no revolutionary unionism. On the contrary, the unionists essentially took advantage of state structures designed to encapsulate, regulate, and control unionists, to lead the unions to ends other than those intended by the state. But they did so over the course of many, many years of careful, slow, "two steps forward, one step backward" union activity.

They embraced the military state's effort to extend some basic social welfare to rural workers beginning in the late 1960s and early 1970s. Many unions were founded with welfare, medical, and dental services in mind. The union movement was divided internally among those who simply were walking hand in hand with the military government's effort to control the countryside, those who wanted to do somewhat more—essentially to make their unions into health facilities—and those who wanted to use the political space the state was providing to truly organize workers. Under cover of such state-sanctioned health care–dispensing activities, this latter third of the union movement raised the consciousness of rural workers, gave them a critical perspective on the dictatorship, and left the rank and file poised to enter democratic politics once the military relinquished power to civilians in a gradual process that ended with the launch of the New Republic in 1985.

These unionists engaged in the "politics of the possible": They took over available political space and resources to use to the best of their creative ability for a variety of progressive projects (land rights struggles, wage struggles, denunciations of abuses). At the same time, they were careful to avoid provoking state actors or rural elites to react lethally. Acre unionists associated with Chico Mendes and his predecessor, Wilson Pinheiro, took part in this progressive wing of the national rural workers' union movement beginning in the early 1970s.

The attempt to avoid trouble did not always succeed, as literally hundreds of rural workers and their leaders were murdered, maimed, tortured, and disappeared during this trying and lengthy denouement of the military dictatorship.[6] Struggles within the national union organization also slowed the march of the union movement. Although the national organization, the National Confederation of Agricultural Workers (CONTAG), was in the hands of progressive unionists from northeastern Brazil, many state federations across Brazil were controlled by right-wing unionists. These unionists either were not really rural workers themselves or were workers interested in taking advantage of alliances with military state actors at the expense of their fellow workers. It was a long, hard struggle, with mixed results for those who wanted to do something for the rural workers.

Much needed to be done, because the state was far from a passive actor, maintaining at the top of its agenda its desire to push ahead Brazil's capitalist development. It played an important role in speeding a disorderly form of developmentalism in the countryside. Massive and costly road and railway building efforts in the interior, for example, served to strengthen landlords whose territories were "improved" by new proximity to means of transportation. Dams were built to electrify the countryside and supply power to mining and other industrial operations. They often flooded immense areas of land where rural workers and indigenous peoples lived, with indemnities coming, if at all, only years after destitute people or tribes had been scattered. The military government offered cheap credit and other fiscal incentives that invariably benefited large interests and not smallholders and small-scale homesteaders (the latter on Brazil's vast stock of poorly regulated public lands).

These developmentalist policies had in common a clear pattern: They fomented an inexorable redistribution of land to fewer and fewer and increasingly large landowners. Already unequal, Brazil became the nation with one of the most unequal distributions of arable land in the world. Furthermore, a huge proportion of this territory was left barely used or completely unused—a scandalous circumstance in land-hungry and impoverished Brazil. In addition to harming ordinary people in the countryside, these policies accelerated an extraordinary urbanization process already under way. People left the countryside for the large and medium-sized cities, creating the contemporary panorama of Brazil's urban areas: immense shantytowns with the pathologies of gangs, drug trafficking, violence, and despair so familiar to contemporary observers.

The rural workers' union movement—internally divided, always closely watched, and often intimidated or attacked—had its hands full. Yet by the time the military dictatorship ended in 1985, just under 10 million workers were organized into more than 2,850 unions throughout Brazil's immense interior, and CONTAG was widely respected as a combative, if necessarily careful and bureaucratic, organization. By the mid-1980s there was an air of expectancy in Brazil: Would the long-overdue agrarian reform finally come about? And if so, *how* might it come about?

As the Brazilian generals had promised, the "long, slow, secure" transition from military dictatorship came to pass under civilian rule in 1985. Tancredo Neves, a centrist and astute politician from Minas Gerais, was to take over from the outgoing military, becoming president of the republic at the climax of an immensely complicated transition process. In the negotiations for the transition, Neves had made commitments to implement some sort of agrarian reform, for no other reason than to defuse the pent-up frustrations of the rural masses. However, in a major tragedy for Brazil and in particular for rural Brazil, Neves became ill and died before taking office. His vice president to be,

José Sarney, a politician from the state of Maranhão who had led the military's civilian elite allies, took office in Neves's stead. He had none of the deft political skills of Neves under the tense circumstances of negotiating the end of a long dictatorship that had perpetrated numerous crimes against its own people. Moreover, Sarney, a member of Maranhão's rural elite and a man of deeply conservative political inclinations, had aligned himself with the military throughout his political career. With Neves's death and Sarney's ascension to power at this critical moment, fortune, it seemed, smiled on the military.

In the confusion and uncertainty reigning in Brazil in the first year of the Sarney administration (1985–1986), many observers thought that Sarney, despite his past, could not avoid some sort of serious agrarian reform in the countryside, given Neves's prestige and promises to do something about rural inequities. Indeed, Sarney's initial rhetoric suggested that he would go ahead with reform. Lines were drawn. The landlords of Brazil—truculent under the best of circumstances—held large auctions of cattle to raise a war chest to buy arms for the defense of their property; or so they maintained. They founded the União Democrática Ruralista (Rural Proprietors' Democratic Union) under the leadership of the inflammatory Ronaldo Caiado, a large-scale rancher from the midwestern state of Goiás. Meanwhile, the Movimento dos Trabalhadores Rurais sem Terra (Landless Rural Workers' Movement) began to emerge in its home state of Rio Grande do Sul, right at the time the New Republic began. Before the emergence of the MST, only CONTAG and the officially sanctioned rural workers' movement could exist without suffering immediate annihilation by the military or gunmen in the employ of landlords. Now, the MST, a social movement entirely independent of the state and tired of the slow but steady approach that CONTAG had painstakingly developed under the dictatorship, began to push for rapid, radical change in the more open circumstances of the New Republic. CONTAG's star began to fade, and the MST began to rise to eventually become what it is today: a nationwide social movement with a radical land reform agenda and socialist ideology.

Yet CONTAG, the MST, and the rural workers' movement were under UDR assault, it seemed, everywhere. Shots were fired. Rural workers fell. Casualties in this unequal struggle were virtually always among the poor and not among their class enemies. Impunity prevailed. The state and the Brazilian legal system invariably found ways to ignore the persecution of and crimes against rural workers. In fact, the first person whose murder, in a land conflict zone, was to be fully investigated—with indictments handed down, a trial of the accused, and the perpetrators sentenced to prison—was none other than Chico Mendes. And in his case, the investigation only happened—to the surprise, no doubt, of Mendes's UDR enemies—because of his worldwide fame, which embarrassed the legal system into doing its job. Caught up in these dangerous times in rural Brazil of the early New Republic, Mendes lamentably paid with his life.

Following an interesting opening description of the way of life of the rubber tapper and the history of rubber in the region, Gomercindo Rodrigues's memoir turns to the circumstances in Acre of the late 1970s and 1980s. The owners of the rubber estates, who ruled the countryside from the rubber emporiums of Manaus and Belém, thousands of miles downstream on the Amazon River, had, in many cases, abandoned their claims to rubber estate zones in areas such as Xapuri in the western Amazon. Although it had had its booms in the late nineteenth and early twentieth century and again during World War II, as part of the Allies' efforts to maintain a reliable supply of natural rubber, the rubber business was in a protracted decline. It was essentially moribund by the early 1970s. Rubber workers were left to their own devices: hunting, gathering, planting subsistence plots, and tapping rubber and gathering other forest products for autonomous sale.

As Gomercindo Rodrigues documents, the military state decided that as a part of its Amazon road-building campaign, designed to provide "land without men" (its perception of the Amazon) to "men without land" in other areas of the country, it would lay out and pave the BR-317 highway. The BR-317 would link eastern Acre to BR-364, crossing Rondônia, which in turn connects the western Amazon to central Brazil and from there to the country's southeastern industrial zones. In my conversations with him shortly after Chico Mendes's death, Gomercindo Rodrigues remarked (and reiterates in the memoir that follows) that to characterize the Amazon as "without men" was a terrible lie the military used to justify two policies. The first was its desire to defuse land conflicts in other regions of Brazil by giving workers a means to travel north and west to the Amazon to seek "unoccupied" land via the new roads. The second was to offer rural capitalists, particularly in the ranching sector, opportunities in the western Amazon to establish large properties near where roads were projected, so they might reap the windfall profits that road building invariably brings to those whose lands lie nearby. This, the military maintained, would constitute "development" of the western Amazon.

Beginning in the 1970s, these two processes precipitated the movement of small- and large-scale interests into Rondônia and Acre. Rubber tappers in Acre—facing well-heeled southern ranchers who typically appeared with armed farmhands, foremen, and, when necessary, *pistoleiros* (professional gunmen)—were expelled by the thousands from the jungle areas where they had gone about earning their modest living. When pushed out of their traditional areas, many rubber tapper families went over the border to try their luck in Bolivia. Others crowded into the urban periphery of the Acre state capital,

Rio Branco, transforming it in a short period from a sleepy provincial town into a bustling, medium-sized city made up mainly of shantytowns (*favelas*). Still others, usually younger, single, and male, traveled to the mining camps springing up around the Amazon.

The small and large property holders entering the region not only devastated the local rubber tappers' way of life; they also destroyed indigenous peoples' lands, infected them with diseases for which they had no immunity, and effectively ended the tribal life of innumerable Indians. Meanwhile, the swidden (slash and burn) agricultural techniques of smallholders and the pasture formation (burning and grass planting) of the ranchers caused the monumental deforestation that brought the Amazon to the world's attention in the late 1980s, when the fires started appearing prominently in satellite photographs of the region.

In an effort to staunch the flow of workers out of the old rubber tapping areas into Bolivia and the Rio Branco urban periphery, CONTAG and the national rural workers' movement came to Acre and organized the first rural workers' unions and the state union federation in the 1970s. Wilson Pinheiro became the leader of the Sindicato dos Trabalhadores Rurais (Rural Workers' Union) of Brasiléia, a municipality near Xapuri, and emerged as the de facto leader of the rubber tappers in the region.[7]

But the devastation of the rubber tappers, the indigenous peoples, and the Amazon forest continued during the last years of the 1964–1985 military dictatorship. The government intended to lengthen, improve, and pave the BR-317, despite common knowledge that this developmentalism caused havoc in the countryside. The dominant ideology was that burning the forest, farm and pasture formation, and defusing extraregional tensions as a result of "opening up this frontier" were signs of Progress. It was at this time that Chico Mendes entered the rubber tappers' movement, joining Pinheiro as a close ally. He emerged as Pinheiro's comrade in his effort to denounce developmentalism and protect the remaining rubber tappers.

In the late 1970s, in a plot consistent with the approach large landowners throughout Brazil had established during the 1964–1985 military dictatorship, the Acre rural elites decided to take matters into their own hands regarding Pinheiro, a leader they felt they could no longer tolerate. They were incensed that he and the Acre rural unionists had begun to organize themselves and make known the catastrophic consequences of the region's developmentalism. Landlords ordered and successfully carried out the murder of Wilson Pinheiro in 1980. Enraged, the rubber tapper unionists took their violent revenge on the alleged perpetrators.

In a facile display of how the Brazilian legal system is almost never impartial in its dealings with the rural poor, the police leapt into action to find and prosecute those accused of killing Pinheiro's murderers, using torture and intimidation to push forward the investigation. It was at this moment, when Chico Mendes was under attack from the authorities and was being prosecuted himself for killing Pinheiro's murderers—a revenge killing for which he was later acquitted—that Mendes took over as the de facto leader of the rubber tappers' movement.

This is where Gomercindo Rodrigues's memoir begins in earnest, with his firsthand account of his slain friend's struggle to lead the movement.

• • •

To reiterate my original questions: What is the broader significance of Mendes's death? What difference did the life of this man from a remote corner of the Amazon make to the rest of us—particularly those who are neither Brazilians nor familiar with the Amazon? To answer, I must point out three parts of Mendes's legacy: his views on the role of violence in the rubber tappers' struggle, his views on development as opposed to developmentalism, and his efforts to build alliances. Together, they serve to render Chico Mendes, and the people like Gomercindo Rodrigues who struggled and continue to struggle along with him, into figures of importance to contemporary world history far beyond the Amazon.

Mendes sympathized with the despair and catharsis of the rubber tappers' violent reaction against Pinheiro's murderers; indeed, he suffered with them the arbitrary investigative techniques of torture normally involved in Brazilian legal "inquiries" involving interclass crimes. But he would develop with his fellows an approach to dealing with the deforestation that would eschew violence: a nonviolent, confrontational technique the rubber tappers termed the *empate*. Gomercindo Rodrigues's memoir highlights the empate as an innovative method the rubber tappers used to face the rural peons in the employ of landlords, sent to cut down trees and brush before burning them to create pastures for the ranchers.

Men, women, and children of rubber tapper communities would simply stand unarmed in the way of tree cutters and their equipment, blocking the destruction and appealing personally to the peons as people of the same social class. While facing the peons, they would explain to them the folly of destroying the forest, pleading with them not to ruin an entire way of life for the pittance the landlords were paying them. It was arduous, tension-filled, tenacious work, requiring persistence and courage, day after day, week after week, at great cost to people always trying to keep a step ahead of a bare subsistence living. But it worked in some, though by no means all, cases. As a result of the successful empates, the peons would withdraw, infuriating the truculent landlords. Fundamentally, it was a nonviolent, communitarian, educational, and consciousness-raising approach to struggle, where all involved on both sides went away thinking that "this is different, this is special."

The most powerful scene, in my view, of Rodrigues's memoir is his description of an entire rubber tapper community at an empate, confronting fellow rural workers cutting down the forest at the behest of landlords. The peons were working under guard by armed state police, sent by a local judge who sided (as is the norm) with the landlord and ordered the police "to protect" the wood cutters. At a certain point, the rubber tappers broke into a rendition of the Brazilian national anthem. And as if on the command of a higher authority, all stood there together in the forest—police, rubber tappers, and wood cutters—and listened or sang together. I can imagine that not a few shed tears—even among the police, poor Amazonians themselves, in formation and at attention—as they sang one of the stanzas: *Nossos bosques, têm mais vida* (Our woods have more life). This was something out of the ordinary for Brazil, following humbly in the footsteps of luminaries in the history of nonviolent resistance such as Dr. Martin Luther King Jr. and the great Mahatma Gandhi himself.

Mendes maintained that through 1985 forty-five empates had occurred, with fifteen partial victories. These guaranteed the preservation of 1.2 million hectares of forest.[8] Meanwhile, Chico Mendes and his followers were under attack for questioning the basic premises of developmentalism. They were accused of wanting Brazil to remain "in the Stone Age." Mendes's opponents asked typically, in denunciatory tones, in the regional media they dominated: What alternatives did the rubber tappers offer? Were Chico and the tappers against Progress?

The ideologues of modernization—ranging from World Bank and Inter-American Development Bank economists in Washington to their military government allies around Latin America—claimed that creating a strong capitalist economy would resolve the problems of all social classes. With a bigger infrastructure of roads, dams, electrification, and communication networks, along with a range of economic incentives (tax holidays, cheap credit, price subsidies for inputs) for those possessing capital, governments could foment capitalist development, and eventually the poor would have more jobs and better lives: a classic version of the "trickle down" theory. In Brazil, officials of both the military government and the subsequent civilian regimes of the New Republic defended a world order in which possessors of capital would play the essential role in national development. They would accuse the rubber tappers' movement of being in favor of keeping Brazil in the darkness of the premodern period. They went so far as to suggest that efforts such as the rubber tappers' endangered the Brazilian nation because competitors around the world, who embraced the ideological vision favoring world capitalism, would overtake and threaten Brazil.

To understand Mendes's response to this powerful regional, national, and international attack on him and his followers, it is helpful to cite his own reflections on how developmentalism had devastated his people and the countryside where they lived:

> When I speak of our resistance against large-scale deforestation, I would like to keep in mind the fact that this deforestation was the result of government propaganda . . . that said that we needed to bring development and progress to our region. And with all this came the opening up of the road known as highway BR-317. The moment that this highway was put into service, the rubber tappers who found themselves living alongside of it were suddenly in the areas of easiest access, and it was in the accessible areas that most of the expulsions of rubber tappers occurred. Large landowners forcibly took over the road-front areas.
>
> Just to give you an idea: From 1970 to 1975, in the period during which the large landowners occupied the areas alongside the road and began widespread deforestation, in my municipality of Xapuri alone the fires and earth movers destroyed 180,000 rubber trees, 80,000 Brazil nut trees, and more than 1.2 million trees of other species, including wood ostensibly safeguarded by the law, and thousands of trees of medicinal value that are so important for us. Various animal species disappeared too as they were burned out. From this point on began the violent [attacks] against us.
>
> And all this happened because of the false propaganda of development and progress. The progress of the opening of the highway only brought ruin upon us.[9]

Mendes and his followers knew, however, that denouncing the destruction and organizing empates would not be sufficient. They had to put their minds to inventing an alternative ideological approach to Amazonian development that would halt the destruction and integrate the dwellers of the forest into the regional development process, ending, once and for all, the developmentalist lie that Progress was destined for "men without land for land without men." They could not afford to accept passively the accusation that they offered no alternatives to the Amazon and Brazil. For that work, Chico Mendes, as well as his fellow rubber tappers and assessores like Gomercindo, turned to social scientists and non-Amazonian activists who also were deeply disturbed by trends under way in the Amazon—principally Mendes's friend from the southern state of Paraná, the anthropologist Mary Alegretti. Together they invented the notion of the extractive reserve. Again, Chico Mendes describes this process:

There was a very serious problem. We were in a very big struggle in defense of the forest, but we did not have in our minds an alternative idea, a proposal, or an argument.

Well, someone would ask, "You are fighting to defend the forest, but what is it that you want to do with the forest?" And many times we would become a little taken aback, encountering difficulty making a response.

At the end of 1984, beginning of 1985, an idea came up at the union of rubber tappers of Xapuri—our idea, to organize the first national meeting of rubber tappers in Brasília. Why Brasília? Because Brasília serves as the forum for decisions at the national level. And because in Brasília the authorities had, until that moment, considered Amazonia a vacuum with nobody living there. We wanted to prove [to them] and the rest of the world that Amazonia had people living there and that it was not deserted.

And so with the support of a few organizations . . . including a person who played an especially important role in the setting up of this meeting, Mary Alegretti[,] . . . [w]e succeeded in making the arrangements for a national conference. . . . By and by, commissions of rubber tappers left for various parts of Amazonia to bring this news to the other comrades, our brothers. In October of 1985, with a great deal of success, we held in Brasília the First National Meeting of Rubber Tappers. Throughout all the history of the occupation of Amazonia by rubber tappers there had never occurred such an event. This was a historic meeting. We got together in Brasília 130 leaders of rubber tappers from all over Amazonia [as well as] observers from Brazil and from other countries too.

Beginning from this point we discovered the idea of creating extractive reserves in the Amazon. This would be the real agrarian reform for Amazonia that we wanted, because we rubber tappers never fought to be the owners or property holders of land. What we want is that the state own the land while the rubber tappers maintain usufruct rights over it. And so this very good idea emerged.

After the meeting, government agencies released this idea all over Brazil and even to environmental organizations overseas.[10]

The extractive reserve, combining state ownership and usufruct rights of the forest dwellers inhabiting it, was an original approach to the problem of Amazonian agrarian reform. For the first time a proposal emerged from, and involved, those who already lived there. The rubber tappers' idea took into consideration the nature of the Amazonian ecosystem, where the "wealth" of the region is not in the soils—all too often quite thin and susceptible to rapid erosion as soon as the protective forest canopy above them is removed—but in the forest canopy itself. Rubber and Brazil nuts are only the most obvious forest products that can be and are sustainably harvested. With further research, innumerable chemicals, medicines, oils, and other products could also be harvested while maintaining the forest in a manner approximating its "original" state. Furthermore, this approach would safeguard the rubber tappers and their families while offering them the economic means to integrate, on their own terms and at a reasonable pace, into the modernizing world around them. Given the enormous bundles of debt, fiscal incentives, infrastructure development, and environmental destruction that the alternative version of trickle-down "progress" entailed, it would also probably be cheaper for Brazil. Mendes made it clear when he promulgated this idea that he was not against development but rather developmentalism that insisted on classism, dismantling of the rubber tappers' communities, genocide of the indigenous people, debt to foreign banks, and environmental degradation as "the only way." He and his allies effectively reframed the problem: No longer was it a matter of *if* but of *how* there was to be development.

Intellectual and political creativity as well as realism were the cornerstones of his agrarian reform proposal for the people of the Amazon. As the rubber tappers eschewed control over the land, fighting instead for control over the resources contained on the extractive reserves, they combined the need for cooperation with scientist allies around Brazil and the world (to research and discover more Amazonian secrets for potentially rational commercialization), the embracing of communitarian values, promotion of entrepreneurialism, and increasingly sophisticated education for their sons and daughters to carry forward this challenging new vision. In telling fashion—since the idea applied in equal measure to the indigenous peoples of Amazonia who were guardians of enormous, untapped quantities of knowledge of the forests' potential contributions to the world— Mendes and his new National Council of Rubber Tappers reached out to their traditional rivals or enemies. With indigenous leaders they successfully forged the Alliance of the Peoples of the Forest to pursue the newly articulated ideology and practical plan of creating extractive reserves across the Amazon.

This set of alliances constitutes the third and crucial reason why Chico Mendes did not die a martyr only for the Amazonian causes he defended but also for like-minded peoples around the globe. While he organized the rubber tappers into effective alliances, Mendes worked as a local politician in the military government's legal opposition party, the Brazilian Democratic Movement (MDB). Later, as the military regime waned, he was one of the national founders of the Workers' Party (PT), personally allying with the urban union leader, now president of Brazil, Luiz Inácio Lula da Silva. He, Lula, and the PT in turn allied themselves with the cause of democratic socialism around the world. Meanwhile, Mendes's National Council of Rubber Tappers, his Alliance of the Peoples of the Forest (bringing together rubber tappers and Brazil's Indians), and his increasing national stature as a man defending not only his people but also the Amazon forest, drew the attention of the international environmentalist movement, which was increasingly horrified by the burning and destruction going on in the Amazon in the 1980s. Mendes of course met and began to collaborate with them also. He was to receive prestigious prizes from the Better World Society and the United Nations, recognizing his work on behalf of the environmental cause. Although it might seem trite in the context of assassination, massive destruction, dislocation, genocide, and ethnocide in which he worked, Chico Mendes embodied the adage emerging in liberal corners across the planet, "Think globally, act locally." He had gone beyond the Amazon and Brazil to become a world figure.

But in the western Amazon, regional logics of the frontier went on undisturbed. Chico Mendes's enemies did not read the environmentalist debates in prominent international newspapers. Nor were they impressed with Mendes's international prizes. On the contrary, the prizes and Mendes's growing ability to influence international bankers and U.S. senators considering support for the developmentalism under way in the Amazon infuriated his enemies. Moreover, these same regional elites—in the landlord class and in media, politics, police, and military circles—were accustomed to the reign of impunity in cases of the murder of leaders from Brazil's rural lower classes.

Chico Mendes was surrounded. However much he organized and forged alliances, he was still at the mercy of the lawlessness and murderous impulses of class warfare in Brazil's rural peripheral frontier areas, where political violence and impunity remained the effective currency. Eventually, a minor landlord stalked and killed Mendes in front of his children and wife. As Gomercindo Rodrigues's memoir recounts, the murderers, from the Alves family, were condemned and served some prison time, but the legal system limited the inquiry regarding the motive for Chico Mendes's dispute with the Alves family over a piece of territory in Xapuri. The allies of these violent individuals and their family live free to this day, still tormenting rubber tappers and indigenous people and burning the forest. There is a widely held belief—and there is little doubt that it is true—that the intellectual authors of Chico Mendes's murder were never questioned.

• • •

Given the importance Chico Mendes has attained, it is no wonder that his work has been adopted as "our work" by both the socialist and environmentalist camps. Because of his socialist utterances and writings, his socialist speeches as a city councilman, his strong unionism and status as a founder of the PT—all well documented in Gomercindo Rodrigues's memoir and else-where—the international socialist movement claimed him as their martyr. Meanwhile, the environmentalists—many of whom remained quite conser-vative politically but were insisting on finding ways to conserve the environ-ment, particularly in the unique Amazonian biome—adopted Mendes as *their* martyr. Many of them would have been shocked at his socialist and commu-nist friends and speeches.

What renders both these camps' claims problematic is that Mendes advo-cated a premodern lifestyle—extractivism, hunting, fishing, subsistence farm-ing—with a postmodern twist—entrepreneurialism, communitarianism, multiethnicity—all within an internationalist framework. Socialists are noto-riously impatient with the peasant worldview, which, in many ways, could be found among the tappers. Karl Marx himself famously denigrated the "idiocy" of rural life in his *Eighteenth Brumaire of Louis Napoleon*. Leftists, from the Lula government to the FARC guerrillas in Colombia, show little understanding of or mercy for the tribal peoples of the Amazon or other regions of Latin America and the premodern production systems involving *caboclos* (descendants of Portuguese and indigenous people) of the Amazon. Yet Chico Mendes was creating his Alliance of the Peoples of the Forest with caboclo rubber tappers and indigenous groups. Environmentalists around the world may love the pristine, but many are preservationist and would have lit-tle understanding of or sympathy for a proposal for *managing* the environ-ment, especially if the managers were in a social formation easily identified as preindustrial and uttering rhetoric—as Mendes did—that could only be characterized as socialist.

Table 1 breaks down, albeit simplistically, the complexities of Chico Mendes the leader, as described by his friend Gomercindo in his memoir and in the literature on the western Amazonian rubber tappers' movement.

As the schematic suggests, Chico Mendes and the movement he led are not easily classified. Mendes was neither exclusively a conservationist envi-ronmentalist nor a socialist. He certainly was not a preservationist environ-mentalist. Nor was he completely a nonviolent pacifist, as he sympathized at one point, early in his political career, with the inchoate rage of his peers when they went after the murderers of Wilson Pinheiro. Nor was he simply the subject of his story: a premodern rubber tapper, focused ethnocentrically on himself and his world. He was self-consciously a protagonist in his peo-ple's struggle, with sophisticated, arguably postmodern ideas. Mendes was attempting to reconcile potentially conflicting ideas of great consequence to his people, and his efforts serve to instruct observers dealing with analogous

TABLE I. CHICO MENDES'S POLITICS

Alliance Mendes Pursued	*Mendes's Posture*	*Allies' Posture*	*Mendes's Role in Building Institutions*
Allied to Brazilian and foreign environmentalists	Environmentalist rhetoric; critique of developmentalism; adoption of international environmentalism; not notably progressive except on environment; largely nonviolent.	Many (though not all) were anti-Communist, even antisocialist; not favoring more rational approaches to Amazonia.	Helped found transregional and transnational coalitions denouncing deforestation and favoring more rational approaches to Amazonia.
Allied to local, regional, national, and international socialist worker movements.	Socialist rhetoric; initially tolerant of his peers' violence, though later not.	Local, regional, and national socialist-oriented political forces at work in Acre, from the traditional Communists (in CONTAG) to the socialists (in the PT).	Founded rural workers' unions in Acre and the National Council of Rubber Tappers; PT on the national level.
Allied to other rubber tappers of the region and indigenous peoples.	Free peasant/rubber tapper outlook; local, regionalist, communitarian attitudes; nonviolent, with few exceptions. Developed tactic of the empate.	Indians were, as the rubber tappers, ethnocentric, trying to break out of traditional insularity for the sake of survival.	Alliance of Peoples of the Forest.
Allied to all the above.	Rooted in premodern social construct while finding places and modernity through politics, creativity and nonviolence. Entrepreneurial, socialist defender of premodern social formations trying to control own modernization; developer of political actions to make coherent these conflicting ideas.	Mendes's allies shared postmodern attitude, especially those who defend premodern social constructs coming into modernity *on their own terms* and *at their own pace*: Amazonian Indians and *caboclos* and national and international progressive activists.	Local, regional, national, international alliances; the first extractive reserves.

intellectual and practical problems around the world. He remained deeply rooted in a past social formation, so much so that he was desperate to find a way to "ease" it, almost intact, and as much as possible under the control of his rubber tapper peers, into the modern world through an innovative, very much present-day approach to agrarian reform: the extractive reserve. And in this important way, he was a man of the future and of the broader world.

He, better than any of us, understood intuitively how these sometimes contradictory ideas held together in a coherent whole. Belying the crisis of paradigms that besets the current moment in history, he fought for the tolerant, democratic society, the rural society interested in the best that urban civilization may offer, the communitarian society, the environmentalist society, the multiethnic society, the educated society, the demilitarized society, the entrepreneurial *and* socialist society, the preindustrial society, the postmodern society, the independent society, the egalitarian society. His was not a pastiche but a workable amalgam, where the forest, the woman, the man, the child, and the creatures might all be noble in their place, with an umbilical cord linking them to the past, present, future, and, above all, one another.

Notes

1. See, e.g., Cockburn and Hecht 1989; Gross 1992; Martins 1998; Maxwell 2003; Revkin 2004; Shoumatoff 1991; Souza 1990; Ventura 2003.

2. Cockburn and Hecht (1989: 206) write, for example, "The objectives of many First World environmental organizations focus primarily on resource conservation and the technical means through which this can be achieved. But the agrarian question that produces the environmental degradation remains largely undiscussed, at least in US environmental circles. Their plans have a timbre that is usually technocratic and politically 'neutral'—that is, conservative in content."

3. See Maybury-Lewis 1990.

4. When the Brazilian generals took over in 1964, the United States, the close and crucial supporter of the military regime in Brazil and the chief ideologue of the western side of the Cold War, was escalating the war in Vietnam, had recently settled the Cuban missile crisis, and was poised to invade the Dominican Republic.

5. See Maybury-Lewis 1994.

6. See, e.g., Amnesty International 1988; Campanha Nacional pela Reforma Agrária 1985; Fajardo 1988.

7. Just before his death, Chico Mendes denounced the state labor federation as in the hands of toadies of the military state. For this reason, the locus of combative unionism practicing "the politics of the possible" was at the union, not the federation, level, particularly the unions of Xapuri and Brasiléia.

8. Maybury-Lewis 1994: 228.

9. Quoted in Maybury-Lewis 1994: 225–226.

10. Quoted in Maybury-Lewis 1994: 228–229.

~~~~~~~~~~~~~~~~~~~~~~~~~~~~~~~~~~~~~

I WAS THERE!

WHY WRITE SO LONG AFTER? How to write? When all's said and done, I am not a "writer," and I have already felt on various occasions that people might want me to write a biography of Chico Mendes. This might not be too difficult: It would require some interviews with some mutual friends who knew him from his early days and would tell some stories and recount some history that might "please the public."

But I think doing that would betray Chico's memory, since he himself would not like to be the center of the story. That was not his way. So I thought it better to write the history in which I was involved, from my point of view, since that way if I make mistakes or say something wrong, I can take responsibility for it.

I don't know much about "style"—it's not my specialty—and I kept worrying about how I should tell my story in the forest, or better, among the rubber tappers, or about how the rubber tappers taught me to be part of their story.

I thought it would be great if I could write like Paulo Jacob in *White Rain*, a fantastic novel by an Amazonian writer many people have never heard of. I quickly came to the conclusion that I didn't have the skill for all that—but, I confess, that's the way I'd like to write.

The story I've tried to write I've already told countless times to Brazilian students and environmentalists as well as human rights activists in various parts of the world. That may be where the suggestion came from that I write the way I talk.

Whenever I start talking with people who want to hear the story, they ask me what I know—first, almost always, about the most dramatic and enduring incident in my memory: the last time I spoke with Chico Mendes. Despite the passage of more than a decade and a half the scene continues to be so vivid in my mind that recently, returning to Chico's house, when I walked into the kitchen, where he was when we last spoke, it was as if I were seeing him again. The pain was searing . . .

It was a little after six in the evening and already dark. I arrived on my motorbike. I stopped in front of the simple shack where Chico Mendes lived. I walked into the wooden house covered with clay tiles, with two bedrooms, a small front room, a kitchen, and a hallway connecting the front room to the kitchen and passing alongside the bedrooms. He was in the kitchen, playing dominoes with two of the three policemen—one had gone to the police barracks to eat dinner—who had been detailed to provide security.

Happy to see me, he said, "Oh, Goma" (that was what he called me, although other friends called me Guma), "it's great that you got here, now we can be partners to beat these dunces. I've already been winning by myself."

"No, Chico, I don't know how to play that game."

"Ah, but to beat these dummies you don't have to know how to play. Sit down, let's play."

"No, Chico, I don't play well enough to help."

"Ah, playing with these dopes without knowing how isn't worthwhile. Sit there, we'll be partners."

"Chico, I'm worried about what I told you yesterday." I had told him I was worried not to have seen gunmen in the city since my return to Xapuri on December 13, 1988, and he had replied that he'd check on the situation in town that day.

"Yeah, I also haven't seen those guys."

At that moment, Chico's wife arrived and said she wanted to make dinner, the soap opera would be starting soon and she wanted to watch it, since it was the next-to-last episode. So Chico said, "Come have dinner with us, Goma."

At first I said no, thank you, because I knew he would have to stand on his head to find enough food in the house. He insisted, knowing that that year I often had nothing to eat and no money because I was unpaid, without even a grant to finance my stay in Xapuri. I survived only because the Amazon Workers' Center (CTA)[1] paid the rent and telephone bill for the house where I lived, which was also the organization's office. Since he insisted, I replied, "I'm going to take a ride around town to see if I find those guys, because I'm very worried."

"Okay, meanwhile I'll take a shower and wait for you to come back to eat, but do come back."

"Okay."

I left, got on the motorbike, rode around Xapuri, passing in front of all the bars where the gunmen used to hang out. They were all deserted. Something tightened in my chest—an indescribable anxiety had been with me since December 13, when I returned from a trip to Rio de Janeiro, where I had substituted for Chico Mendes on December 7, giving a speech at the Brazilian Press Association sponsored by the National Campaign for Defense and Development of Amazonia.

When I returned from that trip, something had changed. Every morning since April 1988, when I opened the window of my house, two gunmen had been in the square. Two also were usually in front of the Rural Workers' Union hall, and two were strolling around town. When I came back, the gunmen had disappeared from Xapuri. This was strange—very strange.

It took five to ten minutes to return to Chico's house. As I arrived, his wife ran out screaming, "Guma, they shot Chico!"

I looked behind me. On the sidewalk in front of the police station, about 50 (yes, 50) meters away, several police were standing. I shouted, "You bastards, aren't you going to do anything?"

At that moment, Pedro Rocha, Chico's friend, shouted, "We need a car, he's wounded!"

In hopes he could be saved, I turned on the motorbike, which I hadn't even climbed off, and went to the Bank of Amazonia office, which I'd passed a little earlier and seen people working. I got there and shouted in the window, "Andrias, we need a car because they've shot Chico!"

Andrias, the bank manager, ran out, jumped in his Escort, and went right to Chico's house. When we arrived there, he was already being placed in a pickup that had been passing. I asked Pedro Rocha, "How is he?" Chico's friend answered, "Ah, he's dead . . ."

But he didn't say it firmly. He left it hanging in the air, making it seem as if he wasn't dead, that there was some hope. I went to the hospital. Since I was wearing shorts, they wouldn't let me in.

I thought, "What good would it do, I'm not a doctor. I can't help here. I'll do something that will help." So I went home and started telephoning. I called friends in Rio Branco, Brasília, Rio de Janeiro. The first reaction was disbelief; they all said I shouldn't joke about something serious, and when they realized I was serious, because I was crying over the phone, they asked if he was dead. I answered that he was so bad that he might die, since I didn't have definitive word.

Among the first calls I made, one was to someone who was not a friend: the superintendent of the Federal Police in Acre at the time, Mauro Sposito. He was not in. I left a message that those who were gunning for Chico Mendes had gotten him. I did this because I had and continue to have great suspicion that the superintendent knew something more about this killing. What I have not gotten yet is any proof of this. Even so, after this call to the Federal Police, by coincidence, my telephone stopped working. So I started making calls from the public phone in Xapuri.

Again I went to the hospital. I went in and saw Chico Mendes lying on a stretcher. He was dead. I went back and made more calls, confirming his death. We started to arrange for an autopsy, embalming, and so on.

A blind rage was consuming me. I got my revolver (.22, with seven shots), which I rarely carried. In the city I had carried it only once: when they killed Ivair Higino on June 18, 1988, six months earlier. On that day I was armed when two of Darli's gunmen—including his son Darci, who later shot Chico Mendes—entered the parish house, where Ivair's body was laid out.[2] They came in, I think to show they were tough guys, but they did not have the courage to look at our comrade's body. For a while after Chico Mendes's death, as an extremely tense situation continued, I carried a licensed firearm. That's how I discovered that this was a big illusion, since one never has time to use a weapon when attacked in an ambush or by surprise; and besides, I'm no gunman. Today I am a fierce defender of disarmament and prohibition of the manufacture and sale of firearms.[3]

On that fateful day of December 22, 1988, when I saw Chico Mendes's body, I took the revolver, put it in a shoulder bag with two extra bullets and, I admit, hoped to encounter any of Darli's gunmen. I think I could have killed them, and I had no doubt I would fire as many shots as possible at the gunmen. But they were not in the city. Everything had been carefully planned.

While we waited to resolve the legal questions, I was standing in front of Chico Mendes's house when, at about 8:30 P.M., a white Volkswagen Gol arrived, and a man got out and started to photograph the house. I asked who he was, and he replied he was a journalist from *O Rio Branco*. Without thinking about it much, I asked, "Already?"

At this point, it is important to mention for readers who might not know that Xapuri is 188 kilometers (113 miles) from Rio Branco, and at that time only part of the road was paved and it was full of holes. Another part was dirt, which made travel very difficult during the Amazon winter (the rainy season in the region).[4] That was the situation that night: The dirt road was very muddy, and the average time to go from Rio Branco to Xapuri during the day was about three and a half to four hours when driving was possible, often only in a vehicle with four-wheel drive. At night the journey normally would take much longer.

The story of the Rio Branco newspaper photographer's quick arrival has still not been explained to this day. The more they try to explain it, the more confusing it becomes for the newspaper and its owners. Strange to say, the fact was never fully investigated by the law, even though the crime has no statute of limitations.

At about 10:00 P.M. we were informed that the doctors from the Forensic

Institute would not come to Xapuri from Rio Branco. If we wanted the body autopsied and embalmed by their personnel, we would have to arrange to have it sent to Rio Branco. This we did. The body left in the hospital ambulance at about midnight.

I stayed in Xapuri. It was the longest night of my life, since I couldn't get to sleep, and at about 5:00 A.M. on the twenty-third the phone began to ring. They were calling from Brasília, Rio, São Paulo because of the time difference (two hours ahead of Acre), seeking more information.

The Story and Actors of a Death Foretold

One year before, in late December 1987, at the general assembly of the Xapuri Rural Workers' Union, the workers carefully analyzed several facts that had begun to worry them:

1) Two lawyers had arrived in Xapuri from São Paulo state (Bragança Paulista) and were preparing to open a law office;
2) Darli Alves da Silva, the gunman-cum-rancher, leader of a genuine gang, who formerly had not owned a car and had traveled frequently by bus throughout the region, had appeared with a new pickup truck;
3) Rumors increased every day that the ranchers were plotting to "deforest at any cost" in the Xapuri region, as a way of wiping out the bad example of rubber tapper organization in the area;
4) Even after receiving two international prizes, Chico was subjected to violent attacks in the press by Acre's traditional politicos. Congress members, who didn't even know Brazil had signed a contract with the Inter-American Development Bank to finance paving of the BR-364 highway between Porto Velho and Rio Branco,[5] also were violently attacking the leader from Xapuri.

The climate already was very tense at the end of 1987, and the Xapuri rubber tappers discussed this. Their concerns included the "spiral strategy," used frequently by gangs to create terror in an area: Movement people would be killed but not necessarily the most prominent leaders. The important thing is to kill to show they are ready for anything, to create generalized fear. This method is used even today, as can be seen in the slums of Rio de Janeiro, for example.

In March 1988 Darli Alves da Silva entered the scene. Until then he had owned the Paraná Ranch, named after the state he had fled in the early 1970s after a crime wave that included ordering the murder of the broker Acir Urizzi in Nova Jerusalém, Umuarama. He appeared with a deed to about

6,000 hectares in the Cachoeira rubber estate. Nobody knows to this day where he got the money for such a purchase. And because this fact never was investigated, it lost its relevance when he was convicted as the author of Chico's murder. Maybe if somebody had followed up on the origin of the funds used to buy part of the Cachoeira estate, they would have found all those involved in the killing of the rubber tapper leader.

After buying part of the estate near the Bolivian border, Darli decided to open a track to the area he had purchased. Rubber tappers had long occupied this area.

To have a legal excuse to enter the area, Darli used a trick very common among ranchers during the 1970s: He "compensated" one of the rubber tappers for a homestead in the part of the estate he had bought.

The rubber tapper, Zé Brito, sold the homestead in the absence of his mother and brother, who also were homesteaders there.

On learning of the deal between Zé Brito and Darli for the Brasil homestead, the rubber tappers of the community met and proposed joining together to pay more than the gunman-rancher had offered. Darli had offered 220,000 cruzados in February 1988, and the Cachoeira rubber tappers were ready to pay 250,000. Zé Brito accepted the rubber tappers' offer and left the estate to undo the deal with Darli. He never returned to the area—and, worse yet, joined the other gunmen in the rancher's gang.

Darli threatened to open a track to take out all the timber in the Brasil homestead (what a coincidence!) and spread the word that he would enter the area, "come hell or high water."

The rubber tappers of Cachoeira and neighboring estates—Ecuador, São Miguel, São José, Porto Rico, and Nova Esperança—met and resolved to camp out at the Fazendinha homestead at the entrance to the estate to wait for the invasion of the "enraged killer."

Darli didn't arrive but did file a legal motion for reintegration of possession[6]—possession he had no right to—against Chico, who was the president of the Rural Workers' Union and did not live in the area, Raimundo Barros, Antonio Teixeira Mendes, and me, as an adviser of the Xapuri union. One of Darli's lawyers in this suit was a state assembly member from the PFL.

As the suit proceeded with an injunction handed down by the Xapuri district judge, whose decisions almost always favored the ranchers, the rubber tappers and their wives and children continued their occupation.

Every time Darli threatened to enter Cachoeira, the occupation was immediately reorganized. This went on for more than a month.

While they were still camped at the Fazendinha homestead, the rubber tappers learned that in the neighboring estate, Equador, the Delta Group[7] was beginning to deforest the Recanto homestead. This action, only 6 kilometers from where they were, made the rubber tappers decide to organize an empate against deforestation of the neighboring area.

So the first empate of 1988 took place. The ranchers, as always, went to court and got not only the right to deforest but also the protection of fifty(!) state police for the ten workers who were cutting down the trees. Even so, the rubber tappers obstructed the deforestation three times. At one point, if it hadn't been for Chico's calmness and steadiness, there would have been a confrontation between rubber tappers and police that could have become a real massacre.

Trying to broaden the struggle in defense of Equador and against Darli's entry into Cachoeira, the rubber tappers decided to move their occupation to the city.

Hundreds of workers spent all night walking 17 kilometers from the Fazendinha homestead to the BR-317, which links Xapuri and Brasiléia, the headquarters of the IBDF (now IBAMA).[8] On May 25, after arriving in the city, the rubber tapper protest completely took over Xapuri.

All during that night of May 25, Darli's sons, Darci (known as "Aparecido") and Oloci, kept riding motorbikes along the road where the rubber tappers were camped out, in a clear attempt at provocation.

At about 1:30 A.M. on May 26, when the great majority of rubber tappers were sleeping on the porch of the IBDF building, three gunmen came by shooting at the people who were sleeping. Some sixteen shots were fired.

Two gunmen went in the back, and a third waited on the side of the building, shooting to stop those who tried to flee from escaping. Two young rubber tappers were wounded. One, fifteen years old, was shot seven times, while the other, seventeen, was shot twice. Much later, when everybody already knew who had fired the shots, the police "discovered" there had been only two gunmen, Darci and Oloci, Darli's sons. They had shot and wounded the workers. The gunman who was supposed to cut off retreat in case the rubber tappers tried to flee was left out of the case, for reasons unexplained to this day; but it might have been because he "cooperated" in clearing up the crime. Even so, at trial he denied everything the police said.

It should be emphasized that the crime at the IBDF was cleared up only in 1989, as the Chico Mendes murder case unfolded.

On June 18, 1988, at about 5:30 A.M., when he was leaving his house for a neighboring settlement to milk a cow because he didn't have one of his own, Ivair Higino de Almeida, a farmworker, leader of a grassroots religious community, and candidate for city councilor, already nominated by the Workers' Party in Xapuri for the 1988 elections, was killed by two shots from a shotgun and six from a revolver.

Ivair Higino was only twenty-six, from Minas Gerais, quiet, without enemies. Because of his openness and kindness he was well liked in his community at Kilometer 26 of the BR-317 between Brasiléia and Xapuri and had a good chance to win enough votes to be elected city councilor.

Next to Ivair Higino's settlement lived Cícero Tenório Cavalcante, also a candidate for city councilor in 1988, for the PMDB. According to the police investigation, which also took place only after Chico's murder, Cícero was involved in Ivair's killing, which may have been carried out by Darli and his brother Alvarino. This is stated in the records of the case, which is proceeding very slowly in the Xapuri district.

In June 1988 the "spiral strategy" was operating with the incident at the IBDF and the murder of Ivair Higino, and it was common to see Darli's gang parading, obviously armed, in Xapuri. On some occasions as many as thirty gunmen would gather.

The question that goes unanswered to this day is: How many more than thirty gunmen were paid and maintained by Darli?

It was more or less at that time that a federal police infiltrator appeared. I tell that story below.

In September 1988, the former rubber tapper José Ribeiro was killed in the middle of the street in the middle of the night. A month earlier he had been beaten by one of the "Minas boys" and other Darli gunmen at a party. These were the same people who would participate in Chico's murder a little later. The spiral strategy continued: Start at the margins and go toward the center. Once they arrived at the main target—in this case, Chico Mendes—so much terror would be generated that nobody would react.

On the same day José Ribeiro was killed in Xapuri, Chico and I, several comrades from the National Rubber Tappers' Council,[9] and people from advisory organizations participated in a meeting promoted by the Institute of Amazon Studies in Curitiba.[10] At that time it was directed by the anthropologist Mary Allegretti.[11] The meeting's purpose was to develop the idea of extractive reserves, in process since the First National Meeting of Rubber Tappers.[12]

Taking advantage of the fact that we were in Paraná and having information that Darli and Alvarino Alves were from that state, Chico asked several lawyers who were sympathizers with the rubber tappers' struggle to check if there was a court case in Paraná against the Alves brothers, as was rumored in Acre.

The search was quick: They discovered that an arrest warrant had been issued for Darli and Alvarino, who were accused of planning the murder of a real estate broker, Acir Urizzi, in 1973 near Umuarama, northwestern Paraná.

Chico obtained a warrant for the court in Xapuri for the arrest of the Alves brothers.

As soon as he arrived in Rio Branco, advised by a lawyer friend and thinking basically about his safety, Chico, Bishop Moacyr Grechi of Rio Branco (coordinator of the Pastoral Land Commission),[13] and a lawyer went to the Federal Police. They personally delivered the warrant to the superintendent of the Federal Police in Acre, Mauro Sposito, with the request that the Federal Police deliver the document to Xapuri, since it could be carried out only with the approval of the district court there.

Taking the request to the Federal Police superintendent as a security measure might well have been Chico's greatest mistake, since the chief kept the document from the morning of September 27, when it was delivered to him, until October 13, when it was sent *by mail* to the judge in Xapuri. There was one small detail: For a few months, the judge in Xapuri was Adair Longuini, but the request was addressed to the judge who had preceded him in the district. It is difficult to believe that the Federal Police superintendent in the state did not know or had no way of knowing who the judge in Xapuri was. The request did not arrive in Xapuri until October 18 and was opened only because below the name "Jerónimo Borges Jr.," was written "Judge of the Xapuri District."

The same afternoon he received the request, Longuini called Chico to the courthouse. I was with Chico. The judge asked him if he had knowledge of the document, and Chico said yes and explained how he had obtained it and how it had arrived at the Federal Police office.

Longuini scolded Chico, telling him he should have brought it directly to him. Chico answered that he was advised not to do that for reasons of personal safety. Dr. Adair then said he had already decided that the warrant would be served early the next morning, because it was already late in the afternoon. In the district, only he, the secretary, the state police chief in Xapuri, and we knew of the existence of the warrant. Nobody else.

The next day, early in the morning, when they went to serve the warrant, the state police from Xapuri were greeted by bullets at the Paraná Ranch, Darli's property. The two wanted men fled. Darli was captured a little while after Chico's murder, and Alvarino was captured only after the statute of limitations had expired on the crime he had committed in Paraná. At that time he returned to Xapuri, where he lives quietly to this very day.

According to Chico's notes in a book he kept for the purpose, "September 27, afternoon. Darli was in front of the Federal Police office. I phoned Dr. Reni from the hotel, asking for Darli to be picked up—nothing was done."

Two clarifications: Reni Graebner was a Federal Police captain and assistant superintendent of the Federal Police in Acre at the time; the letter with the warrant for Darli and Alvarino had been delivered that morning to the Federal Police superintendent.

At a meeting in Brasília in 1989, after Chico's murder, I spoke with the former justice minister, Oscar Dias Correa, in front of several members of Action for Citizenship[14] and Congress members Plínio de Arruda Sampaio (PT-SP), Nelton Friedrich (PSDB-PR), Sigmaringa Seixas (then PSDB-DF, now PT-DF), city councilor from Rio de Janeiro Alfredo Sirkis (PV-RJ), and members of the Chico Mendes Committee of Brasília. I asked if on September 27, 1988, already knowing Darli was sought by prosecutors in Paraná, the Federal Police could have arrested him and sent two agents to Xapuri with the request for the district judge to legalize the arrest they already had made. It should be recalled that at that time, the federal Constitution of October 15, 1988, had not yet been promulgated. The minister's reply was affirmative.

Asked about the delay in the request reaching Xapuri, Captain Mauro Sposito said he had received an open envelope, the judge in Xapuri could have considered that a violation of privacy, and the CPT had delayed sending the official document.

The captain's claim is backed up only by the handwritten receipt of the Federal Police, stamped with the date October 13, 1988, against the postmark on the official letter sent by the CPT, dated September 27, 1988—that is, the same day the captain requested the delivery. Why would the CPT put the date September 27 on the letter if it were sent on October 13, or any other date between then and now? No reason! The CPT delivered the official letter the same morning, and the person who confirms this is the lawyer who took care of it. So aside from acting in a very strange way during the whole proceeding, Mauro Sposito, or somebody under his command, committed fraud by putting a different date from the one on which the document arrived at the Federal Police office.

Another small question: In such a secret matter, would it be prudent for the letter delivering the request to the Federal Police superintendent to be entered in the office record? Evidently not. The same person who received the letter received the warrant: Mauro Sposito.

At that point, Sposito's responsibility became obvious: If he received a request to deliver to the judge in Xapuri, and if he knew the contents of the document because it effectively arrived open from Pará, where it had been delivered to lawyers who would serve it, the fact that he did not order the immediate arrest of Darli only increases suspicions about his behavior in the entire situation.

It would be funny if it weren't tragic that the Federal Police captain, with a choice between arresting a wanted individual and demanding a sealed envelope, should choose the latter, assuming the judge in Xapuri would think it more important to have the envelope sealed than the criminal in custody!

Suspicions multiply in the search for the real story of Mauro Sposito and Chico Mendes. Chico himself denounced the long and difficult interrogations the captain had subjected him to when Chico was a city councilor in Xapuri.[15]

The situation became still stranger when, in the first week of December, under the pretense of responding to Chico's denunciation of his conniving with Darli and Alvarino, Sposito tried to smear the rubber tapper leader by branding him a Federal Police informer, releasing a dossier containing several documents without ever explaining how he had obtained them. He had no shame making public the documents, which, in truth, did not document anything and were not obtained by legal means. Among them was a letter from the Ford Foundation to Chico as president of the Xapuri Rural Workers' Union.

Another document he released was Chico's weapons permit with a "canceled" stamp, exactly at the moment when Chico was receiving the most intense threats.

Chico came to Rio Branco countless times seeking renewal of his weapons permit, and he was always told it hadn't yet arrived. All of a sudden, the permit was published in the Rio Branco papers with the "canceled" stamp—that is, the document was there, but the Federal Police, then under Sposito's command, did not deliver it. This was a way of undermining Chico's security, especially when he traveled to Rio Branco and other towns in Acre and even in other states.

Another question is important to raise: At the time, Sposito was responsible for the potential expansion of the Calha Norte project into Acre.[16] This project was strenuously opposed throughout the country, since it aimed at the militarization of the border areas in the Amazon region. This would cause great problems for indigenous communities in various areas.

Speaking of militarization, one more question is appropriate here: Why was the Federal Police superintendent, and not the military commander in Acre, responsible for promoting the Calha Norte project?

Much certainly remains to be explained about Sposito's involvement in the incidents preceding Chico's murder.

As I've already mentioned, the captain sent the official request that had been delivered to him by hand, in the interests of security, by ordinary mail, which was totally inappropriate because of the gravity of the matter.

In reference to the strange actions of Sposito or the Federal Police he commanded in the state, more than two thousand pages of court records in the Chico Mendes case contain very important information.

In a deposition during the instruction phase of the criminal case (Act No. 5929/89 of the Xapuri district), confirmed during the jury trial, the civil and criminal notary clerk of Xapuri, Mr. Raimundo Dias de Figueiredo, recorded the following:

> That the accused Darli was in the local notary's office and asked the witness against him for an official request from the state of Paraná; that the witness replied to Sr. Darli, in his role as clerk of the Civil and Criminal Notary, that he did not know anything about the arrival of an official request in this district; that the clerk also told Sr. Darli that all the letters to the judge passed through his hands and he had not seen anything of the kind; that he also replied to the defendant Darli that the person who could give better information about the existence of this letter was the district judge, president of this hearing; that on that occasion Darli said to the witness that he already knew the official request was in Acre and the deceased Chico Mendes possessed a photocopy; and *Darli also said the request could be found at the Federal Police office*; that Darli said to the witness that neither Chico Mendes nor his wife would live long, and he could wait and see what would happen.[17]

Now I can go back to a question that has never been answered and has never stopped reverberating for me for more than fifteen years: How did Darli know there was an official warrant for his arrest at the Federal Police office, if not even the judge in Xapuri knew about such a document?

Everything related to Sposito was brought to the attention of Romeu Tuma, then director general of the Federal Police, and José Fernando Eichenberg, then secretary of the Justice Ministry, at a meeting in Xapuri on December 26, 1988, four days after the murder and one day after Chico's funeral.

When he received the information, Tuma said he would look into it, since he hadn't known about this matter of Chico and Sposito, but this information could not be mixed with other details so as not to prejudice the investigations they were carrying out about the intellectual authors of the murder.

Tuma promised he would look into everything about Sposito and send the information to the union and the organizations that participated in the meeting in Xapuri. Even today no such information has arrived in Chico's hometown.

It must be pointed out that Sposito, even though under suspicion, was sent to Brasília by Tuma and became Tuma's adviser for many months.

One more "coincidence," among so many others about Sposito: Soon after Mendes's death, after Sposito had been transferred to Brasília, the former superintendent of the Federal Police in Acre met informally with Sueli Bellato, one of the lawyers who worked on the Mendes case for the prosecution, and politely introduced his companion, the lawyer João Branco, president of the UDR in Acre at the time of Chico's murder and director and shareholder of the newspaper *O Rio Branco*. He also had acted suspiciously, as I recounted above.

At this point, I would like to emphasize that there is no doubt whatsoever as to the planner of the crime. The depositions and Darci Alves Pereira's own confession are rich in details. The only divergence is that Darci insisted the whole time that he was alone when he committed the crime. This is not true, since he was seen fleeing accompanied by another person: "Mineirinho."

It is interesting to consider some more obvious details: When they reenacted the murder, before going to the site where the murderer retraced his path, the special investigators from São Paulo carried out a meticulous interrogation of Darci, in which he confessed details and precisely described the location of the crime, showing he had perfect knowledge of the site.

During this interrogation, Darci repeated to the police from São Paulo, "I did it myself, the man kept threatening my father. Every day in the papers, on the radio . . ."

He also outlined his actions on the day of the murder, saying he had decided to "do the crime" at about noon. He said he left home at about 1:00 P.M., walked some 25 kilometers to Xapuri, where he arrived at about 5:30 P.M., staying in town until it got dark. "So I arrived there. It was the time that the church bell rang. . . . It must have been about six o'clock. So I stayed about 20 or 30 meters [from the house]. There I committed the crime."

Asked where he was when he fired, he answered, "I was behind a coconut tree. In his backyard is where it is. . . . Well, I stayed behind the coconut tree. I arrived, there was a gate there. I went into his backyard. I saw the coconut tree there, got next to it, and stayed there, waiting. Soon after, he walked out."

Asked if he had taken anything with him, he was categorical: "I took a black rain cape." The description was of a rain cape found in the bushes behind Chico Mendes's house, between the house and the Acre River, close to the entrance to his backyard.

Asked how he shot and what the location was like, he did not hesitate: "I was sitting down on a pile of tiles next to the coconut tree."

He described Mendes at the moment of the crime: "I saw he had a towel on his shoulder. And he had a flashlight in his hand. Just a light. And I don't know if it was a towel he had on his shoulder . . . When he opened the door, the light from his house was on his face. That's how I knew it was him."

About the location of the house and its surroundings: "It's near the riverbank . . . I went down by the river . . . There's a fence where they stop cows from crossing the river. At the back of his house there's a grotto."

It is important to point out that Darci hid in the woods and ranches of the region until he was arrested after Chico's murder. It was impossible for him to know so many details that coincided with what the police had found without actually having been at the site at the time of the crime. At the back of Chico's backyard there was a wooden fence, with a small gate. Inside the backyard, a little behind the outhouse, about 9 meters, there was a coconut tree and next to it a pile of tiles.

Dr. Eduardo, of DEIC-SP, and Drs. Nelson Massini and Badan Palhares, both forensic scientists at Unicamp at the time, carried out the reenactment.[18]

Dr. Eduardo: Okay. What did you take with you?

Darci: The rifle.

Dr. Eduardo: What else?

Darci: The rifle, the rain cape, and a bag.

Dr. Eduardo: What did you have in the bag?

Darci: The cape.

Dr. Eduardo: Oh—you put the cape inside the bag?

Darci: Yeah, that's right.

Dr. Eduardo: What color is the bag?

Darci: The bag is black.

Dr. Eduardo: The black bag, Darci, what was it? A carryall that you'd put on your shoulder?

Darci: The kind you put on your back.

Dr. Eduardo: A backpack?

Darci: Yeah.

. . .

Dr. Eduardo: The weapon you carried in your hand. The backpack on your back. So you ran out, fired . . .

Darci: No. When I fired, I'd left the backpack in the bushes.

Dr. Eduardo: Ah! You'd left the backpack in the bushes.

Darci: Here, more or less around here. Here it's clean . . . and I'd left it on the edge of the woods, hanging on a branch (as he spoke, he gestured to exactly where he had left the backpack, and it coincided exactly with the place where it was found by police the day after Chico's murder).

Dr. Eduardo: Why?

Darci: When I ran away, I forgot it.

The clarity of the description of the crime and the site is obvious; the only thing that does not fit with other testimony in the case is the fact that two people were involved in carrying out the crime. (The other was Jardeir Pereira, "Mineirinho.")

When Darci reenacted the crime, he indicated the route he had followed, as well as places where he had stopped, where he had hidden the backpack and rain cape, details only somebody who was there at the time of the crime would know. Another important detail is that Darci always insisted he had been alone when he fired and had taken that route only once. These claims are belied by his thorough acquaintance with the place, the grotto between Chico's backyard and the Acre River, and the pile of tiles.

Another interesting fact, apparently small but which shows how well Darci knew the route, is that along the trail in the woods where he walked to get to Chico's house, there was a mango tree and below it a nylon bag on the ground. Darci said on the day of the crime it was hanging on a branch of the mango. Until the day before the reenactment it was there. While going over the route before the reenactment, Dr. Palhares cut the cord that tied the bag to the branch, to find out if anything was inside that could serve as evidence. There was not, but Darci knew where the bag was—that is, there is no doubt that he is one of the perpetrators of Mendes's murder. It would be interesting to know why he always protected Mineirinho.

The path in the woods bordering the river behind Chico's and neighboring houses showed signs of having been used countless times. And next to the place where Darci said he had left the backpack with the black rain cape was a 5-liter water bottle and various cigarette butts of different brands, showing that the gunmen had been lying in wait for several days, belying Darci's claim that he had decided to commit the crime on the same day he carried it out.

It is possible Chico was being targeted from the beginning of December 1988 and was not shot before then only because he was traveling to São Paulo, Rio de Janeiro, and later Sena Madureira, where he went to coordinate the meeting of the rubber tappers of the Purus Valley.

On December 15, when he celebrated his forty-fourth birthday, his friends gave Chico, who had arrived in Xapuri the day before, a small surprise party. At this party he received as a gift the towel he had on his shoulder at the moment he was shot. Perhaps he was not killed that day because several people were with him, and they could have reacted immediately. The gunmen must have decided to wait for another opportunity.

From a technical point of view, it should be emphasized that the experts from Unicamp who went to Acre after the crime analyzed a hair found on the black rain cape Darci mentioned in his deposition. Comparing it with a hair pulled out of his head by the gunman himself, they determined that the two were identical.

Several depositions said that after the fatal shot two people ran along the street a little above Chico's house. The mistress of one of the "Minas boys" confirmed this, testifying that she had heard her brother-in-law and Darci at about midnight on December 22 saying everything would be quieter because they had taken care of Chico Mendes. At trial this witness denied what she had said to the police; but she ended up contradicting herself so many times that the judge ordered an inquiry to investigate her for perjury.

As for the participation of Darli Alves da Silva, it became clear not only in the declaration of the court clerk but also because everybody knew that in the family the order to carry out any kind of "work"—or "corn-shucking" in the argot of the gunmen—always came from above. None of the sons of Darli or Alvarino would make any decision without his father's order. The testimony of a former cowboy on the Paraná Ranch makes everything clearer:

> Last December, he was doing his work [as a cowboy] on the Paraná Ranch, the property of Darli Alves da Silva. Two days after the killing of Francisco Alves Mendes Jr. [Chico Mendes], at about 3:00 P.M., the witness and Oloci Alves da Silva, went on horseback on the ranch to herd cattle. At this place, as they took care of the herd, Oloci Alves da Silva told the witness that those who had killed Chico Mendes would have been the people of Darci Alves da Silva, known as "Aparecido," and "Serginho" Jardeir Pereira, on the orders of Darli Alves da Silva. The witness also says Darci and Jardeir were afraid to commit the crime, *but at the insistence of their father, they decided to do it, and Darli Alves da Silva told them they would have to earn their long trousers.* [My emphasis.]

This deposition was transcribed from page 950 of Case No. 5929/89 and confirms a preliminary deposition of this witness during the police investigation that was disallowed before the judge of the Senator Guiomard district, where Alício Dias de Oliveira lived. To explain why this testimony was disallowed, the witness said Darli's lawyer had coached him. In court, in front of the lawyer, he did not have the courage to repeat this, but he stood by his testimony incriminating Darli.

The Alves da Silva family has an extremely bloody history, with many pages marked by lead and blood, from Ipanema, Pocrane, and Conselheiro Pena in Minas Gerais to Umuarama and its outlying areas in western Paraná, until they arrived in Acre, where their bloody and cowardly acts continued.

In Xapuri a story circulates that when the family arrived there in the early 1970s, the family patriarch, Sebastião Alves, now dead, introduced himself as the pastor of an evangelical church he had founded and even spoke on the radio about the "goodness of God," claiming this as an example of his conversion and saying he had killed many people until he was converted. The pastor said he actually had not killed anybody, because "we pull the trigger, and if it fires it's because God let it, because He is the source of life."

The crimes perpetrated by the Alves family in Xapuri, especially those immediately before Chico's murder, were all registered during the trial in depositions by the witness Genésio Barbosa da Silva, who was fourteen years old at the time, and whose sister was Oloci's wife. He was being trained to be a gunman. But he decided to make a different choice.

I should repeat that the possible participation of some local ranchers and politicians interested in the elimination of Chico Mendes, as financiers and/or intellectual authors, was never investigated.

Darli, the Gunmen, and the Plot to Kill Chico Mendes

The empate at Cachoeira in March 1988 has always been cited as the main reason Chico Mendes was killed by Darci Alves Pereira, son of Darli Alves da Silva, at Darli's orders in December of that year.

It's important to know that Darci and Darli were only the snake's tail in a plot that was well under way at the time. It included important participants who never have been exposed or held responsible for the assassination of Chico Mendes as they should be, since they were the true intellectual authors who financed this crime, directly or indirectly.

The year 1988 was one among many when the "Alves family," which already had killed people in Minas Gerais during the 1950s, then in Paraná in the 1960s and early 1970s, committed violent acts. They also are suspected of many other unsolved crimes during the 1970s and 1980s in Xapuri township.

This family, whose patriarch, Sebastião Alves da Silva, died a few years ago, arrived in Xapuri around 1973, on the lam from Paraná, with three members suspected or accused of crimes: "Old Man" Sebastião himself, suspected of planning several crimes in Minas, and Darli and Alvarino Alves, also accused of crimes there and in Paraná.

The Alves are still feared, decades later, in all these areas. In 1996, when Darli was sent to Umuarama to be tried for a crime he had ordered near there in the 1960s, it was possible to see how much he was feared. To give an idea of the terror he aroused, a witness who was a retired policeman showed up for the trial in disguise, wearing a wig. I heard many stories about the violence of the Alves family, both in Xapuri and in Umuarama. To this day the family has been tried only for the assassination of Chico Mendes and the attack on the rubber tappers' occupation of the IBDF in Xapuri at the beginning of 1988, after the Equador empate. In that case Darci and Oloci, Darli's sons, were sentenced to twelve years each. Names of members of this family or gunmen linked to them appear in several other cases, but the proceedings have been stalled in Xapuri for more than a decade.

After the events at Cachoeira, Darli, financed by unknown people, kept about twenty-five gunmen permanently at his ranch. I counted them once. This was when state police from Xapuri detained four of them because they were bathing in the river wearing only their underpants. They were taken to the police station. Soon after, Darli went to his ranch and returned with the gunmen and his brother Alvarino. He left them in front of the station, on the other side of the street, and went in alone. He came out with the four who had been detained.

I was in front of my house in Xapuri, talking with two friends, when Alvarino and twenty-five gunmen came along. I counted them one by one. Darli was walking around town with several more.

After May 1988, almost every day, two gunmen were in the square in front of my house. Or if they weren't, they arrived soon after. It was the same in front of the union hall, where it was common to see Darci, the guy who killed Chico Mendes, and one other. They didn't do anything; they merely watched everything we were doing. They were always armed, but the police never approached them.

The gunmen kept changing during 1988. We always were very attentive to this, since it could be a matter of life or death. It was very easy to identify a gunman who was new to the area. They always arrived dressed as gunmen. They had their own way of speaking, with a backwoods accent, rolling their *r*'s like northeasterners or Paraguayans. Also, they used to eat tapioca (a typical regional food made from manioc) with Coca-Cola for breakfast.

We monitored the presence of these gunmen all the time. So when they "disappeared" the week before Chico Mendes's killing, I got worried because I had no way to check on them, and I knew they were plotting something terrible. I sensed this.

1988: "The Presence of Death"

During 1988, in light of the tension permeating Xapuri, all of us knew we could be killed at any moment. There were lists of those marked for death. Several of us were on all the lists, almost always headed by Chico Mendes but always including others from the movement or Moacyr Grechi, the Catholic bishop of the Rio Branco diocese.

There was a scary, foreboding atmosphere, since every day gunmen were in Xapuri—five, six, ten of them walking armed through the town. At any moment a murder could be committed, since the police did nothing or pretended they saw nothing.

The first time I thought seriously that I could be killed was on June 6, 1988. I was going from Xapuri to Rio Branco to arrange for the printing of

Ventania, the newspaper published by the Workers' Party municipal committee in Xapuri, and to have my motorbike fixed. I was alone and unarmed. When I arrived at Araxá, a restaurant on the road where the bus stopped, I decided to stop and see how the motorbike was doing, since it had an oil leak, and have a snack.

When I went into the restaurant, I felt a chill go up my spine. Waiting there was José Brito, who had gone to work for Darli after selling his holding to him, plus a gunman I didn't know. I saw death in his eyes. His gaze was as cold as a razor. I thought to myself, "I'm dead." Nobody else was there.

Zeca Brito, who knew me, pulled the other gunman to the porch in front. I thought, "Good, since they're going to kill me, they'll kill a guy who didn't run. I'm going to have a bite to eat and pretend I didn't notice anything." I asked for a meat pie and a soft drink. The unknown gunman came back in by himself and sat next to me. Perhaps feeling the chill in the air, the server, who wasn't doing anything, asked, "Is something going on?" With a harsh northeastern twang, the gunman answered, "No. We're just waitin' on a creep finish what he's a-doin' to see how we'll settle things with him."

Obviously the gunman was referring to me as I ate my snack. I felt it was a provocation. He was waiting for me to ask him, "Is it with me?" He would answer yes and perhaps empty his revolver into me. Well, "a creep" in those circumstances wasn't me, nor did it have to be, you know? I kept quiet, calmly eating as if nothing was happening. I knew Zeca Brito was a big zero. I didn't have to worry about him. I was totally ready for an attack by the gunman who was three feet away from me. If he moved, I'd jump him, and if I was going to die, I'd die fighting.

If anybody had tested my nerves at that moment, it might have been possible to play the violin on them, but outwardly I stayed calm. I finished eating, paid, grabbed my helmet, put on my backpack and helmet, and left walking normally. Feeling the bullets in my back, I went to the motorbike, looked idly at him and thought, "Good, I'll try to make the gunmen's work harder." I got on the bike, turned it on, accelerated as hard as I could, and let out the clutch. The bike jumped forward and I left zigzagging. Nothing happened, but I believe that day I escaped death by a little, very little.

Another time, during the second half of 1988, after they had killed Ivair Higino, I caught the "big crow," the night bus from Brasiléia that stopped in Xapuri on its way to Rio Branco. In Xapuri only three people got on: me, a local rancher, who went to his ranch about 10 kilometers outside town, and a young gunman, who was put on the bus by "Little Darli," Darli's son.

It was beastly hot, maybe about 85 degrees, late at night. I was in shorts and a T-shirt, and, as always, with my bag on my shoulder. The gunman, aside from his costume—jeans, a belt with an enormous buckle, cowboy boots, a hat—had a jacket rolled up in his hand. This was very strange considering how hot it was. I saw Little Darli buy him a ticket only as far as Quinari, as Senator Guiomard township, 25 kilometers from Rio Branco, is known to those from Xapuri.

I got on the bus. In the seat where I was going to sit, a passenger who had come from Brasiléia and gotten off in Xapuri had left a news magazine. I picked it up. The gunman got on and sat in the seat behind mine. I thought, "OK, I'll play a mind game with him." I sat across both seats, since the bus was almost empty, pushed one of the seats back and left the other one upright, put my hands on my shoulder bag, and looked at the gunman, as if I were saying, "Draw your gun!" Like every other gunman I've ever met, this one wouldn't look me in the eye. He looked up, saw I was facing him, and lowered his eyes. It was a cat-and-mouse game until Araxá.

The bus stopped and we got off. The gunman got back on before me, and when I came on, he had the magazine I'd picked up in Xapuri. He asked in a loud voice, "Does this magazine belong to somebody?" It wasn't mine. I'd found it on the bus. I kept quiet. Once again it was a provocation that I didn't rise to. He didn't know what to do and said, "So if it doesn't belong to anybody, I'm going to read it!" He shouted so that the bus driver would turn on the reading light, leafed through a couple of pages of motorcycle ads, as I could see clearly because I was watching him from the seats on the other side of the bus. He shut the magazine and let it go.

Didn't I say that the magazine was only a provocation?

We kept going, and I suddenly realized the gunman was dozing. I took advantage of the fact that it was dark inside the bus and went to the back, keeping an eye out. After a few minutes, all of a sudden the bus hit a pothole. The gunman woke up and immediately looked at the seat where I'd been sitting. I wasn't there. He got upset, stood up, walked through the whole bus, only calming down when he saw me, watching him from the back. He returned to his seat and turned around from time to time to make sure I hadn't changed places.

We arrived at Quinari. The gunman didn't get off the bus at the bus station. I thought, "Things are going to get complicated." When we were almost outside the city, he got up and asked the driver if he could get off the bus, saying he'd been sleeping and missed his stop. This was not true. I'd watched him the whole time and knew he hadn't dozed off again. What happened in fact was that he hadn't succeeded in carrying out his "agreement" with Little Darli. He got scared because he thought I was armed. The worst thing was that I had no weapon on me. But he didn't know this, and since he saw I was very secure, he decided not to take the risk. Gunmen are almost always quite cowardly, so they take people by surprise or in an ambush. Those who show courage when they kill somebody are rare.

The Story of the "Federal Police" Infiltrator

Sometime in 1988, between the killing of Ivair Higino in June and Chico Mendes in December, a woman I didn't know approached me in front of the Rural Workers' Union hall in Xapuri, saying she needed to talk with me. I said she could talk right there. She said she couldn't and asked me to look for her.

I didn't think much about it. About three days went by. I met the woman in the street, and she asked why I hadn't sought her out. I said I didn't know her name or where to find her. She repeated that she needed to speak with me. I invited her to go into the union hall. She said it couldn't be there. I asked if we could meet in the CTA office, where I lived. She answered that I should go there and she would join me there soon. I went. I turned on the radio because the office was cheek by jowl with the house of a right-wing city councilor and waited for the woman.

When she arrived she was nervous and wanted to know if the house was safe. I answered no, but the sound of the radio would ensure that the neighbor wouldn't overhear what she had to tell me.

So she told me she was a Federal Police agent working undercover and had made friends with Darli's daughters. Having gone to his ranch several times, she already knew he had heavy weapons and machine guns.

I asked why nothing had been done if the feds already knew what all of us knew. She answered laconically that she "only wrote reports." Then she said in fact that wasn't what she wanted to tell me but rather that I was running the risk of being killed. She said several of my comrades were on a death list.

She said on one of the visits she had made to Darli's Paraná Ranch, Darci, Oloci, and other gunmen were target shooting and she had picked up a revolver and brought down a bird at a considerable distance. When he saw this Darci took her aside and asked how much she wanted to kill me. She said she'd replied that she wasn't interested and she'd hit the bird only by chance.

According to her, Darci had asked how much she would want to get close to me and take me to a place in Rio Branco where they would arrange for me to be killed. She said she didn't have the courage to do that, but Darci gave her a deadline, which was about to expire, for her to give him an answer. She told me the next day she'd answer that she wouldn't do the job, but she wanted to warn me, since another woman could be contracted for the same purpose.

She also said Darci and Oloci were learning how to shoot from a moving XL 250 motorcycle, one driving and the other firing, to get me on the road, while I was going to or coming back from Rio Branco. She begged me to be careful, because she would have to disappear from Xapuri.

I never did find out if the story was true or if it was just an invention, but at that time it was very possible that there really was such a plan.

Why Did They Kill Chico Mendes?

There are various responses to why Chico Mendes was killed, depending on one's point of view and political or administrative position.

In my opinion Chico's murder has extremely complex aspects that go far beyond the official version embraced by the media, in which Chico was killed in "revenge" because he went after Darli Alves, and this motivated the crime, according to the testimony of his son, Darci Alves Pereira, convicted as the executioner of the rubber tapper leader.

This version was the most plausible at that moment because it closed the Chico Mendes case, leaving it "completely clarified," explaining who the killers and the intellectual author were and leaving nothing more to investigate.

That Darli could have been encouraged to plan Chico's death is quite probable, but for him to have done it without any kind of support or encouragement already has been shown to be extremely unlikely, since he was not representing his own interests in the conflict over the Cachoeira rubber estate.

For the media and the authorities of the time, with the case closed as it was, many questions that they still present as crystal clear and official sources do not bother to answer could be left unexplained. I will deal with these questions further on.

To trace a brief history of the background of this crime, which had national and international repercussions, it is necessary to tell the story of the twenty-five years before Chico's murder.

For many years concern about the Amazon had been increasing around the world and was by no means irrelevant to the Brazilian government. Perceiving all the attention that the region already was getting, the armed forces, which governed the country from 1964 to 1985 through a dictatorship, soon sought to include Amazonia in its planning as a very important geostrategic region.

Since Amazonia is a strategically important area, the military developed megalomaniacal projects implemented during the period known as the "Brazilian Miracle" with the opening of highways and the occupation of the region, which remained "of interest to national security."

Also long-standing is the world's great financial and industrial conglomerates' economic interest in the Amazon's riches, such as timber and mineral deposits, including radioactive ores. The process of internationalizing the region, accomplished with the military's agreement, connivance, and participation, permitted these multinational capitalist groups to acquire immense forested areas in an unprecedented way.

Brazilian economic interests also acquired immense landholdings in the Amazon region during the military dictatorship, with the aim of promoting speculation and even mineral extraction on their "properties."

Besides allowing the acquisition of millions of hectares by large economic enterprises, the Brazilian government increasingly financed—with funds borrowed at subsidized rates—the entire process of the region's occupation, consistently favoring the big landowners and the economic groups that acquired Amazon lands at an extremely high economic and social price, as may be seen today.

The environmental degradation that continues in Amazonia—especially along the highways included in the Brazilian government's strategic planning, such as Belém-Brasília, Cuiabá-Santarém, the Transamazon, and, most recently, the BR-364 from Cuiabá to Porto Velho and Rio Branco—became so blatant that environmental organizations around the world became increasingly concerned. For their part, they started pressuring the multilateral development banks (the World Bank and the Inter-American Development Bank) to stop financing devastation.

In October 1985, the Rural Workers' Union of Xapuri, then directed by Chico, organized and carried out the First National Meeting of Rubber Tappers in Brasília.

During the meeting, the rubber tappers discussed their problems and the difficulties they faced and sought solutions, especially to the land question and the government's support for the big landowners. In opposition, the participants in the First National Meeting of Rubber Tappers launched a proposal to create extractive reserves, which gave them full visibility, first internationally and later nationally.

This proposal for extractive reserves was a great discovery for all those who were extremely worried about the devastation of the Amazon and who always ran up against the same argument from the Brazilian government: "We can't let 54 percent of our territory be transformed into an 'ecological reserve.' It's necessary to develop that area."

The rubber tappers' proposal made clear that the forest would be used productively, and thus it advanced a plan that had already existed for a long time but was neither known about nor disseminated: development of the region by its traditional populations. The National Rubber Tappers' Council's defense of this propose and its worldwide promotion of the rubber tappers' struggle to defend the forest led to Chico Mendes's receiving two international prizes during his lifetime.

For Acre at that time the big project was the paving of the BR-364 highway from Porto Velho to Rio Branco, completed in the early 1990s. A third of the financing for the work came from the World Bank.

Pressured by environmental organizations around the world but especially groups in North America, the World Bank required that to receive financing the Brazilian government must develop a "Program of Protection of the Environment and Indigenous Communities" (PMACI) in the entire area affected by the paving, which included part of Rondônia, half of Acre, and part of southern Amazonas state.

An interministerial working group was created to plan PMACI. Its coordination was the responsibility of IPEA, part of the president's planning secretariat. As time passed and as a result of pressure by the World Bank, which was continually pressured by the environmentalists, and the mobilization of rubber tappers and Indians, the working group had to listen to local communities. That was when the force that was really behind the planning, the National Security Council (NSC), as revealed by the agreement with the World Bank, entered the scene. For the NSC, Amazonia, even in "transition," would continue to be considered "an area of national security interest," understood as an area of military interest.

As for "private enterprise": Looking to take back lands conserved until then as reserve value in financial capital, the ranchers energetically resumed attempts at massive deforestation not only as a way to expel squatters from the areas but also to increase the land's value by creating pasturage.

These attempts at deforestation, especially in areas such as Xapuri and Brasiléia, where the rubber tappers were more organized, always encountered resistance in the form of empates. The rubber tappers already had gained exposure in the national and international media. Thus the empate stopped being an action with limited, local repercussions and began to acquire importance as a form of resistance supported beyond the regions where it occurred.

With the empates, Xapuri was the focal point of rubber tapper resistance. In that township, where Chico was president of the Rural Workers' Union and had already become known and rewarded internationally, the ranchers were always threatening to use brute force. But many did not believe they would go so far as to kill someone because of this organized resistance.

It must be kept in mind that at that time Acre's traditional politicians, who kept alternating in power for decades under the old "father to son" system, began to view the political ascent of Chico, an "illiterate rubber tapper," as they used to call him, with considerable anxiety. Meanwhile, the struggle in defense of the forest began to worry the region's old-time politicians, all of whom were connected to national and international economic interests.

Chico represented the "other side," and the traditional politicians feared outright confrontation with the Workers' Party (PT).[19] After the PT's victory in several state capitals and big cities in 1988, this concern grew considerably. In their opinion it was necessary to prevent Chico's possible candidacy for the governorship of Acre in 1990.

In early 1988 Darli Alves da Silva, the gunman who doubled as a rancher, "bought" 25 percent—about 6,000 hectares—of the Cachoeira rubber estate in Xapuri township and prepared to enter the area at all costs.

The rubber tappers of Cachoeira and several neighboring estates organized and discussed resistance. The union's mobilization, which developed while the occupation of the estate was already taking place, brought rubber tappers to the area from almost the entire township. This organized resistance discouraged Darli from even trying to enter the estate. This reduced his prestige as a bad man, a killer.

So as has been shown, a series of "interests" would be served perfectly by Chico's death. Any of those involved could do the crime, but if all of them got together it would be easier to kill the rubber tapper leader.

~~~~~~~~~~~~~~~~~~~~~~~~~~~~~

Chapter 2

A VERY DIFFICULT BEGINNING

PEOPLE ASK ME if I'm from Acre. I say not by birth but by choice, since I was born in Mato Grosso do Sul, where I trained as an agronomist. So they ask how I came to be in Xapuri. This is a long story. Maybe by telling it I can recover a little of the history of the rubber tappers' movement in Xapuri.

January 1986: The meeting had already been delayed too long. The atmosphere was extremely tense, and making the situation worse was the fact that Chico Mendes and other members of the union's central committee were not there, although the meeting had been scheduled long before.

The purpose of the meeting was to evaluate the activities of the Rubber Tapper Project over nearly five years of existence, analyzing two of its key aspects: the literacy project on the rubber estates and the establishment of small cooperatives in those areas.

I was to try to make a technical (and political!) diagnosis by analyzing everybody's comments about why the experimental cooperatives hadn't worked. This was my first experience of working with the rubber tappers. I had not been acquainted with Xapuri until that day in January 1986. For all intents and purposes, I was a "neutral bystander" and therefore could not understand the reason for so much tension at that early date.

Only three members of the central committee, along with some others, were there, but the leader, the president, Chico Mendes, was absent. Aware of the atmosphere of the meeting and determined to avoid a direct confrontation with comrades he had worked with until then—a conflict that, in his opinion, was absolutely unnecessary and could be overcome in time—he had decided not to participate and had gone to his homestead. (This is the rubber tapper's production unit, where he lives and works, extracting latex for production of rubber, collecting nuts, cultivating subsistence crops, raising animals, such as chickens, pigs, a few cows.)

This increased the difficulties of having a quiet meeting. The person who had to take charge was "Big Raimundo" (Raimundo Mendes de Barros, Chico's cousin and his deputy on the committee).

During the meeting, what I heard was worth a whole specialized course on rubber tapper organization, adult education, the history of the occupation of Amazonia by extractivists, and the search for solutions to the crisis that had been obvious to the forest's inhabitants for a long time.

The diagnosis by the rubber tappers and their coworkers on the Rubber Tapper Project was very realistic and, at the same time, rather worrisome to somebody participating in such a meeting for the first time. What caught my attention was the obvious honesty with which the analyses were made. I'll reproduce parts of two analyses, taken from the transcript of the meeting on file at the Rubber Tapper Project.

Raimundo: "All I want is for the comrades not to get disgusted over time. I'll try to say some of the many things I'm feeling and thinking about what has happened during the four years since we started this work with the staff of the Rubber Tapper Project, and with the schools, since we union members already have seven, going on eight, years' experience.

"I remember well that about five or six years ago, I decided to leave town and go to the rubber estates, and about seven months later we met two comrades, Marlete and Fatima, at our house. That in itself impressed me, since I hadn't thought that one day they'd arrive there and say they'd come back again. That made us very happy.

"And in fact, two or three months later, only one comrade returned, Marlete, this time with Ronaldo, who I'd met for the first time on the road to Boca do Acre, where I was involved in a working group called Catch the Gunman, because we managed to catch a few of the hired guns who were leading a reign of terror. . . .

"A little while later, we started a school in Nazaré.[1] This got attention in Floresta and São Pedro.[2] During that period, we had already met and discussed union matters and how to generate more profit from rubber, which still was being delivered to the boss at the time.[3] That's how things went out there, and the one thing that's clear is that the school at Nazaré started up at the homestead known today as Already Hungry.

"Those of us from Floresta, who were also interested in a school, started contacting them to take care of these matters, asking for help because they were linked to others in Rio Branco. We started making demands.

"At that time disagreements had already emerged, and we started to encounter problems. Perhaps because we weren't close by or because they were threatened by our wanting to do things by ourselves, we didn't get along with them, and so there were problems.

"It's clear that in all our work, whenever hassles come up, we can learn to meet, sit down, discuss what's happening to improve our work. But mostly, and maybe always, it has been otherwise: One person starts listening to somebody over there, and another starts listening to somebody over here, and everybody gets annoyed, and everything falls apart.

"If the method that's starting today, of meeting and discussing the problem to see if it's possible to find a way to improve the work, had been applied from the beginning . . . but no, people have a falling-out as a result of gossip or something else. . . .

"I recall I was alone at home, and when they arrived, they treated me differently than they had before. They arrived and stayed by themselves in the front room, because I was very busy in the kitchen. I had to take care of the kitchen, take care of the animals, take care of one thing or another, and they stayed by themselves in the front room.

"When I laid out the food and stepped into the front room, it was completely dark, and they were sleeping on the *paxiuba*[4] benches. I thought the comrade would remember, and I said, somewhat disgusted, 'What are you doing this for? Here you are in the house, you don't have to do something like this. Why don't you come into the kitchen and ask for a hammock? If you haven't brought one, we've got one here, and you don't have to do something like this.'

"The schools in Floresta and São Pedro were built, and the one at Nazaré was operating, and the one at Nova Esperança was built, and frankly, as a native of Xapuri and a rubber tapper, I've never seen a project like this ever before, and I thought we were making a great step forward.

"They were responsible, the initiators. And who knows, perhaps it was because of the change in our union in Xapuri, which gave an opportunity to these outsiders, which met these new people and tried to get to know them and started working with them. So the last time we were talking, when I proposed that the union shouldn't break with the Rubber Tapper Project staff or the schools, and that the schools and the project staff shouldn't break with the union, it was because it was work based on the union's work, and one was helping the other.

"I don't see why the moment has arrived when it's necessary for one to go his way and the other to go the other way. I think this is ridiculous. Depending on the outcome of our meeting today, I insist we try to unify this relationship and this work and, who knows, improve it.

"As for continuity, for some time we've noticed a certain neglect—whether deliberate or inadvertent, I can't say—by our comrades of the Rubber Tapper Project."

Pedro Teles:[5] "Mary asked Raimundo if the union had grown since the schools opened. I didn't think it has, because most people don't recognize that the schools were the union's work. It was the people who arrived here and went to the forest, accompanied by interested union people, who were responsible for the schools on the rubber estates. And even today, not even the students themselves are aware of this. They think the people from the city had this in mind, that they dreamed up the idea of putting a school in this or that place.

"They don't think it was a joint project, that the people who fought for the school really were from the union. And so the union hasn't grown. In my opinion, it's fallen down when it could have grown, because there was this development and this point in its favor that could have been considered.

"The union fell because it was certain that these schools would make the union grow. The union fell because while the schools were appearing the union's central committee forgot to do the outreach work it used to do."

So the whole day was taken up with washing dirty linen, evaluations of all the steps and obstacles the Rubber Tapper Project was encountering. I participated as an observer of everything related to the schools. As for the idea of a cooperative, which should have been the vanguard of the project—after hearing everybody, in a very quick and obviously superficial evaluation resulting from my deep ignorance of the situation, I summed up: "I haven't followed the Rubber Tapper Project. But from what I've seen here in relation to a specific topic and the questioning of cooperativism itself, I want to say that cooperativism is not the system that resolves the problem and is only a way of ameliorating problems.

"From what I've heard here and now, and from the little I've discussed with Nonato[6] today, I believe there were some obvious conceptual distortions that led to this. A cooperative for Marlete and a cooperative for Nonato are two completely different things.

"First, this cooperative is being proposed as a solution, as a socialist form of work within a capitalist system. That is, it grows out of a completely incorrect assumption. So either everything is changed or this cooperative is set up to work within a capitalist framework, because you can't work with the cooperative in a socialist way and in relation to the state, to business, and have a capitalist relationship. It won't work, because the two things don't go together; they can't fit into the same box.

"As for the question of paternalism, I spoke today with Nonato. The money is there, and if we have the project, we can set up a storage facility and the whole business. So let's go out and do it. The cooperative will work out, we can buy this and that, it's very easy, and the rubber tappers will have a front-row seat. It's fine, the motor[7] and other things are on their way, and they'll applaud when it's there, when they're earning without greater involvement.

"And the problem is exactly that. If the rubber tapper doesn't gain maturity by understanding this as the beginning of an entire process that's intended to develop something, that it isn't being built for its own sake—if he doesn't have this conception, as long as he's getting what he needs, it's fine. But later, when he has to start using it and making it start producing on its own and working on its own, then everything gets complicated. Because he was only receiving, and all of a sudden he has to put something of his own into it—then the business gets complicated.

"If it starts out like this, it's coming from a false assumption.

"In relation to the issue of outside actors, the members can and must decide: If we have a surplus, what are we going to do with it? Are we going to divide it among all of us, or will we invest in the cooperative? This is the role of the member. But to coordinate, gather the product, do the accounting, bring the merchandise to the city, that's not the rubber tapper's role. If it were, he'd have to leave his work of tapping rubber to be a cooperative worker—an unpaid worker, because during the time he lost in the cooperative, he'd earn nothing.

"So he starts questioning this. To succeed, the cooperative will have to have somebody administering it who would be paid for his work. The cooperative itself should pay for it. Now the problem has to be discussed from the beginning. If the guy dividing his time loses a week of work or four weeks of work, how much would each one lose as a result of the work he didn't do? If each loses 60 kilos of rubber and there are three people, that's 180 kilos of rubber per week and 720 per month, which means, at today's prices, a little more than 7 million cruzeiros. If a person were paid to do this at 3 million, that would be good pay, with an accumulation of 4,200,000 cruzeiros for the work he stopped doing. So this has to be discussed with him.

"In fact, there was a very puritanical concept of a cooperative. When it began to have a very pure concept, that wiped it out. Why are we going to have a stranger working in the cooperative? It has to be the rubber tapper who's running it. But the rubber tapper never had a concept of a cooperative, he's never seen it, how is he suddenly going to absorb this understanding and put it in practice? Then everything gets mixed up in his head.

"This issue of professionalism, of somebody who works, who manages, could even create prospects for the rubber tapper's son, to be trained as a manager. If his son can study there or even outside—I don't know what kind of school this would be, that's also something that has to be thoroughly questioned and discussed—afterward he'd return to work in the cooperative. The rubber tapper's dream is that his son not be the same as he is. Every farmworker, every rubber tapper, every poor man dreams of being rich. This is their big dream, because the whole society creates this. So there are possibilities of creating prospects for his son.

"Are the prospects the cooperative opens up only to market and buy rubber, to transport the merchandise, and so on? Couldn't this cooperative open up the possibility of seedling and seed production, crop cultivation, technical assistance? The initiative starts to get complicated, but either it creates these prospects or its momentum stops.

"So what prospects does the cooperative create? What does the cooperative have that I can make use of? The cooperative has to open this window. And I think that's where the issue of an entity that could advise comes in.

"I've felt this in a short time here. What I've heard is that there really was a lot of puritanism in this concept. The obstacle really was this obsession with purity. And it's good that it exists, because we have to search for it. The problem is to get to the point of really having it from one moment to the next. You can't do it."

That is how I entered the lives of the rubber tappers—or rather, that's how the rubber tappers entered my life and taught me much of what I know today.

Baptism of Fire (with Lots of Water!)

Since the afternoon of the day before, I had been preparing to endure the boat trip on the Xapuri River to the São Pedro rubber estate, seven hours upriver. My expectations kept growing; at last I'd enter a rubber estate for the first time, an experience I believed would be interesting.

But it wasn't only that. We'd take a survey that could result in a diagnosis of the situation, so we could find out why the experimental cooperatives had failed on the rubber estates, comparing them with areas where no such organizations had existed. As we had discussed with the union's central committee, the evaluation would try to take an "X-ray" of the rubber tappers' situation in their areas. For this reason the questionnaire was very open-ended and had a total of ten pages, in addition to a manual that included regional terms and would comprise part of the experience accumulated by our comrades Manoel Estébio and Armando of the Rubber Tapper Project, which I was monitoring. I also had to take an "intensive course" from the two comrades to be able to understand the local situation in a general way, so as not to compromise the work.

The questionnaire that we took tried to provide a detailed look at the rubber tapper's life—for example, what radio station he listened to, how many hours he liked to work, and what kinds of home remedies he knew about and how he used them, as well as what kind of crops he grew and his cultivation techniques. In short, the questionnaire was intended to be a diagnosis of reality.

On the morning of February 12, 1986, in the middle of the Amazon winter—which, as I already mentioned, is the rainy season in the region—I woke up early and full of expectations, but the journey was delayed. We left at about 9:00 A.M. on a boat piloted by Negão. I had never traveled by boat, and water is not my element, and I didn't feel safer in a small boat.

About an hour and a half later, going up the winding river, which did not present many navigational problems because it was quite high, we passed the ranch belonging to the Bordon Group, one of the ones it had deforested most extensively in Xapuri township in recent years. The company was one of the rubber tappers' greatest enemies in the region. For three hours I watched ruined shacks, especially on the left bank. On the right side was the area that had been the Nazaré rubber estate, which was not completely destroyed thanks to the rubber tappers, who had carried out countless empates there.

The deforestation I saw in passing was criminal, with the upper forest clear-cut. Consequently the riverbanks were extremely eroded. The pasture, which went on as far as the eye could see, was full of weeds. Cattle, the justification for the deforestation, were nowhere to be seen.

Farther ahead was the deforested Tupã rubber estate, more or less in the same condition, and a little farther along was the Vista Alegre Ranch, which had practically destroyed the Tupinambá rubber estate, part of the Full Moon estate, and all of Vista Alegre. The legal requirement to conserve half the area was completely ignored.[8]

Lunch was cheese, a sweet, crackers, and a banana. Afterward I began my apprenticeship in getting water from the river to drink while the boat was moving. The first few times I succeeded only in getting wet when I tried to put a can in the water. So they taught me to make a quick movement with the can held tight, banging it hard and straight into the water so it would go under the surface.

At four in the afternoon, I was already sore all over, since the small boat didn't offer many options for changing position. I was sitting down almost the whole time, burned by the strong sun that beat down on us during seven hours in the boat. Then the comrades who knew the region told us we were arriving at the borders of São Pedro.

We landed and disembarked with our backpacks. As a result of inexperience, I was carrying a very heavy pack, with several changes of clothes, a hammock, and a sheet, in addition to the questionnaires. This would have bad consequences and teach me something else: When you walk in the forest, especially the Amazon forest, the less the weight of the bag you carry and the more waterproof it is, the better it is for you.

After arriving and greeting the owner of the house, Jaci, a longtime rubber tapper in the area who had become a *marreteiro,*[9] we went to take a shower and put up our hammocks. There I had another technique to learn. Not only didn't I know how to tie the rope of the hammock, I didn't know how to sleep in one. Two lessons at the same time. First they taught me how to put up the hammock. Obviously I didn't get it right the first time. In the days after I kept asking the comrade who went with us as a guide to help me with this task, which seemed as difficult to me as tying a tie, which I learned a few years later when I absolutely had to, when I was graduating from law school.

Before sleeping we were faced with a big dinner, which included "toasted" (fried) wild boar meat and monkey in Brazil nut sauce. It's said this was Chico Mendes's favorite dish as a rubber tapper. It really is delicious. And for the ecologists who might be horrified by this information, I have only one excuse: Hunting to eat, as the rubber tapper does, does not exterminate a species. It's predatory hunting done by people from the cities who invade the rubber estates, using trained dogs, that decimates animal species.

Does sleeping in a hammock require skill? I guarantee it does. I learned this precisely because I doubted the instructions of the comrades and slept with my body following the hammock's curve. It was hard to sleep. So I decided to follow their instructions and slept on the diagonal. It felt like I was lying on a spring mattress, and I slept extremely well.

The next morning, as we had arranged the night before, the three of us, Manoel Estébio, Armando, and I, went out, each following a different line,[10] agreeing to meet two days later at the Itapissuma homestead, where Simplício, one of the community leaders of São Pedro, lived, three hours' walk from the Xapuri River along the main line.

Naturally, since I had no knowledge of the rubber estate, I went with Raimundo—"Tatá"—a rubber tapper from the area, as a guide. Administering the questionnaire was not difficult, although each one took about an hour to fill out completely. As for the walk, I had to go fast to keep up with the rhythm Tatá imposed. After some time I discovered he was only testing me. It was a way of establishing the superiority he knew he had over me, since I had no experience walking along landings, fords, or even a dogleg. Years later, after my apprenticeship, I managed to pay back Tatá, when he couldn't keep up with my pace on a hike. I didn't pass up the opportunity to remind him of this.

As for landings, fords, doglegs, I didn't know how to distinguish one from another. For me, the forest was all of a piece; sometimes it seemed as if we were walking in circles, since we would go through places similar to ones we had already passed. Gradually I put together the explanations Manoel Estébio and Armando had given me with the information collected from the rubber tappers themselves.

A landing is a main trail, normally more open and frequently traveled, with bridges (which are sometimes tree trunks no more than 15 centimeters around that cross tiny tributaries). The landing makes it possible to more or less follow a line between homesteads located varying distances apart, sometimes fifteen minutes, sometimes ninety minutes.

The landings are located inside a rubber estate and formerly were the supply and product collection trails for the bosses. These trails used to accommodate pack animals, making them different from fords. The latter is a shortcut that usually links homesteads on different lines or even different estates. Normally it is a smaller trail, less traveled, and pack animals or vehicles don't use it.

A beach often includes doglegs, which are parts of rubber estate trails. Since the rubber trail is usually full of turns, the ford bypasses them because its purpose is to arrive more quickly at a neighboring homestead. Usually a ford includes the doglegs of two homesteads and sometimes even of a third homestead between the other two.

The homestead is the productive unit inside the rubber estate. It is where the rubber tapper lives, builds his house, has his rubber trails (at least three, in the Xapuri region), plants his crops, hunts, fishes, chops wood and gathers straw to construct his house, and collects fruits—in sum, fully exercises his rights of ownership. A rubber estate is made up of several (sometimes dozens) of homesteads. Each homestead is bounded by several rubber trails.

Once I heard someone saying the rubber estate is a "big expanse of land." I corrected him right away. The estate is a big expanse of forest, since for rubber tappers, "land" is what's least important. The most important thing is the *forest* from which the rubber tapper extracts his sustenance. This correction is absolutely necessary because it involves an ideological component: For the ranchers who arrived in the region at the end of the 1960s and the beginning of the 1970s, what was important was the thousands of hectares of land. For the rubber tappers, what is important is the forest, the rubber trails, the homesteads, and their ownership. It is a different way of seeing the same world. In fact, these are two worlds, since one seeks to preserve while the other doesn't know how to produce without destroying.

It is interesting to recall that each homestead has a name, often completely incomprehensible, for the area, such as Switzerland, Japan, Europe. Sometimes the name is a combination of words: "Already Hungry," "Start Right Away," "Whoever Wants, Goes." Others describe the great distances between the old barns, such as "Moon Tower," "Desert," "Hell." The names are very varied and often repeated, although this is more common on remote estates.

Between the homesteads each rubber trail[11] has a name, usually the direction where it is and referring to the closest homestead in that direction. But sometimes the trails are named after events, such as "jaguar trail" (related to the fact that some rubber tapper at some time met and confronted or had to run away from a jaguar on that trail). Large trails, with more than two hundred trunks, have names like "Limp Prick" and "Pee Walking" (referring to the fact that to cut all the trees, the rubber tapper cannot stop for anything except to make a small incision, called a cut, in the bark of the rubber tree, or risk staying through the night to collect latex). Trails with many obstacles (stream crossings, steep slopes, etc.) have names that indicate their difficulty, like "Sacrifice." Giving names to the trails helps people at home in case something unexpected happens. On leaving home, the rubber tapper tells his wife what trail he'll be cutting, so if he has to be called even the children know where each trail is.

Tatá was teaching me about all this as we walked at a moderate pace of about three miles an hour in the forest along the landings and fords. It's worth reemphasizing that on the estates distance is not measured by kilometers but rather by hours or minutes. When asked the distance between one homestead and the next, the rubber tapper always answers in minutes or hours. When it's a little less than an hour (fifty to fifty-five minutes), they say it's "a short hour." When it's a little more than an hour (one hour and five or ten minutes), they say it's "a long hour."

On that first day of work on the estate we traversed almost the line that we'd expected to cover in two days. At lunch and dinner I found out about the rubber tappers' food, usually very simple but always in quantity and quite nutritious. They eat a lot! The basic menu includes rice, beans, and manioc flour, always with some sort of meat, especially game. When they have no game, they kill pigs, chickens, or even, more rarely, eat eggs. During the winter, when Brazil nuts are harvested, they use a lot of Brazil nut milk, which is very nutritious, to season meat or rice or with couscous. It gives needed energy to those who have to walk a lot.

I ate venison, boar, monkey, and even tapir, which is more difficult to find but which the rubber tappers like to hunt, because besides providing considerable meat, it is a very intelligent animal, causing many difficulties for the hunter. It is a challenge, and the rubber tapper, like any human being, likes challenges.[12] In addition, it is in danger of extinction and found only in remoter areas, on the estates farthest from the towns or the large deforested areas of the ranches, following the big *igarapés*.[13] Restocking is necessary before the species disappears.

In midmorning of the second day we met Manoel Estébio and Armando, who still had not arrived at the meeting place on the Itapissuma homestead. We joined forces, since I had already finished my part of the work, and went to Simplício's house, where we had lunch and redivided the work, arranging to meet again three days later at the Maloquinha homestead on the Tupã estate, the third to be studied, since I was going to give the questionnaire at the Full Moon estate, where only four homesteads were occupied at the time of the research. We left in the afternoon on the next leg of the journey. This was my "baptism of water" during the Amazon winter.

Soon after we left the Itapissuma homestead, it started to rain torrentially. This was a typical "white rain," as Paulo Jacob would say, but they don't use this expression in Acre.

We went toward the Full Moon estate, but first we had to pass three other homesteads, still in São Pedro. At one of these homesteads we would meet Chico Nunes, a longtime rubber tapper in the region, who lived alone and presented an additional problem for us: He was afraid of "souls," as they call the spirits of the dead who return and appear to people in this region. In other areas they are known as phantoms.

This "problem" of Chico Nunes introduced me to rubber tapper culture and taught me a little more about their customs. He was afraid only when some tragedy had happened, such as the case of one brother who had killed the other sometime before in the area where I was working. Since the day of the crime each night Chico had slept at the house of a different neighbor. Tatá knew about this, because he lived on that estate and helped us search for him, passing through the homesteads where we might find him. This detour obviously increased our travel time and thus the amount of rain we encountered. We found Chico Nunes in none of the homesteads before his own, which made us conclude we would only find him later.

It was already starting to get dark, and we were drenched by the torrential rain. Night came and we had not reached any inhabited homestead. On the beach the water was up to our knees. The soaked backpack was terribly heavy. (Note to backpack makers: I've never found a backpack, even the waterproof ones, that could withstand the rains of the Amazon winter without getting everything inside wet!)

We were going solely according to Tatá's rubber tapper instinct. It was impossible to see the trail. Suddenly a bigger danger: a creek flooded over its banks, about 6 feet deep. We crossed it holding the backpack above our head and swimming. A short way ahead, the creek was about 15 feet deep and had a bridge, a tree trunk about 15 centimeters in diameter, and it was about 60 centimeters underwater. Tatá cut a staff about 15 feet long to help us cross the bridge (which we couldn't see!). The water was moving with considerable force. Trying to be a bit more balanced than usual, I managed to cross the creek (whew! Did I say water isn't my element?).

We walked for about half an hour until we arrived at the São Francisco homestead on the Full Moon estate. Chico Nunes was there, spending the night in Cesar's house so he wouldn't have to be afraid of "souls." I took my things out of the backpack (even though they were in plastic bags, they got wet) and hung the pack over the stove, to see if it would dry out before we continued our journey the next day. This was my "baptism" on the rubber estate.

The Knife's Blow

The first phase of the work ended on February 18, 1986, at the Malo-quinha homestead, where I had arrived the day before and waited for Armando and Manoel Estébio. Tatá returned to the São Pedro rubber estate. Before he left he taught me one more secret of the forest: On February 16, when we got up very early, Tatá heard the song of the caboré, a forest bird, and said it wouldn't rain that day. I asked him why, and he explained that the way the caboré was singing was predicting that. It was cloudy the whole day, but it didn't rain.

On the nineteenth I moved to the Nazaré estate, which was claimed by the Bordon Group and where rubber tappers had resisted the big clear-cutting operations for several years. It was a place where union organization was so strong that the Rubber Tapper Project's first school was built there.

I had arranged to wait for the two comrades at the Desert homestead, where the school that had started on the Already Hungry homestead was operating. There we would reallocate the work.

The next day Armando and Manoel arrived. We reallocated the work, and an additional problem came up: We hadn't managed to find a guide to go with me on that stage of the research. The only solution was for me to go alone until I could find someone to accompany me.

We left after lunch. My first stop was at the Boa Vista homestead. Up to that point everything was fine, the landing was good, and I didn't get lost in the forest. I administered the questionnaire and continued on my way. The next stop: the Already Hungry homestead. When I arrived the rubber tapper who lived there was harvesting rice with two neighbors.[14] I went to the fields carrying only a clipboard with the questionnaires. I introduced myself and explained my work. I was received with considerable coldness and even hostility. I sensed the atmosphere and tried to explain specifically with whom I was working and the reason for the research, but I didn't succeed in breaking the ice. Valderi Vicente, the owner of the homestead, Rocha, and "the old chief," neighboring rubber tappers, subjected me to a veritable interrogation. Only after they were convinced that my work had union approval did they invite me back to the house, and there, after a long conversation, we became good friends.

The interesting thing about this episode is that a long time after, talking with some comrades from that community, I learned that when I arrived at Valderi's field with the clipboard and started introducing myself, he and his neighbors assumed right away that I was putting them on and that in fact I was associated with the Bordon ranch. Believing this, they were preparing to give me a beating with the side of a knife.[15] I'd be assaulted without knowing why, but for them it would be a way to show they didn't accept any sort of conversation with the ranchers. This fact is still remembered by Rocha, who is quite elderly and living in Xapuri. I spoke to him recently and he recalled the episode.

In 1986 the tension in the entire Xapuri region was considerable, and the rubber tappers had already been fooled several times by INCRA[16] technicians and the ranchers. So it was better not to take any risks. This explains the "interrogation" I was subjected to and the mistrust of the rubber tappers.

In its annual general assembly at the end of 1985 the union was already warning its members about the risks of deforestation and that the Bordon ranch was threatening to carry out a big clear-cutting operation on the Nazaré estate that would affect a great number of homesteads, evicting many rubber tappers, as they had done before in deforesting more than 3,500 hectares.

But everything went well with the survey I was conducting, despite the difficulties and the wrong turns I made in the landings, sometimes having to double back for half an hour to find the trail I had mistaken for a dogleg.

Our work was finished in March, after Armando and Manoel administered the survey at the Boa Vista estate and I did one at Barra (with João do Nande, a local rubber tapper, as my guide).

Afterward we went back to Rio Branco and tried to arrange to tabulate the data with several people at the Federal University of Acre (UFAC). This final phase never was completed because of the great amount of information collected and the difficulties systematizing it. This was a result of our technical inexperience in putting together a questionnaire, but it was extremely useful. If it had been done within technical requirements, most likely we would not have succeeded in collecting all the information we got. The survey we did was later useful in discussions about establishing a cooperative for rubber tappers and small farmers we wanted to reach in Xapuri township and even the entire Acre River valley.

My Wanderings on the Estates

Talking about my walks on the Xapuri rubber estates is a way of telling the story of my time there. I learned everything, or almost everything, by walking on the estates, participating in community meetings, getting to know the schools and homesteads from the farthest to the closest ones.

During these walks, I learned how difficult it was for the rubber tappers to organize, since the distances almost always hindered meetings. As I've mentioned, the rubber tappers lived on homesteads on the estates along the landings, as much as two days' walk from one to another.

By walking I discovered that distance is not measured in kilometers but in hours and minutes. With the only means of travel being walking or taking a boat, it isn't possible to figure out precisely how many kilometers one is from a place, but it is possible to say how many hours or minutes. Even so, it depends on who's counting, since one hour's walk for me could be two hours for somebody else. This makes it even harder to determine the distances. To give one example, the Rio Branco homestead where Big Raimundo lived was about three and a half, or at most four, hours from Xapuri for me. For Mariazinha, who lived there, the trip never took less than six hours, as she told me.

That's how it was when I walked on the estates. Sometimes someone would tell me I was almost at my destination when I still had to walk another two or three hours. This was at the beginning, because later on I became an excellent walker, if I do say so myself. Even today I'm famous on all the Xapuri estates because few rubber tappers managed to keep up with me during the time I was walking there.

When I was working in Xapuri I often walked twelve hours in one day without a break, stopping only for a drink of water at the houses along the trail before arriving at my destination. One time I made a bet with Jorge Capoeiro, who lived at the Caboré homestead on the Boa Vista estate, about eighteen hours' walk from town, as everybody says in Xapuri. The first time I went to Caboré, I walked about ten hours the first day and slept two hours away from there. When I arrived I told Jorge the next time I'd leave Xapuri and arrive at Caboré on the same day. He doubted it. The opportunity came for another trip. I prepared carefully, even packing a snack of chicken with toasted manioc flour to eat on the trail so I wouldn't have to stop to eat.

I left Xapuri at 5:50 A.M. and walked a long way while the sun was "cold"—so far that by about 11 o'clock I was already at Porongaba, a homestead that usually took about seven hours to reach from Xapuri. Dona Antonia invited me to lunch. I ate quickly and got back on the trail, saying I was going to Caboré. She also was dubious. I walked and walked and walked. At

6:00 P.M. I arrived at Jorge Capoeiro's hut. He asked when I had left Xapuri. I said I had started that day at 5:50 A.M. He didn't believe it, but it's the honest truth. The result of my forced march was an injury to my right knee that made it necessary for me to return on horseback.

I honestly don't know how many thousands of kilometers (it was several thousand, I'm sure) I walked on the Xapuri estates. To give an idea, Caboré must be about 60 kilometers or more from Xapuri. Each time I went to Caboré I continued as far as Espalha, another 15 kilometers farther along. Thus each round trip was about 150 kilometers (every time I went, I had to return, right?). I made about five trips to Espalha. So right there we have 750 kilometers. At least two times I walked and went another two hours by boat to São José on the Xapuri River, something like 170 kilometers, halfway on foot and the other half by boat, going down there "inside," through the estates. That's 340 plus 170, for a total of 510 kilometers on those journeys.

I made four trips to Deserto, located about 45 kilometers away. Round trip 90 times 4, that's 360 kilometers.

In July 1987 I went from the São José estate on the Xapuri River to the Already Started homestead in Two Brothers, on the Acre River below Xapuri. That was something like 80 kilometers. Ah! On that trip, when I arrived at the Already Started homestead, I saw my wife (we have been together since 1997) for the first time, when she was a fourteen-year-old girl (and beautiful, I must add).

At least three times I went to the Barra estate, about 30 kilometers from Xapuri, adding another 180 kilometers.

I made countless trips inside Cachoeira from Nova Esperança, going back and forth between the two, something like 500 kilometers just on these estates.

I made several trips to the Rio Branco homestead, about 15 kilometers from Xapuri, walking more than 150 kilometers just on that stretch.

Among the many journeys I made, one, when I was living in Rio Branco studying law at UFAC, was especially notable. Contracted by CNPT-IBAMA, I went to talk about extractive reserves with the rubber tappers of the Chico Mendes Extractive Reserve. I left the banks of the Xapuri River and walked with others to the banks of the Iaco River, five days walking an average of ten hours per day—something like 150, 180 kilometers. Afterward I traveled another day and a half by boat and walked about 80 kilometers from the banks of the Icuriã Creek to Assis Brasil.[17] That is, on this walk I started from Xapuri township and walked to Assis Brasil. If I had gone on the highway, it would have been about 180 kilometers. Through the forest, it must have been about 260 kilometers.

Have you added up all the distances? Not even I have, so the numbers I'm giving are approximations and could be greater or fewer. But they add up to something like 2,700 kilometers in the Xapuri forests. You've got to agree, that's a lot of ground covered. To give an idea, it's like going from Rio Branco, Acre, where I am, to Campo Grande, in Mato Grosso do Sul, the capital of the state where I was born.

I forgot several trips I made to the Remanso estate, traveling "inside" from Xapuri, more than 100 kilometers away. Maybe if all the distances I walked are added up they come to about 3,000 kilometers.

Why am I telling you all this? Am I trying to look like a superhero? I don't think so. I'm doing it to show how difficult it is to do the organizational work we set out to accomplish, taking into account only Xapuri township and one trip to other areas. Chico Mendes, Big Raimundo, and other comrades did this almost crazy work for years.

How many kilometers must they have walked? It would be very difficult to count them, since one would have to estimate how many kilometers they walked when they cut and collected latex, at least 15 kilometers a day, five days a week, for a total of 75 kilometers, 300 kilometers a month, 2,400 kilometers a year. Then there's walking to hunt, to go back and forth to the fields, to the meetings of the union, the cooperative, parties. In a year a rubber tapper certainly walks as much as I walked in the seven years I worked in Xapuri. So I didn't accomplish such a great feat.

In the case of the leaders, in addition to this normal work over decades, there was also the work of visiting union halls, conducting meetings, and so on, and so on. That adds all the treks through countless estates to the 2,400 kilometers a year. That should help you understand the difficulties of organizing unions, schools, and cooperatives.

Walking the forest involves a profound apprenticeship. I discovered this over a period of years, and although I became a great walker, I didn't learn half of what I needed to know to survive in the forest, something I surely couldn't do if it were necessary.

My first trips were pretty dangerous. On the very first day of my travels, I ran into a lot of rain and crossed flooded creeks on "bridges" that were round tree trunks with a diameter of no more than 20 centimeters. In addition, crossing these "bridges" required skills that I never did acquire: walking like a parrot across the trunks. Usually I'd fall in the water. My balance is terrible, and I never managed to improve it much, even over several years.

Aside from the risks I've already mentioned, I didn't have much practice paying attention to the ground where one treads; I stepped on snakes a couple of times, luckily in ways that they couldn't bite me. With the techniques I learned from the rubber tappers, I can report that on another occasion, when I was walking in front of a group of comrades, including rubber tappers and other advisers, to a meeting on the São Luiz do Remanso estate, I saw a snake moving. I jumped and warned them that a snake (it was a jararacucu, whose markings look like dead leaves) was ahead. A rubber tapper walked ahead and killed the snake. Even after it was killed, those of us from the city still couldn't see it on the ground. The comrade had to lift it up to show it to us. This demonstrates the animal's marvelous camouflage skills.

They wanted to know how I had seen the snake if I was walking so quickly. I answered that I was paying attention to the ground and saw a slight movement, enough to alert me to the snake's presence. That's how it works for the rubber tappers.

Walking the forest requires one to pay total attention to the spot where you're going to put your foot when you take your next step. Looking at the branches while you walk is extremely dangerous, but it's still important to look all around, scanning the ground, the trees, the obstacles farther ahead if you're not walking on a trail (a landing or a ford), the sky to figure out where you are—but to do this you have to be an experienced rubber tapper. In seven years I didn't manage to learn all this.

On many trails, I must add, on many occasions I walked through places where nobody knew me, but I was always well received and well treated by the rubber tappers (with the exception of that incident of the "knife blow"), because the rubber tappers are affable, hospitable, and good at passing the time of day.

I'd like to point out one notable episode: In 1994, when I made that trip from Xapuri to Assis Brasil, as I was going along the banks of Icuriã Creek toward Assis Brasil, past the Primavera homestead, I was walking alone through an area where few people knew me. I stopped at each homestead, drank water, and asked for directions to a completely unknown trail that I had never walked before.

I arrived at a homestead at about 4:00 P.M. A talkative rubber tapper received me. I asked for a glass of water and directions to Assis Brasil. He said at that time it wasn't very safe to continue on, because nobody might be at the next homestead, and the one after that would be another hour and a half along. That is, I would arrive there at about 6:00 P.M. In the forest it's already dark at that time. I told him I'd keep going anyway.

The rubber tapper, who said his name was Jonata, asked me if I were "Italian," because I was wearing a backpack, and periodically some Italians associated with the Catholic Church visited the inhabitants along the Icuriã. I answered no and said my name: "I'm Gomercindo."

With shining eyes he exclaimed, with a northeastern accent, "I don't believe it! So now you won't be so rude as not to come in. I didn't even know you, but I voted for you. Now you're going to stay here and have dinner with me. Come in, I'll show you I'm not lying. Come in, come in!"

Very moved, I took off my backpack, because in 1990 I had been a Workers' Party candidate for federal deputy and had won a significant number of votes in Assis Brasil township—that is, about 10 percent of the valid votes. I went up the steps. I begged his pardon. I went in the house. On the line[18] behind the door, covered with DDT spray from SUCAM,[19] was a little ceramic figure of me from the 1990 campaign. I admit I almost cried. This was something I've never forgotten.

Sr. Jonata called his wife and children and merrily introduced me to everybody. He asked his "woman" to make country-style chicken because I was going to have dinner at his house. I thanked him and stayed there. Everybody was extremely nice. I took a welcome bath, put up my hammock, and listened to Sr. Jonata, since he wouldn't let me get a word in edgewise (and believe me, this isn't easy!). I heard many stories, and afterward we ate and then I went to sleep. The next day I walked from 7:00 A.M. until 3:30 P.M., when I arrived at Assis Brasil.

"I'm a Serious Man, Don't Fool Around with Me!"

I could remember and tell many stories from my walks, but since I didn't record all of them, I might make many mistakes, especially about some comrades' names. I intend to make a collection, recording these stories, for another book—who knows?

There's one story whose main character is "Mr. Little Rock," an elderly rubber tapper who lives in Xapuri now. But when I was there he lived like a hermit about fourteen hours from town on the Nazaré estate. Mr. Little Rock was one of the three men who had thought about hitting me with the side of his knife.

Well, Mr. Little Rock, as his comrades affectionately call him, lived alone at Cacoama homestead on the Nazaré estate for many years. He produced enough to be able to eat, he had a pension, either from FUNRURAL[20] or as a rubber soldier,[21] that he'd periodically pick up in town, and he lived on the estate, sometimes participating in collective work crews but not wanting anybody to live with him.

Despite his age, Mr. Little Rock tried to participate in all the Rural Workers' Union assemblies. To do this he had to leave home three days before the meetings, because the fourteen-hour walk stretched to more than thirty hours for him.

Mr. Rock, as I respectfully called him, was one of the first to support the cooperatives on the estates, having participated actively in the one at Already Hungry and later at Desert. He knew how to read and write, and he managed the first cooperative for a while, until he felt he didn't have the confidence of some comrades. This made him quit directing the association, which ended up going broke a little later, according to his report.

Once some comrades who had known him longer told me the reason he lived alone, like a hermit, was some disappointment, perhaps the infidelity of a woman when he was young. He never wanted to talk about this, and I sensed it was a subject that troubled him.

At the same time these comrades told me the reason for Mr. Little Rock's solitary life, they also told me a story that he called a lie but never strongly denied. Half-smiling, he said they had made it up.

The story—and I say "story" because I don't know if it's true or only a joke of the comrades who lived in the neighborhood—is that knowing he lived alone and was a hard worker, a woman from town decided to go and live with him. He accepted. The woman went with him from Xapuri.

Arriving at Cacoama just before nightfall, Mr. Rock went to put up his hammock. Quickly the woman put her hammock up next to his. As silent as ever, he got up, took the woman's hammock, and put it up in the kitchen. The woman didn't complain.

The next night, to avoid problems, the rubber tapper went to put up his hammock in the "parlor" of the house, actually an open but covered area. The woman came out to put up her hammock next to his. He got up, looked seriously at the woman, and supposedly said, "Listen here, lady. A woman for me is for helping in the field, making food, and washing clothes, not to mess around with me. I'm a serious and very respectable man. And madam, tomorrow you'll pack your things and you can leave."

To this day he denies the story and says it's invented. I've never met the woman who was said to be the subject of the story, so I record it as a tale, knowing that Mr. Rock never wanted anybody living with him on the estate. And besides being a hard worker and an active member of the union, he is very kind, a good conversationalist when others want to talk or quiet for hours on end, something he's used to because he has lived by himself for more than twenty years with nobody to talk to.

For the Record Book?

Another story I heard is confirmed by the protagonists, brothers "Joca" and "Tamborete," who were well known when they were younger for eating a lot. They even say the two could eat a whole paca[22] at a sitting. Miguel Mendes told the story that once upon a time, when there was still a boss on the estate, at the Cachoeira trading post, Tamborete, who was already famous as a glutton, made fun of him because he was drinking a tin of condensed milk

(395 grams), saying he could drink a dozen tins at a time. Miguel or somebody else nearby made a bet: If Tamborete drank twelve tins of condensed milk at one sitting, he would lose; if not, the glutton would have to pay him. The barn manager immediately grabbed a dozen tins of condensed milk and opened them all, meaning they would have to be paid for in any event.

Without ceremony Tamborete drank all the tins of condensed milk one after another. When he finished he asked for one more, "just for a taste." That is, he drank thirteen tins of condensed milk at a sitting, the equivalent of 5.13 kilograms (about 6 quarts) of the sweetened drink. Without a doubt this is one for the record book.

~~~~~~~~~~~~~~~~~~~~~~~~

Chapter 3

RUBBER TAPPERS: A CENTURY'S STRUGGLE

THE AMAZON HAS ALWAYS BEEN COVETED, ever since the "discovery" of Brazil. As early as the sixteenth century Spaniards made their first journeys on the river they called the Amazon because, it is said, when they went up the river, they met indigenous populations that included women on horseback, and so they called it "the river of the Amazons."

The vastness of the forest and its secrets inspired greed. Everybody imagined that in a region so teeming with trees, greater riches would be hidden underground. They were right, as we've seen in recent years (gold in Yanomami territory, at Serra Pelada,[1] and in the Carajás Mountains). In addition to gold there are dozens of other minerals, some important for nuclear fuel processing, manganese, porcelain, bauxite, and so on—almost all looted, especially during the military government and continuing during the post-dictatorship governments. That is how the myth of "Amazonia, the great Eldorado," began that has been cultivated and reinforced over the centuries up to the present.

The history of rubber tapper occupation of the Amazon stretches over about one hundred fifty years. On the explorers' many journeys in the region, a product of great elasticity, used by its traditional inhabitants, the Indians, attracted their attention: It was natural rubber, produced by extracting latex from a regional tree later called the rubber tree. The explorers thought it might have some commercial value in Europe, which was in the midst of the Industrial Revolution.

Sent to Europe, rubber came to have multiple uses that kept increasing as new technologies were discovered: vulcanization (by Charles Goodyear) and pneumatics (discovered by chance by Dunlop, a veterinarian), among others.

These discoveries, in conjunction with the needs of young industries in

Europe for transmission cables with greater durability and resistance and especially for a raw material with multiple uses, created a sizable market for rubber produced in Amazonia. The problem was that the Indians did not produce it on a commercial scale, as industry required. To respond to the demands of the consumer market, it was necessary to have a workforce dedicated exclusively to its production.

how rubber tapper began)

Thus were encouraged the first migrations of people from the Brazilian Northeast to the Amazon, and the *aviamento*[2] system was set up to finance the influx of these populations.

As early as the middle of the nineteenth century the number of northeastern migrants in the Amazon forest was considerable, but "official history" claims that the main factor responsible for the massive arrival of northeasterners in the region was the great drought that devastated the Brazilian Northeast around 1877. Nothing could be further from the truth. This was only one more reason. What encouraged the influx were industrial interests, especially those of the British. They were also behind the big disasters in South America during the nineteenthh century, such as the Paraguayan War.[3] As we will see, they did not consider the consequences of their greed when they cultivated thousands of hectares of rubber trees in Southeast Asia, which has had deadly implications for the Amazon populations up to the present. This was the first great act of biopiracy in the Brazilian Amazon.

For their part, the rubber tappers came from the Northeast with the expectation of quick riches—rubber was "white gold"—and they wanted to return as quickly as possible to their home region as rich men, so they wouldn't have to suffer anymore from the problem of chronic drought.

When they arrived in Amazonia they were selected by the rubber barons, or bosses, who controlled vast areas of the forest. They were called "colonels of the riverbanks" because the rubber estates were normally located along the rivers, the only roads to the heart of the forest. From the moment they were chosen, practically bought, the rubber tappers were in debt to their new bosses for the costs of the journey from their homes to their arrival on the estate, as well as all the necessary equipment for settling on the homestead and starting to process the rubber.

The rubber barons were "dispatched" (financed and supplied) by the dispatch houses[4] (in great part financed by English industrial capital) and had to deliver the crop every year to these financiers.

The relationship between the rubber baron and the rubber tapper was like master and slave. The rubber tapper could sell the fruit of his labor—in this case, rubber that he processed at the homestead—only to the owner of the rubber estate, from whom he had to buy everything he needed to continue living in the forest, from food to ammunition and kerosene to rum and clothing. The rubber tapper was forbidden to cultivate any crops so he would not lose time from the work of producing rubber and would keep depending on the trading post for everything, including food.

Periodically the rubber tapper was visited at his homestead by a clerk sent from the trading post[5] to list the purchases he needed. It should be emphasized that provision of goods was related directly to the rubber tapper's production. If he was sick or produced little, almost nothing was provided. The decision to furnish supplies or not was the manager's or the boss's. This situation was repeated in the case of the rubber tapper who owed a great amount to the trading post. It is important to point out here that it was exclusively the boss who set the price of the goods and the rubber. After the clerk came the rubber tapper received a visit from the oxcart driver, who delivered his supplies and took away the rubber he had produced.

Also, the inspector came to verify that the rubber tapper was not cutting the tree so as to kill or burn it—that is, to make it unproductive. When he cut the tree the rubber tapper had to follow a rule (perhaps the only positive thing, as it prevented destruction of the trees) that determined the deepness of the cut, which must not reach the heartwood, and its height. Each rubber tapper had to cut up to the height he could reach without taking his feet off the ground. The rule also determined the shape of the cut. It was forbidden to cut in the shape of a herringbone, the most common form in illustrations of rubber tappers at work.

The rubber tapper had to cut a "band"; that is, the cut had to be horizontal and be the length of one palm and a finger to one-and-a-half palms, always leaving one band's space between each cut. After about three years, the time the rubber tapper took to "lay down a band," or cut to the place he could reach without taking his foot off the ground, he reached exactly the band that was free and started to cut. The period of three years used to be sufficient for the previously cut area to recover, so the same tree would produce for more than fifty years. Therein lay the sustainability of the activity. The circumference of a rubber tree was covered by a number of "bowls" (used to collect the latex) attached to it. Thus the rubber tree, or any other tree, had a circumference of, say, six bowls, with each bowl placed more or less three palms from the others.

At the end of the production season (from approximately April or May to November or December), with all the rubber stored in the warehouse, inventory was taken. By this time the rubber had already lost all excess moisture and was dried, with no risk of cracking. Even so, when weighing it, the boss charged for "weight," discounting 10 percent of the weight on the assumption that the rubber would crack. Not only that, the trading post's books were normally rigged so they could steal several kilos from the rubber tapper each time the rubber was weighed.

The boss determined the prices of goods and rubber. It should be pointed out that the majority of rubber tappers could not read, write, or do arithmetic, so they were always at the mercy of the manager. Thus the rubber tapper was always in debt for the next season. This is what present-day scholars customarily call "debt slavery." The dream of returning to the Northeast was thus only a dream that became increasingly remote from reality. In spite of everything, at the cost of superhuman work, some rubber tappers managed to make a profit. When they thought they were free and could return to their homeland, it was not uncommon for them to be attacked and killed by trading post employees, so they literally buried their dreams in the forest. There were exceptions to this pattern, but not a few owners used this expedient to keep money from leaving the estate.

Life on a rubber homestead was extremely lonely. The rubber tappers met only on weekends, sometimes once a month, at the trading post. This was also a way for the boss to maintain absolute control over the entire estate. The dispersion of the rubber tappers and the fact that they could get together only under the surveillance of the boss and his guards meant they could not organize any kind of revolt. There were few women on the estates. The rubber tapper who managed to find one always ran the risk that another would "take" her or simply hang around his house while he was out or, worse yet, that he would be killed so the other could take his "prize." Not to mention the fact that the trading post employees almost always believed they had rights to the rubber tapper's wife. Woe to the woman who dared not satisfy the demands of these gunmen; she would lose her husband.

The rubber baron was the absolute authority on the estate. It was he who married people or arrested them when a serious crime occurred, and he set the punishments to be inflicted on rubber tappers who broke the law.

In such an exploitative situation, it was logical that a few rubber tappers would try to find a way out. Often this meant selling the crop to the *regatão*[6] or another boss. But if he were caught doing this, the rubber tapper would undergo the most terrible punishments, even being burned alive with a *péla*[7] of rubber tied to his back. Another very common punishment on the estates was to tie the rubber tapper to a wooden frame near the trading post and torture him in front of everybody, as was done with black slaves during the period of slavery in Brazil.

Selling the rubber off the trading post involved high risk. The rubber baron would offer rewards to other rubber tappers if they informed him of any "irregularities" in the area near where they lived, as a way to protect control of the estate. Thus one's neighbor could be an enemy or a spy. This made everybody distrust everybody else, a trait of rubber tappers. Even today mistrust is always part of the rubber tapper's consciousness—thus the difficulty of uniting and organizing them.

Wealth and Poverty, Two Sides of the Same Coin

During the second half of the nineteenth century and the first decade of the twentieth, "white gold" made a few rich and thousands poor. The traces of this era of the rubber barons' opulence can be found today in Belém and Manaus, for example, in the Amazonas Theater, built so the rubber barons, the managers, and the owners of the commercial houses could see theater companies that were successful in Europe.

The rubber barons, those feudal lords who controlled all the production of immense forests, would insist on showing off their wealth when they went to Manaus or Belém but would never say where it really came from. To support such luxury and ostentation, the rubber tappers were forced to work harder and harder. Since they could not read or write, their debts would increase instead of diminish every year. The more they produced, the more they owed.

The sons of the rubber barons, like those of the coffee barons of southeastern Brazil, studied in Europe or at least in Rio de Janeiro, and had all the benefits of this.

On their vacations in Manaus or Belém or even Europe, the wives of the "colonels" didn't make only small purchases; they insisted on buying the best. Their dresses came from the world of the rich or were made to order by the most famous couturiers of the era.

On the estate, where they almost always spent the rest of their lives without even reaching the nearest town, the rubber tappers had as their only entertainment drinking rum at the trading post on weekends. This increased their debts even more. On rare occasions a party took place, after the marriage of a rubber tapper's daughter, the visit of one of the boss's sons who was studying in the city or overseas, or at the end of the annual production process.

At the parties, because of the few women available to dance, some rubber tappers would tie a cloth around their heads and play the part of a lady—but only to dance. I've never heard reports of homosexuality on the estates, but I have heard many stories of sex between rubber tappers and mares, cows, or donkeys. Women were rare.

Another obstacle for the rubber tappers was the enormous distance from their workplace to the nearest town, along with the fact that the boss exercised rigid control over the rubber tappers' departure from the estate—when he allowed them to leave at all.

In the cities at the height of rubber production, the "colonels" were greeted with lavish parties and were considered part of the local elite because they had money. These colonels wielded influence over politics and the local judiciary.

The trading houses treated the most prosperous rubber barons who delivered the greatest quality of rubber each winter with special deference. Winter is the season when the rivers flood, making it possible for boats to go upriver to collect the rubber stored in the warehouses.

The rubber tappers were not, however, the only or the greatest victims of the greed of the rubber barons and the industries that used rubber. The Indians, who had lived in the Amazon region for millennia, were killed or expelled to remoter areas, the "general lands," so that the landlords could increase their holdings.

Looking at the past of the Amazon is like rereading the present: a few enriching themselves while the majority keeps dying little by little, abandoned to a miserable fate.

The "Forays"

Getting rich, earning more and more money no matter what the social cost, was the raison d'être of the "colonels," the feudal lords of recent times.

In this context, the Indians, primeval inhabitants of the forests, were obstacles to be removed. The forest itself was to be conquered by the warriors of a "holy war" whose most important holy relic was the wealth, luxury, and greed of the new landlords.

The new warriors were the ragged, undernourished men from the Brazilian Northeast. It was their job to carry out the conquests that would make their already prosperous bosses even richer, at the cost of thousands of Indian and rubber tapper lives.

To increase their holdings, the rubber barons needed to conquer the land of those who already lived there. Thus it was necessary to convince their "soldiers," the hillbillies or "tough guys" who came from the Northeast, that the Indians were not even human beings but rather "wild animals," savages who had to be exterminated because of the danger that the rubber tappers themselves would be wiped out if they let the Indians live. Their hatred was deliberately fueled by terror.

So they promoted "forays,"[8] extermination expeditions against the Indians who lived in the areas the rubber barons intended to add to their estates. For these hunts the rubber barons armed the rubber tappers and furnished the ammunition and even an experienced woodsman (guide) to take them to the villages and organize massacres.

The term "foray" may refer to what happened on these expeditions: The rubber tappers were armed with repeating rifles and the Indians with only rudimentary weapons (arrows, blowguns, lances that were sometimes tipped with poison), so the latter, taken by surprise, would rush into the forest in different directions. The order given the rubber tappers, however, was *to kill*, not take anyone alive, not even children. Using their knowledge of the forest, whenever possible the Indians would respond in kind, setting up ambushes or raids, as in a guerrilla war, thus increasing the terror and hatred even more.

More recently, in the twentieth century, the forays resulted in the "domestication" of some indigenous groups, and it is still possible today to meet Indians who carry on their bodies the brands of their bosses.

Thus for more than a century Indians and rubber tappers were deadly enemies. This hatred benefited only the rubber barons and was only in their interest.

Without realizing it, however, the rubber tappers themselves learned a great deal about the forest from the Indians—how to use medicinal herbs, how to move about in the forest without getting lost.

It's worth remembering that the discovery of rubber itself is owed to the Indians. If not for them, perhaps the Industrial Revolution would have been delayed for decades—who knows?

It is important to point out that until today the majority of indigenous peoples that remain in Amazonia do not have demarcated territories that they can be sure nobody will take away from them. For them the struggle continues in an extremely unequal way. The weapons available are still very unequal, and these groups are being decimated little by little but much more quickly than could have been predicted. Some are being exterminated by diseases brought to their people by contact with the "civilized" people who prospect for hardwood, gold, precious stones, and strategic minerals.

The Story of Rubber Tree Seed Smuggling

The domestication of the rubber tree, native to Amazonia, was a carefully planned scheme of the British government, especially the Ministry for India, through its agent, Clements R. Markham,[9] as Warren Dean recounts in his book, *Brazil and the Struggle for Rubber*. For a long time, Markham, who had already planned the transfer and domestication of cinchona, native to Peru, for the production of quinine, sent reports that persuaded the ministry to try to domesticate the rubber tree. According to Dean, Markham succeeded in arranging for the British consulate in Belém to acquire rubber tree seeds from Henry Wickham, who lived in Santarém.

Dean challenges several of Wickham's accounts of how he got the seeds out, but the most important thing to note is that, shrewdly or not, the British adventurer managed to transport about seventy thousand rubber tree seeds to Kew Gardens, where they arrived in June 1876.

In his account Dean says:

> It has also been claimed that, contrary to Wickham's version, the Brazilian authorities were aware of what he was doing. O. Labroy and V. Cayla, who in 1913 wrote a semiofficial study of rubber in the Amazon, said that he had succeeded "thanks to the good offices of the Brazilian government, which had these seeds collected by Indians in the rubber groves of the uplands." These authors were most likely engaged in face-saving. No one else has repeated this assertion, or provided proof, yet it does seem odd that Wickham could have collected rubber seeds for a period of a year or more without authorities, at the local level at least, becoming aware of it. There were, after all, a police chief and judge in Santarém, and they were not ineffectual. . . . Local authorities may well have been aware of Wickham's purposes, then, but they did not hinder him. (1987: 20–21)

With the available information it would be very difficult to confirm or challenge the issues Dean raises. Even so, a few years earlier the Brazilian government had allied with the British government during the Paraguayan War. So if the smuggling of the seeds was one more game in which the Brazilian authorities participated, that would be no novelty. On the other hand, it would be much easier for official British history to justify such actions if they did not seem to be directly involved in an international theft, which is what really happened.

Dean tries to justify this situation in an almost naive way when he describes the myth the English adventurer cultivated:

> Essential to Wickham's tale was the element of duplicity. Had he not experienced danger, there would have been no triumph; had his exploit not appeared to have constituted a theft, paradoxically there could be no honor. For the retired servants of the Empire who gathered at the Royal Colonial Institute, where Wickham customarily held forth in later years, much of the charm of his narrative lay, no doubt, in a victory slyly won over the natives. (1987: 21)

To try to justify the theft of the rubber tree seeds from Amazonia, Dean cites several examples of importation of products to Brazil, most important, coffee, imported from French Guiana.

From this point of view, product for product, everything becomes very simple. It is based on theft for its own sake and the popular saying that "the thief who steals from a thief receives a hundred years' forgiveness." The important thing to discuss is what the practical result was for the Amazon of the extraction of the rubber tree seeds for cultivation in Southeast Asia. What were the consequences one hundred years later for the region's inhabitants? And how does this affect the planet's environmental condition today?

If we leave behind the tree itself and its product, rubber, to consider its importance in the modern world and how the people live who have depended on extractivism in Amazonia for more than a century, then perhaps we can have a more human, and more impassioned, discussion. Not to mention the very important and timely subject of biopiracy.

Since 1912, when rubber produced on plantations in Southeast Asia began to enter the international market, the story of the Amazon's inhabitants has changed radically. The bankrupted rubber barons moved to the city, abandoning the trees and the rubber tappers to their fate on the remote estates, days if not months from the cities, with no way to stay or leave.

The price of rubber fell in the international market after 1912. Thus rubber tapping stopped being of interest to international investors. The commercial rubber houses closed their doors. The rubber tappers went on to sell to the peddlers, who paid wretched sums for the rubber they produced.

Only in 1940, with the closing of Asian ports by the Japanese, did the Amazon once again have some importance in the production of natural rubber. The allies had a great interest in investing in the production of this precious raw material. The Amazon was again almost empty of rubber tappers. Once again the Northeast provided the labor power necessary for the industrial production that the war required.

Another important point: Today the rubber tapper is seen as a "guardian of the forest," but he still competes at a disadvantage with the rubber plantations and official subsidies for latex and rubber production in Southeast Asia. What is the incentive for the guardian to stay at his post?

The Revolution in Acre: A Rubber Tapper Struggle

Even during the first rubber boom, responding to the need to produce increasing amounts of rubber for the international market, Brazilian migrants were sent beyond the imaginary border between Brazil and Bolivia, because the international treaties governing this question were not very clear and provided such opportunities.

With the open market for rubber, the Bolivian government also began considering the possibility of earning money by exporting this raw material. Therefore, it tried to pressure the Brazilian government to reopen negotiations to delineate the border between the two countries, as Brazil and Bolivia still had lines drawn up by Portugal and Spain.

In 1867 Brazil was pressured to sign the Treaty of Ayacucho, which defined the frontier. Brazil was weakened in the negotiations because Bolivia could have allied itself with Paraguay, with which Brazil was at war. Even so, the treaty increased the territory of our country. After the treaty was signed Bolivia began to press for demarcation.

Despite Bolivian pressure, demarcation began only at the end of the nineteenth century. It was exactly at that time that the Brazilian representative discovered that if the demarcation were done according to the Treaty of Ayacucho, Brazil would lose extensive areas already occupied by Brazilians. Therefore, the principle of *uti possidetis*,[10] established in the same treaty, had to be respected. Obviously the Bolivian government did not want to know about this.

For the big Brazilian merchants in their Manaus and Belém commercial houses, this was an additional worry. Many had already backed rubber barons beyond the borders claimed by Bolivia, in the watersheds of the upper Purus and Aquiri Rivers.[11]

Seeing their interests threatened, the merchants made resources available to support a struggle by the inhabitants of that area against the Bolivian government, should that prove necessary. With the opening of a Bolivian customs post on the Aquiri River, the government of the province of Amazonas decided to do the same so that it would not lose the sizable proceeds of taxes on the sale of rubber.

Because of all these factors and especially because Bolivia decided to place customs posts in areas it considered its property, the first raids, financed by the Amazonas government and the large commercial houses, began.

The first expedition to fight for Acre was led by a Spaniard, Luiz Galvez Rodriguez de Aria, a journalist and adventurer in Pará, where he found work because of his legal training. As a journalist he found out about deals between Bolivian representatives and North Americans for the latter to provide weapons and money so that Bolivia could keep control of the area from which its agents recently had been expelled by the rubber tappers, led by their bosses.

After arranging for wide publication of the documents he had obtained, Galvez left Pará, counting on the support of the Amazonas government for arms, ammunition, funds, and supplies.

On arrival in Acre, Galvez created the Republic of Acre, with a town where a Bolivian customs post had operated as its capital. Naturally the president of this republic could only be Galvez himself, with the early support of the local rubber barons. As president, the Spaniard Galvez proclaimed a series of decrees putting local commerce under Brazilian law. He also adopted the language and currency of Brazil. This adventurer's dream lasted only a short time; he failed in his attempt to bring the rubber barons under the control of the laws of this "republic" and was deposed the same year he came to power.

The Bolivian government was careful to occupy the entire region of Acre with forward military posts to ensure its sovereignty over this coveted part of Amazonia. The Brazilians made ready to fight, and the Amazonas government financed a new expedition, inciting a nationalist claim when in fact merchant capitalist interests were at play in the region. This expedition was defeated.

For its part, certain that it could not keep control of the region, Bolivia decided to hand over these lands to international—especially North American—economic groups. According to an agreement the Bolivian government signed with the Bolivian Syndicate, the financial management of Acre would be the responsibility of this organization, whose headquarters were in New York. Brazil's response was not to wait. Numerous Brazilian diplomats traveled to England and the United States to try to annul the agreement.

War fever overtook the region. This time, as a result of the failure of the previous expedition, the Amazonas government tried to find someone who understood military strategy to lead the raid. They hired a gaucho working in the area as a surveyor, Plácido de Castro, who had studied at the Military College of Porto Alegre, Rio Grande do Sul, before going to the Amazon.

Plácido de Castro also had the much more important support of the Acre rubber barons, who put at his disposal men, weapons, money, food, and boats for the expedition. As a result of his bellicose and authoritarian temperament, he put the simple rubber tappers through tough training and transformed them into soldiers.

Plácido de Castro used guerrilla tactics to win the war decisively against Bolivia. With their knowledge of the forests and rivers, the rubber tappers played a fundamental role in the war. The leader was only a mercenary who decided to accept the mission for which he was hired.

The war started in Xapuri on August 6, 1902, Bolivian Independence Day, and lasted until January 1903. At its end the Independent State of Acre, governed by Plácido de Castro, was established. A short time later he was assassinated by one of his officers. The state lasted a short time before being abolished and annexed to Brazil, which acquired legal rights to the region with the signing of the Treaty of Petrópolis at the end of 1903.

The Rubber Soldier

It was not only in the Acre revolution that the rubber tappers were important actors. During World War II, with the closing of Asian ports by the

Japanese, Amazonian rubber went back to being a strategically fundamental product. The allies needed it for the pneumatics of their planes, vehicles, tanks, and so on, and now it was possible to get it only in Amazonia.

Because of the very low prices for rubber in the international market before this time, the Amazon had lost considerable population. It was necessary to repopulate it with northeasterners who would produce rubber in the quantity the Allies required.

Since it was a wartime effort, the Americans financed it and the Brazilian government took responsibility for promoting the production of rubber in Amazonia. To do its part, the Brazilian government carried out a recruiting campaign in the Brazilian Northeast and used a term that was extremely useful at the time: It was recruiting rubber soldiers. It promised that everybody would earn a lot of money and would be officially recognized as soldiers, in addition to the fact that those who went to the Amazon would not run the risk of being sent to the front in Europe. No such guarantee was made to those who failed to produce the necessary rubber. Recruitment started around 1940 and lasted until the end of the war, with the result that Amazonia was again populated by thousands of hillbillies who had come from the Northeast to produce rubber.

The incredible aspect of this story is that once again the rubber tappers were left behind. The money sent by the United States to finance the war effort in rubber production was either lost in the bureaucracy or channeled exclusively to the rubber barons who, once again, simply exploited the rubber tappers.

To give an idea of the cruelty involved, thousands of northeastern men, the great majority of them youths or adolescents, traveled in ships trailed and often directly threatened day and night by German submarines until they arrived at the port of Belém. There they were "selected" by the bosses and sent to the rubber estates.

Instead of being paid as rubber soldiers, when they arrived in the estates they discovered they were in debt for everything from the fare from the Northeast to the clothes on their backs, as well as all the equipment needed for production. They also discovered they could leave the estates only after paying these debts.

Official recruiting campaigns took place in northeastern cities, with "posting" of rubber soldiers by Brazilian authorities; but when they arrived in Amazonia, the hillbillies discovered they had nobody to complain to, no official would listen to them, because all the authorities were related to the bosses.

Thousands of northeasterners died in the war effort to produce rubber in Amazonia. Millions, if not billions, of American dollars financed the production of rubber without one penny going directly to the true producers, the rubber soldiers. The dollars enriched either state technocrats or rubber barons; not one rubber tapper received any pay for his contribution to the war effort.

It was not until the Constitution of 1988,[12] in its Temporary Provisions, that the rubber soldiers were officially recognized by the Brazilian government and given rights to a pension of two minimum salaries per month. But now the Social Security Administration requires that in order to be recognized, a rubber soldier must present a written document from the time of World War II proving he produced rubber. However, the rubber barons were the only ones who kept records of production, and almost all of them have died. Those who are still living destroyed all such records, as keeping them would provide a confession of guilt of their appropriation of rubber tapper payments.

Requiring that rubber tappers have written documents or notes from that era means no rubber soldier will ever be recognized as such, since this proof is absolutely impossible to produce.

The cruelty of this requirement by the Brazilian government can be seen when one meets these rubber soldiers, now at least seventy years old, and hears their accounts of everything they suffered, transported like slaves in steerage, forced to eat scraps, running the risk of being attacked by German submarines, and then everything they suffered on the rubber estates, learning the work, facing the diseases common to the region, always having to produce more rubber without ever being able to pay their debts. It is very rare to talk to a rubber soldier and not cry along with him, seeing the irresponsibility of the Brazilian government, since they were recruited officially and then abandoned to their fate in Amazonia, where they experienced conditions as difficult as those they had left in the Northeast.

Speaking of the rubber soldiers, I remember Cabo Veio, from Ceará. In his home state he would have been a "cornet corporal" in the army who came to Amazonia as a rubber soldier. He worked for the Xapuri Rural Workers' Union in 1988. He always talked about his home with great nostalgia. He would describe his father's ranch as if he had visited it the day before. He would have returned to Ceará, but he never managed to go back. His life was remembering his home with nostalgia. I know that there are so many others like him that it would be impossible to mention here all those I encountered during the years I traveled in the Xapuri estates.

I consider what the Brazilian state did and continues to do to the rubber soldiers a profound injustice. I remember one time, when I was studying law in Rio Branco as an intern, I attended a hearing in federal court. It was a "justificatory hearing," where elderly rubber tappers tried to prove through witnesses that they had worked in Amazonia during World War II.

I sat at the back of the chamber, as was appropriate for interns according to the presiding judge, who didn't like interns very much. An elderly man came in and said he had worked around 1941 in the "dispersion." Acting as if he didn't understand, or perhaps really not understanding, the judge asked, "Dispersion, what is dispersion? Is it a city, a ranch, a village?" (Note that although he was questioning a rubber tapper who was trying to explain his activities, His Honor did not ask if "Dispersion" was a rubber estate.)

"Dispersion is a rubber estate, St. Francis of the Dispersion, near Dispersion Creek," answered the old rubber tapper, with an expression of surprise. It was obvious to him that when he spoke of "Dispersion" he was referring to the estate of that name, and it didn't seem right that an authority like the judge would not know this.

"Where is this near?" asked the judge.

The rubber tapper didn't know what the judge wanted to know. In fact, what His Honor wanted to know but didn't explain was what township the estate was located in. But the way he asked the question, it was impossible to answer for a very simple reason: the Dispersion estate isn't near anywhere. On foot to Xapuri it would be a fifteen- to eighteen-hour walk. On foot to Rio Branco, it would take about the same time. By boat to Rio Branco, it would take about two days. By "speedboat" (an aluminum craft with a 25 or 40 horsepower motor), it would take about ten hours. Or so. Dispersion is far from everything!

How did the judge expect the rubber tapper to answer his question in the form he asked it?

Soon after, a witness, another rubber tapper, about eighty years old, came in. The judge gave the customary warning that he was speaking as a witness and if he lied he would be prosecuted for perjury. The old guy answered "in the can," as they say locally; that is, straight up, "I know, Your Excellency can ask me."

The judge began questioning:

"Does the gentleman know the plaintiff (indicating his name) present here?"

"Yes, Your Honor."

"Since when?"

"Since 1940."

"Where did you meet him?"

"At Dispersion."

"What is Dispersion? Is it a city, a ranch, a village? What is it?"

"Dispersion is the estate!"

"Do you know if he tapped rubber trees?"

"Yes, sir! He was my neighbor."

"Did you tap rubber trees?"

"Yes, sir!"

"How is it that you saw him tapping trees if he was at another homestead. Did you stop tapping to look at him?"

"No, Your Honor, there was a rubber trail that was an extension of mine, and we always saw each other when I was tapping on my trail and he was tapping on his."

The judge then tried to find out the names of the boss, the clerk, and the inspector who worked on the estate. The witness got everything right. As he dictated to the stenographer, the judge deliberately reversed the names. The witness quickly corrected the judge: "No, Your Honor, that was the boss. The other one was the clerk, and the third one was the inspector." This took place around 1996, that is, about forty-five years after the fact. Trying to cast doubt on the witness, the judge said, "The gentleman has a good memory, doesn't he?"

The witness didn't mince words: "Listen up, sonny, you are trying to say that at the age of eighty, never having lied in my life, I am lying now, in front of an official? Is that what Your Excellency is trying to say?"

I admit I almost applauded the witness, since the judge shut up and ended the hearing. But the striking thing is that the judge, as far as I could understand, was trying to cast doubt on the witness.

This was when oral pleas were allowed. Imagine now, when written documents from the time under dispute are required.

The Magical World of the Forest

Having traveled into the past to try to understand what is happening in the present, and before coming to more recent times, I will go back to my first apprenticeship in the forest.

When I was walking with Tatá as my guide, the day he went back to his homestead, in the morning he heard the song of the caboré and said it wouldn't rain that day. By coincidence or not, it did not rain. But as we walked through the forest he told me about its magical aspects. Since I am not very credulous, I tried to explain these stories by referring to actual situations that happen in the forest, but it is not always possible to do this.

I don't know if the forest's magic resides in its grandeur, its biological diversity, the thousands of sounds and colors that inspire reverence in its inhabitants. I do know there are many stories and legends about the forest. I can say that in the seven years I frequented it, I never encountered confirmation of any of these legends. But the older rubber tappers all insist on telling these stories, which grow out of the relationship between human beings and the magic of the forest, reinforcing superstitions and creating beings and godlike creatures that become part of the culture of this immense region.

One of the beings the forest's inhabitants fear most is the Mapinguari, a large animal in the form of a human, with round feet, like the bottom of a pounding stick, one eye in the middle of its forehead, and a very bad smell. It likes to eat people alive—especially their heads—and is therefore greatly feared.

Another respected creature, as I heard from Tatá, Simplício, and other older rubber tappers, is the "Mother of the Rubber Tree" (whom some call the Queen of the Forest), a beautiful woman whose face is all cut up, the way a rubber tree is scored. She helps only bachelor rubber tappers who try to increase their production of rubber. To do this one must make a "bargain" with the Mother of the Rubber Tree. To work, the agreement has to include several basic actions: On a night with a full moon, the rubber tapper must go to the "mouth" of a main rubber trail, that is, the one farthest from the house, and call the Mother of the Rubber Tree three times. When she appears, he must propose the agreement ("the rules," as the rubber tappers say when they tell the story). One of the goddess's basic requirements is that the rubber tapper remain single. Marriage breaks the rules, and the Mother severely punishes the traitor, sometimes even killing him. According to the older rubber tappers, only with an agreement can they succeed in paying off their debts to the boss by increasing their rubber production.

The "Little Forest Half-Breed," also known to the Indians as "Curupira," is the great protector of the animals. If the rubber tapper kills game only to feed himself, there is no problem; but if he kills for its own sake, the Little Half-Breed feels the pain of the animals and beats the hunter with tree branches, leaving him bruised all over, in addition to making him lose his way in the forest. Several accounts of things that had happened were told to me during my first job. Whether they were true I don't know, but they were certainly told in great detail.

"Miraculous souls" are spread throughout Amazonia and normally are "rubber tapper saints" or angels that protect and help the inhabitants of the forest. In Xapuri, for example, they have St. John of Guarani, who is commemorated on St. John's Day but has nothing to do with the Catholic saint. He is the "miraculous soul" of a rubber tapper who died in the middle of the forest, at the Guarani homestead on the Boa Vista estate. One day a rubber tapper who was lost came there and made a vow to light a pound of candles if he could find the way home. He found it soon after, and thus the myth was created.

True or not, a small chapel at the place is full of messages from people who went there to fulfill a vow to the rubber tapper saint. In case of any further problem, people go back to St. John of Guarani. I myself had to go with several people to fulfill vows they made when I was shot in 1991. The rubber tappers made many vows, all of which included my journey to the Guarani homestead, about nine hours' walk from Xapuri, to accompany them. When I recovered, out of respect for my rubber tapper friends, I went with them.

Every year on St. John's Day (June 24) thousands of people from Xapuri, from townships near Rio Branco and even from other states, go to the chapel of St. John of Guarani to fulfill their vows. The Catholic Church takes the opportunity to honor St. John, but it is not the Catholic saint the faithful are visiting.

So the forest certainly has its magic and strength, demanding respect from those who live in it. For them, these beliefs or superstitions justify their fears.

Party on the Rubber Estate: Forgetting Day-to-Day Hardships

Especially during the first two periods of the rubber boom (until 1912 and after 1940, during World War II), the rubber tappers always lived in isolation in the forest. Their neighbors were far away, and they often could not rely on their coworkers who lived nearby, since they could be "spies" who received payments from the bosses to spy on the other rubber tappers and prevent them from selling rubber to other rubber barons or small traders.

This situation usually created only one meeting place on the estate, the trading post. In this place the rubber tappers got together on the weekends for a few hours of leisure. The basic form of entertainment was drinking rum.

Sometimes parties were organized, usually in the trading post itself. Under the influence of alcohol, the festive atmosphere would last all night long under gas and kerosene lanterns. The main rhythms came from the Northeast, where almost all the region's rubber tappers were from. Those who hadn't been born there were descendants of northeasterners and identified with the music.

Sometimes somebody there played a musical instrument, and he was the life of the party. Or the parties were organized by the boss, who was also the main authority in case of a fight.

The parties provided a golden opportunity to get acquainted with the daughter of a married rubber tapper and "keep an eye on the girl." It was not rare for fights to the death to take place because of women, precisely because it was so hard to find one on the estate.

Religious holidays always provided a good excuse for dancing and drinking all night to forget the hardships of everyday life in the forest. On these occasions there was first a religious ritual, such as saying the rosary or a mass, when the boss played a very important role and ordered the vicar of the closest parish to officiate.

To attend a party, sometimes the rubber tapper walked more than ten hours that same day; so rare were these opportunities that the sacrifice was worthwhile. To this day, a *forró*[13] that happens after community work or a football game is the main leisure activity on the estate, with the rubber tappers walking many hours to participate.

Today parties are much more common and take place for various reasons. Religious rituals are still traditional, and some places are well known for their annual events: Saint Lucy, St. Francis, and St. John are usually the most honored Catholic saints—the first two because their days come close to the end of processing, when it is easier to have a party. Another common reason today is a cooperative workday. Another is a political rally during an election campaign. Usually during the day a soccer tournament is held and at night they dance the forró. A wedding always provides an opportunity for a big party, because even today a formal wedding is rare on the estates.

From early on children and adolescents learn to dance, participating actively in the festivities on the estate. Almost everybody over nine years old dances, especially the girls.

A "Wedding" on the Estate

Family structure on the rubber estates follows very peculiar rules. "Marriage on paper" or in church is very rare and, according to the rubber tappers themselves, unnecessary and expensive, since you have to give a party when you get married.

To avoid this expense but perhaps also to make marriage more dramatic, it is better to "carry off" or "steal" one's future bride and establish the marriage as a fait accompli in this way.

The rubber tappers tell many stories about these marriages. But the majority of couples are not formally married; they just live together. But here's an interesting fact: Even though he has stolen his wife, the rubber tapper won't admit that anybody stole his daughter. When this happens the reaction is always quite violent. It seems necessary to manifest lack of approval of what the daughter did by calling the son-in-law a "horny goat" for not having had the courage to ask for her hand.

When the rubber tapper's daughter "flees," her father makes a huge scene. He vows never to forgive her or see her again. After about a week, however, the daughter returns home, rarely bringing her lover on this first visit, to see the lay of the land. Normally, as in every similar situation, the mother is sought out first to calm things down, and after delivering a long sermon, the father blesses his daughter. Thus the situation is resolved and the marriage formalized or accepted. The son-in-law then comes to visit the parents to show he intends to take responsibility for the new family. This whole situation can be explained by the fact that usually everybody knows everybody else on the estate, so there's no way to perpetuate a hatred that in fact does not exist; it's only momentary.

Escapes of women from the estate often take place without forethought and even without prior courtship. The two become interested in each other and arrange the girl's "theft." It is almost a ritual in the forest. The more difficult the flight, the greater the proof of true love.

The parties are also excellent opportunities for flights of women because they bring many people together, and despite the mother's vigilance, the father lets down his guard after a few hours of heavy drinking, making escape easier. Also, the mother often has to divide her attention between the daughter, who is in the room where everybody's dancing, and helping in the kitchen, as all the women help one another on these occasions. Not to mention the fact that the mothers themselves also like to dance.

The young men start working on the estate as "half-timers" with a rubber tapper who has trails available. When he is already thinking of getting married, the young man finds a way to get his own homestead, which sometimes is inside his parents' holding.

Because diversions are so rare, "marriage" takes place very early on the estate, with men about twenty years old and the girls considered ready from the age of twelve. This means families are large. A couple normally has six to eight children, and some have as many as fifteen or twenty. Recently the number of children has declined because of the information that has arrived at the estates about health and natural means of birth control. On the remoter estates, however, the practice is still to marry early and have many children.

Formal marriage happens only many years later, when the couple takes advantage of a priest's duty visit.[14] After such a marriage, it is not necessary to have a party, although this usually happens as a social occasion organized by several people to celebrate baptisms and godparent relationships on the estate.

Chico Mendes a few months before his death in 1988. Photograph © Miranda Smith, 1988.

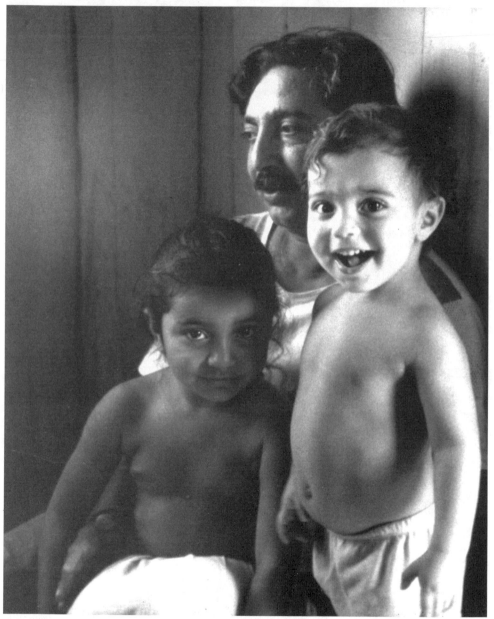

Chico Mendes and his children, Elenira and Sandino, July 1988. Photograph © Miranda Smith, 1988.

Chico Mendes by the side of the BR-364 highway. Photograph by Pilly Cowell.

Police try to enforce a repossession order with tractors and chainsaws. Photograph by A GAZETA do Acre.

Local musicians play forró. *Photograph courtesy of Conselho Nacional dos Seringueiros.*

Chico Mendes's funeral procession in Xapuri. Photograph by A GAZETA do Acre.

His comrades express their grief at the burial of Chico Mendes. Center, with arms raised, is his cousin, Raimundo Barros.

Headquarters of the Xapuri Rural Workers' Union. Placed there after Chico Mendes's killing, one banner on the front reads "Enough!" Photograph by A GAZETA do Acre.

Gomercindo Rodrigues, 2006. Photograph courtesy of the author.

~~~~~~~~~~~~~~~~~~~~~~~~~~~~~~~~~~~~~

Chapter 4

A GENOCIDAL OCCUPATION

AT THE BEGINNING OF THE 1970S the military dictatorship in Brazil developed an Amazon policy based on geopolitical and geostrategic principles conceived by General Golbery do Couto e Silva[1] and his disciples. This policy was based on several false premises, such as the Amazon being a demographic desert and an unproductive region that should be incorporated into the productive process in the interest of national and multinational capital, with the justification that this occupation would generate surpluses to pay the foreign debt.

On the other hand, the occupation of Amazonia was important strategically because the frontiers in a remote region would be protected in this way. So it was necessary to encourage migration to the region, which, it was already known, was extremely rich in strategic minerals. Obviously this was not part of the official rhetoric.

With the incorporation of Amazonia as an area of agricultural development, it was possible to resolve, or at least minimize, the problems that the concentration of landownership in the Center-South[2] was creating so as to specially benefit large economic enterprises and landholders in the region.

For their part, the rubber barons in Amazonia were completely bankrupt, and many suddenly found themselves likely to be able to sell their holdings. Thus they escaped the burden the rubber estates represented, despite all the government support and incentives the Rubber Bank (later the Bank of the Amazon, a private company)[3] had given them, with no concern for the rubber tapper.

The purchase of vast areas of estates by ranchers, businesses, industries, and financial conglomerates from the Center-South led to the complete destruction of traditional occupation of the Amazon region, since those who bought estates intended to use them for speculation.

To support this new Amazon policy and take care of the interests of the big construction firms and national and multinational investors, the dictatorship's strategists arranged for the opening of superhighways to "facilitate the occupation of the region," always using the argument that they were protecting national security. From this period come the big highways—the Transamazon, the Northern Perimeter, Belém-Brasília, Cuiabá-Santarém, and the BR-364 from Cuiabá to Cruzeiro do Sul, Acre.

The frontiers of farming and ranching expansion were forming along these highways, involving thousands of small farmers, landless rural workers, or unemployed urban workers from the Center-South. They went there after hearing the government propaganda that Amazonia was the Brazilian "Eldorado," a move reminiscent of the nineteenth-century westward migration in the United States. The dream of easy wealth, fertile land, and the possibility of quickly becoming a "rancher" took over.

The government itself took on the task of creating the integrated colonization or directed settlement projects to accommodate the migrants. Thus Amazonia served to alleviate tensions in the Center-South by receiving thousands of workers. Left in remote areas without means of communicating, they ceased being a potential risk to the military dictatorship. Thus the occupation of the Amazon comprised part of a complex geopolitical strategy conceived as part of the policy developed by the mentors of the 1964 military coup.

This entire occupation was extremely damaging to the Amazon, fundamentally harming the native populations or those who had lived in the region for a long time, as well as producing profound and irreversible environmental changes in the regional ecosystem.

Another expanding activity was cattle ranching. To increase the value of the vast land areas they had purchased in Amazonia, the big ranchers developed the so-called Cattle-Raising Projects financed by the federal government through SUDAM[4] and SUDECO through highly subsidized interest rates; the projects were economically viable only because of these concessions. The application of capital through loans to "productive projects" in the financial markets ended up paying out borrowed money, which could be paid off only with interest.

The expansion of ranching—basically pastures, as ranching could not be developed with the level of financing provided by the federal government—expelled thousands of rubber tappers from the Brazilian forests to the urban slums or even to Bolivia and Peru. The same thing happened to other extractive workers or collectors in other regions, where colonization took over with greater violence, as, for example, in southern Pará. That is, the entire process of occupation in Amazonia impinged violently on the local populations. Indigenous groups that were still uncontacted, such as the Uru-Eu-Wau-Wau in Rondônia, were practically exterminated, and the same thing happened to the Cinta Larga, the Caxarari, the Kayapó, and other groups that were "integrated into civilization" without consideration of the costs in destroyed lives and cultures. The same thing happened to the rubber tappers pushed to the slums or outside the country. Thus it can be claimed that this model developed by the military for Amazonia was effectively *genocide.*

Colonization: "Rationality Squared"

The shipping of large population contingents from the Center-South and the Northeast to Amazonia, under the aegis of official propaganda about the new Eldorado, easy wealth, and abundant fertile land, was part of a policy of taming the region, opening it to capital investment and creating a reserve army for the concentration of Amazonia in capitalist hands.

The colonization projects, developed first in southern Pará and later in northern Mato Grosso, Rondônia, and Acre, did not strictly obey basic norms for projects that would involve human lives and profound environmental changes.

Developed almost always by technobureaucrats in Brasília, the projects did not take into consideration information about topography, hydrography, soils, farming practices, and other local factors. It seems as if the technocrats grabbed a map of an area and divided it up on paper in the simplest way by drawing straight lines.

If studied in a more thorough way, this failure of the technocrats and regional reality itself would show that colonization was and is completely unviable in Amazonia. The extremely fragile soils left after the removal of the forest canopy are rapidly degraded in almost the entire region, making colonization projects impossible.

On the other hand, drawing straight lines that created identical rectangular lots in vast areas, without considering the topography and hydrography of each locality where the projects were set up, created ridiculous situations—for example, lots with a great amount of water, sometimes mostly underwater, and completely dry lots, where even drinking water was hard to find during the dry seasons. This is what we customarily call "rationality squared," still part of the mind-set of the majority of INCRA technocrats in the Amazon or Brasília, despite the great technological advances that allow them to obtain detailed information from satellite photos of any area in the region. The problem is one of theoretical conception and not lack of information. Even today the lots laid out by INCRA in the region follow the dictates of "facilitation," as opposed to more consistent technical criteria.

The conditions of the people sent to the colonized areas—who, according to the official propaganda, would receive prefabricated houses, medical

care, and schools for their children as well as roads for shipping out their produce—were, and continue to be, the worst possible. Nothing that was promised was delivered.

Deforestation to create fields on a scale much greater than had been done
by previous inhabitants, the extractivists, as well as the concentration of population, led to the appearance and spread of diseases such as malaria, yellow
fever, and hepatitis. The workers were discouraged from remaining on their
smallholdings and encouraged to migrate to the urban slums. This resulted in
overcrowding in cities with almost no infrastructure or services. In addition,
the lack of jobs in the region meant that the ever-increasing excess of
labor power could not be absorbed, greatly worsening the poverty of these
populations.

On the other hand, this migration resulted in states such as Rondônia seeing population increases of 700 percent over the past twenty years. Dozens of
cities grew out of nothing and became extremely crowded in a decade.
Regional centers sprouted up overnight, as happened in Marabá, Belém,
Manaus, Porto Velho, Ji-Paraná, Ariquemes, Vilhena, and Rio Branco, where
the number of neighborhoods and inhabitants quintupled during the same
period.

This population increase brought with it terrible devastation. Up to 1982
about 10,000 square kilometers of Rondônia had been deforested. By 1985
deforestation had already reached 27,000 square kilometers, corresponding
to 11 percent of the state's total area. During the 1990s deforestation reached
more than 22 percent of the area of the state. More recent studies claim that
the speed of the devastation is increasing considerably, doubling the deforested area every two years. This process is absolutely suicidal.

The same thing that happened in Rondônia happened in southern Pará
and now is happening in Acre—even after Chico Mendes's murder, which
drew attention to Amazonia as a whole. Every year about 77,000 hectares are
deforested in Acre, according to the most recent data.

It should be noted that since a good part of this deforestation is done to
create pasture, each year the area of burning increases in the entire region,
stopping air traffic out of Cuiabá and affecting the entire northern region of
the country during certain periods, especially during August and September.
These are the driest months of the year in Amazonia.

Highways: Arteries of Devastation

As part of its "occupation" policy and in cooperation with the economic
interests of the big contractors, the military government developed a
broad highway construction program in the Amazon to "create the roads of

progress." The biggest of all these projects was the Transamazon Highway. According to the official propaganda, it should have been the road that would take thousands of landless northeasterners to the "empty" lands of the Amazon. This highway actually linked nothing to nowhere, and thirty years after its construction it is almost abandoned. Along some stretches it could not even serve as a track for motocross or a race car rally.

Highways like the Belém-Brasília or the Cuiabá-Santarém paved the way to full occupation of the Center-West and southeastern Pará. This chaotic and violent occupation of southeastern Pará, southwestern Maranhão, and northern Tocantins state, in the area known as the "Parrot's Beak," is having repercussions to this day, with the "law of the strongest" prevailing. Even now this region is the most violent in the entire Amazon. In its turn, northern Mato Grosso was favored for settlement; there a different kind of colonization predominated: private projects with private firms purchasing vast expanses of land and dividing them later into smaller lots that were sold to small farmers in the Center-South.

It is still difficult to measure the devastation caused by these highways up to the present. One could mention the almost total extinction of the Brazil nut stands in southern Pará, especially near Marabá. The southern migrants brought with them the same practices that had led them to devastate the pine forests of Rio Grande do Sul, Paraná, and Santa Catarina, the savannas of Mato Grosso do Sul, and even part of the Minas Gerais rainforest.

The BR-364 highway, especially between Cuiabá and Rio Branco, has been causing the complete devastation of Rondônia since it was opened and paved. Not to mention the extermination of local indigenous populations, since it serves as the main route into the heart of the forest, with other roads branching off to lead the way to devastation.

The nonindigenous traditional populations—rubber tappers, nut harvesters, gum tree pickers, river dwellers—living along these highways either changed their occupations or moved away. Most were expelled to the urban slums, where they became cheap labor because they had no training for the new occupations that emerged from the expansion. Or they migrated to countries like Bolivia and Peru, where they live under constant threat of expulsion or have to give up their sons to serve in the armies of these countries.

On the other hand, according to official propaganda, the highways would not only bring "progress" to the remotest areas of the Amazon, they would also lower the cost of living for local people, since they would facilitate shipping of industrial products to the Center-South. This was a bald-faced lie. Today Rondônia has some of the highest prices in the country, as does the entire Amazonian agricultural frontier.

The other important factor to consider is that all the megaprojects and the construction of the roads to nowhere cost billions of dollars, which considerably enlarged the Brazilian foreign debt without benefiting the people. On the contrary, these highways, aside from leading to devastation, helped perpetuate the most recent cruel ethnocide in Brazil, financed with dollars from the World Bank and the Inter-American Development Bank.

The worst part is that this insane policy of opening highways to "promote progress" still prevails, without the discourse of those that defend them having substantively changed. In their opinion it is still necessary to promote "national integration" or guarantee our borders or even "integrate Amazonia into the nation's productive processes." Not to mention, obviously, improving the living conditions of the local people.

In questioning the opening of the big highways I do not want to defend isolationism. I think it is possible and necessary to discuss a transportation model that is viable for the Amazon and that benefits its local populations and guarantees a self-sustaining development model at the same time.

Highways can be built, but it is necessary first to guarantee that the land alongside them remains in the hands of the people who already live there, thus ensuring that the highways do not become migration routes to devastation but a means to regional agricultural and extractive self-sufficiency. This model already exists, but it obviously does not interest the big economic enterprises that want the highways to be for the export of high-value hardwood to the international market.

It is necessary to find a development model that really benefits the Amazon and the planet, combining defense of the forest and water resources to maintain global equilibrium. This does not mean putting the Amazon at the service of international interests but rather of greater interests, including the local populations, which could actually help to protect our international frontiers without additional cost to the country. This does not mean Amazonia should be a sanctuary; on the contrary, it should be exploited for all its potential without, however, being destroyed.

This is what the local populations are proposing through the extractive reserves, the use of agroforestry systems, the diversification of the forest with economically viable species. Nobody in his right mind defends the untouchability of the forest but rather its self-sustaining use while respecting the traditional populations.

Megaprojects: Megacatastrophes

At the same time that it was developing highway projects in Amazonia, the federal government launched big programs to support migration into the region to accompany the projects.

With resources obtained by an astronomical increase in the Brazilian foreign debt, Polamazônia and Polonoroeste[5] were supposed to finance infrastructural projects for the towns sprouting up alongside the highways, as well as private "development" projects such as ranching and regional industrialization. Riddled with corruption, SUDAM and SUDECO were responsible for the administration of most of the resources sent to the region via these big projects.

The results of the application of these resources—a few billion dollars—were so damaging that the World Bank itself, which financed Polonoroeste, decided to temporarily suspend the release of final program funds in light of the evidence of uncontrolled devastation it was causing, principally in Rondônia. In addition to suspending release of its resources, the World Bank required development of an ecological-economic zoning plan as a condition for releasing the $200 million remaining in the program fund. As a result, the Rondônia government developed Planafloro, a controversial zoning program for the state.[6]

The indigenous groups of Rondônia, some of whom had had no contact with white "civilization" until the early 1980s, are now, at the beginning of the twenty-first century, almost extinct. Such has been the violence of the government-sponsored occupation of the region.

Large areas of rubber stands, in the Ariquemes region of Rondônia, for example, have disappeared, becoming colonization projects or large cacao plantations. Settlements or even cities have rapidly multiplied in the state, with increasing pressure on the environment and total collapse of the existing urban infrastructure, such as energy, sanitation, and transportation.

In the Xapuri region, thanks to cattle-ranching projects financed by SUDAM, about 120,000 rubber trees and 80,000 Brazil nut trees disappeared in ten years. These had been sufficient to maintain about three hundred rubber tapper families who were forced to migrate to Rio Branco or Bolivia.

Special projects were developed in the Amazon to support industrialization, such as construction of huge hydroelectric projects, most of which caused irreversible ecological damage. For example, the Balbina dam in Amazonas state flooded a vast area belonging to the Waimiri-Atroari Indians, but today it is completely inefficient: It does not have the capacity to generate enough energy to supply even half the needs of Manaus, the state capital.

Tucurui, in Pará state, was a hydroelectric project constructed basically to supply electricity to the industrial park that developed as a result of the Grande Carajás mining project. In principle Tucurui supplies electrical energy to two giant aluminum-processing plants, ALBRAS, which is Brazilian owned, and Alcoa, 100 percent foreign owned. Local populations, those affected most by the ecological problems caused by its construction, take second place.

The water dammed by these hydroelectric projects always affects areas occupied by local people, causing considerable trouble, since resettlement is always a "secondary problem." Thus the workers who used to have enough to survive no longer have any place to work and end up depending on odd jobs.

Mineral exploration projects in the Amazon are also responsible for great catastrophes from both the social and the ecological point of view. In the former case, this is because vast areas previously devoted to self-sustaining activities by traditional populations are closed, expelling the families that have lived there for more than a century. In the latter case, mining is highly predatory but justified by its technicians.

In Carajás, for example, it is common to hear from a technician of the Rio Doce Valley Company (CVRD)[7] that it contains enough iron to be mined for four hundred fifty years. But they do not say what they will put in place of the iron-bearing mountains that will be destroyed or how they will "fill in the hole." In the opinion of the technocrats, this is not a current problem. "Let the future take care of itself!"

This project, pompously called Grande Carajás, foresees mining not only of iron, the mineral in the greatest quantity, but also of gold, nickel, aluminum, copper, manganese, and so on.

There is a serious problem inside the CVRD area—about two thousand families of rural workers who already lived in the Carajás Mountain region well before the discovery of minerals in the area and who are continually threatened with removal by the firm. Not to mention that the entire area is, or at least was, guarded by a private army, much better equipped than the Pará state police and certainly, according to the workers, no less truculent.

This private army controls the entry and existence of all those inside an area determined by CVRD, which allows the entry only of the contractors' employees, subcontractors, and officials of the "Valley" or people specifically authorized by the company directors.

As a result of these big hydroelectric and mining projects, the great Brazil nut stands of southern Pará have been almost decimated by a forced, disorderly occupation without government support. Another problem that especially threatens the Brazil nut trees of southern Pará is the installation of pig iron kilns fueled by charcoal. Every year the area devastated to provide wood increases.

Linked to the lack of government support of the region's traditional populations is the predatory logging of tropical hardwoods such as mahogany from the entire region. These species have already disappeared in many places where they used to grow in great quantity. Thousands of cubic meters of this wood are illegally extracted every year and exported to the rich countries.

On the other hand, the same government that systematically declined to support sustainable development of the forest has been directly or indirectly financing (through fiscal incentives, subsidized electric power, and transportation infrastructure) all the agricultural and mining megaprojects in the region since the 1970s. One need only cite the ill-fated Jari project,[8] which cost several billion dollars. I hope this changes radically now.

Perhaps what is most impressive is that this model of development emerged from the closed military offices and their schools of strategic planning. Since the military dictatorship and continuing until the present decade, Amazonia is still considered of strategic interest by the military. With this vision and the same discourse of "preserving the integrity of our borders," they insist that indigenous areas in border regions not be demarcated, as well as seeking and obtaining resources from the G7 (now the G8) for a broad project of monitoring the Amazon region, whose name says it all: Amazon Vigilance System (SIVAM).[9] Their interest is not, in fact, in preserving the region. If it were, they would not have allowed the transfer of millions of hectares of Amazon forest to multinational capital during the dictatorship.

The military always had its own projects for the Amazon. To this day, they have not deigned to explain the strange "hole" in the Cachimbo Mountains[10] in Pará that was supposedly for nuclear testing. To ensure that the information does not reach the public, they invoke the whispered term "national security" to justify all these secret projects, whose costs are paid for by the long-suffering Brazilian people.

A more recent invasion, which, strange to say, has not been commented on, wears civilian clothes: a big project with the strange name 2010, referring to the year it is supposed to be finished. It was planned by Eletrobrás[11] and proposes the installation of several big hydroelectric projects in the region to guarantee the electric supply in Brazil for most of the twenty-first century. At least that is how it is justified.

Without discussing the hydroelectric potential of the Amazon region, the fact remains that this is a flat region, and the lakes created by dams cover extensive areas of forests, causing considerable ecological and social damage.

In this context, it should not be considered strange that the recent regulation in the Forest Code (Decree No. 1282, of October 19, 1994, regulating articles 15, 19, 20 and 21 of Law 4771/65) opened the possibility, before it was vetoed, of using dead Brazil nut trees in areas where "projects of public interest" (such as hydroelectric plants, highways, railroads, electric transmission networks) would be built.

Mining: Destructive Illusion

From the time of the country's discovery, interest in its mineral wealth was one of the bases of colonial Brazil. It is no different today in a region whose previously unknown mineral potential was discovered only recently.

Poverty, unemployment, lack of land for rural workers in the Center-South, and official propaganda that Amazonia was the new Eldorado led to the migration of a huge group seeking easy wealth on abundant and cheap land.

On arrival in the Amazon, everybody realized that the propaganda was much more positive than what the region had to offer; the soils are abundant but fragile and not very fertile once the forests that cover them are removed. Infrastructure for the migrants was almost nonexistent. Diseases spread rapidly, especially malaria. So Eldorado gleamed much less brightly than the propaganda indicated.

Then the mineral discoveries began in the region. Serra Pelada, in southeastern Pará, was compared to an anthill, given the great number of miners who went there. Gold and tin mines appeared in Rondônia. The gold frontier moved to the extreme north of the country, Roraima, where rich lodes of gold were found in Yanomami[12] territory. Always searching for quick and easy money, the miners went to the region, causing big problems for the Yanomami, whose lands were recognized but had not been demarcated because they stood in the way of regional geopolitical and economic interests.

The trail of devastation left by mining is impressive. One need only look at the settlements that grew up around this activity, big slums with no infrastructure, with important rivers such as the Madeira contaminated by mercury, or the huge craters at Serra Pelada. In Roraima the drama has become even greater, as almost ten thousand Yanomami, who had little or no contact with white "civilization," are being decimated by various epidemics because they do not have antibodies against diseases they had never even heard of. A genocide is going on with government connivance; no practical actions have been taken to prevent it.

Human life is worth little in the mining camps. If somebody succeeds in striking it rich, he might soon be found dead without anybody seeing anything. According to the miners themselves, life in a gold mining area is always hanging by a thread.

In truth, mining is a great illusion that leads to devastation. The dream of easy wealth never becomes reality for the miner, but it makes the gold buyers and their agents richer and richer. Meanwhile, entire regional populations are malnourished. Much more quickly than expected, the forest falls. The pure waters of the rivers become polluted. The incidence of prostitution, especially among girls twelve to fifteen, criminality, and disease increases geometrically.

The 1970s: The Ranchers Arrive and the Violence Begins

During the entire military dictatorship and up to the present, the Amazon was and is considered a national security problem by many interests throughout this immense region. In this context, one of the military's policies was to promote the occupation of the region, as a way of guaranteeing sovereignty over this piece of national territory. Thus the strategists of the time made plans that involved the installation of infrastructure (roads, cities) and broad incentives and financing for those who decided to invest in the region.

One of the most important aspects was the creation of big agricultural and ranching projects completely financed and supported by state banks. This project, which combined cheap and easy financing with low land prices, was broadly publicized throughout the country. In this way the bankrupt rubber barons sold immense holdings, most with disputed titles. This was not a big problem for the *paulistas*[13] who came to the region. They always sought to solve the problem using the traditional Brazilian maneuver of "finding a way." One mega-holding became the biggest property in Brazil, with about 2.1 million hectares. After INCRA investigated, the owner was left with "only" 40,000 hectares, a reduction of 98 percent.

The arrival of the ranchers not only was a developmental event for the region, as the defenders of the predatory ranching model tried to claim; it also increased the level of violence many times, especially in Acre. Violence took place because the land sold by the rubber barons almost always was completely occupied by rubber tappers who, despite the failure of the estates, still lived off extractive production, with the small trader or peddler who brought goods in exchange for rubber along the rivers replacing the boss.

As a result of their long occupation of the land, the rubber tappers were legally considered homesteaders, but they didn't know this at first. The ranchers, however, knew very well that it was necessary to clear the estates and drive out their inhabitants to avoid lawsuits. With the estate cleared of homesteaders, the value of the land would increase.

Having brought gunmen disguised as guards from their home regions, the southern investors tried right away to expel the homesteaders from their areas. In the process, everything was possible: laughably small compensation for the rubber tappers' improvements or expulsion pure and simple in most cases—setting fire to the traditional occupant's home and evicting him at gunpoint—using gunmen or even state police transformed into a private army that acted with or without judicial authorization when the occupants resisted.

Disorganized at first, the rural workers began to seek ways to resist. Early on they counted on the support of the Catholic Church via the grassroots church communities and later, in the mid-1970s, the Agricultural Workers Confederation (CONTAG), which set up an office in Acre and encouraged the formation of the Rural Workers' Union.

The organization of the rural workers gave them the strength they hadn't had when they were isolated. Forms of resistance, such as the empates against deforestation and collective action against the violence of the gunmen, began. This cost the workers dear over time, as their comrades, especially the leaders, were assassinated.

~~~~~~~~~~~~~~~~~~~~~~~~

Chapter 5

"OUR VICTORY DEPENDS ON OUR ORGANIZATION AND DISCIPLINE"

SOMETIME AFTER BEGINNING TO WORK with Chico Mendes, I saw the phrase in the title of this chapter written on a blackboard during a general meeting of the Xapuri Rural Workers' Union. It sums up the entire political method that directed the actions of the union under Chico's leadership. It looks like a simple slogan. And organizing a union seems simple to workers. In the Center-South unions have existed for decades. In the Amazon, the first ones sprang up in the mid-1970s.

As victims of the violence of the paulistas' hired guns, the rubber tappers began to discuss how to resist, initially with the support of the Catholic Church through grassroots religious communities. They had discovered that if they continued to be alone and isolated, they would be fair game. The first meetings took place around 1973 in Brasiléia, after a group of rubber tappers tried to stop a clearing operation on the Carmen estate, protesting against use of the herbicide Tordon, which poisoned several people in the area.

In 1975, still in Brasiléia, this time with the support of CONTAG, the first Rural Workers' Union in Acre was founded. This union became the cradle of organized resistance among the rubber tappers, where the strategy of the empate was created. In this first union were two great future leaders of the workers who would be tragically murdered some years after: Wilson Pinheiro (killed July 21, 1980) and Chico Mendes (killed December 22, 1988).

In 1977 the Xapuri Rural Workers' Union, which became the second organizational base of rural workers in the Acre Valley, was started. At the same time other rural workers' unions sprang up in other townships in Acre: Sena Madureira, Tarauaca, Cruzeiro do Sul, Rio Branco. The tradition of struggle extended from Brasiléia and Xapuri to Tarauaca and Sena Madureira during that period.

At this point I'd like to bring up the issue of isolation among the rubber tappers and the favors the bosses gave certain rubber tappers so they would serve as spies. This was done during the era of the traditional estate but did not exist during the 1970s. So what was its relationship to the organization of the rubber tappers?

This is a crucial question because the bosses fomented mistrust among the rubber tappers, and this became a cultural personality trait among them. This created problems in organizing unions. Since everybody mistrusted everybody else, it was very difficult to start rural workers' unions. First it was necessary to break through this cultural trait, and only then could we manage to bring together and organize the rural workers.

In truth, organization was somewhat forced on them from outside, since the violence of the paulistas and their gunmen made the rubber tappers think they had to join together in order not to be wiped out. At this point it was especially important that the Catholic Church, along with CONTAG and its advisers, but especially several leaders such as Wilson Pinheiro in Brasiléia, could count on Chico Mendes's support. He already knew something about unionism, which he had learned from Euclides Távora, the Communist who was his great teacher of reading, writing, and Marxist theory, which was of great value in getting him to join the Brasiléia Rural Workers' Union, where he was a member of the first directorate.

In 1977, as an MDB[1] council member in Xapuri, Chico Mendes helped set up talks to start the Rural Workers' Union there. He became its president in 1983, when he left the city council, until his death in 1988.

The founding of the unions was very important for organizing resistance among rural workers. It could be said it was responsible for preventing the catastrophe in Acre from reaching the same level as in Rondônia, where the rubber tappers are in remote areas, most of the estates having been destroyed by "progress" or occupied by big ranchers or mining operations.

It was the rural workers' unions that began to develop the empates. In Brasiléia several were carried out as the union was being started. This meant that the ranchers who succeeded in clearing forest, or deforested less than they wanted, began thinking that the best solution would be to finish off the "agitators."

The Assassination of Wilson Pinheiro:
A Plan to Destroy the Union

Obviously the resistance of rubber tappers organized in unions worried the ranchers, who could not clear as much forest as they wanted. In many areas they could not deforest at all because of the workers' mobilization. As a result, the ranchers thought up and executed a plan to "show" the rubber tappers in Brasiléia and undermine the new union. They were going to "make an example," by doing something forceful to show who really had the power in the region. So on July 21, 1980, Wilson Pinheiro, its great president, was murdered inside the Rural Workers' Union hall in Brasiléia.

But the carefully constructed plot did not stop there: The same people who ordered Wilson Pinheiro's murder hatched a more macabre plan, to kill the ranch manager who possibly knew something about Pinheiro's murder and put the blame for his death on the rural workers. They would kill two birds with one stone.[2]

All this occurred and is recorded, strangely enough, in the record of the Brasiléia court on July 28, 1980. Jesus Matias, a farmer who had a good relationship with Nilão, the ranch manager, went early in the morning in a rented pickup truck to the ranch where the manager was staying and had breakfast with him, according to information provided by Nilão's widow's lawyer.

It is important to emphasize that the strange thing about the journey of Jesus Matias is that the union truck was transporting workers for free the same day at about 9:00 A.M., but he didn't wait for it. He went early, paying for a rented vehicle, expensive for a farmer.

After making Nilão lose some time and with information about when Nilão would leave the ranch, Jesus Matias went back about 8 kilometers and waited for the arrival of the workers who were returning from a ceremony honoring Wilson Pinheiro, whose murder had taken place a week before.

When he went to this place Jesus Matias was accompanied by two strangers, unknown to any of the workers who were coming back from the city. Jesus Matias said the two were chainsaw operators, and they had Paraguayan accents, according to a witness's testimony.

When the workers who came from the city arrived where Matias was, it was no longer possible to go to the union hall in the truck, since it had rained and the road was in terrible condition. He said Nilão was going to flee and it was necessary to detain him and deliver him to the authorities. The workers agreed, but when Nilão arrived Jesus Matias and the two strangers had him killed, putting the blame on the workers.

In this way a potential witness was eliminated and at the same time the death of a ranch manager was pinned on the rural workers. Politically speaking, nothing could be better for the ranchers, who deflected the investigators' attention from Wilson Pinheiro's murder.

So it was that Lula, Jacó Bittar, Chico Mendes, and others were indicted, tried twice, and found not guilty in the Manaus military court, having been accused under the National Security Law[3] as "inciters" of violence against Nilão. But nobody, absolutely nobody, has been accused in the death of

Wilson Pinheiro to this day. Recently seventeen rural workers were tried for the death of Nilão. They were exonerated because the jury in Brasiléia understood that the story told above was much more convincing than the version the police and the prosecutor gave them. An appeal is in progress.

It is appropriate to mention that about two years later Jesus Matias himself was killed by someone who was having coffee with him—the same modus operandi.

The impressive thing about this whole story is that it is recorded in court documents in Brasiléia. Witnesses testified, described the possible plotters, and even mentioned that one of them had a Paraguayan accent. Instead of looking for them, since none of the rubber tappers accused in Nilão's death had a Paraguayan accent, and investigating the men who were with Jesus Matias at the crime site before it happened, the police preferred to close the proceedings, indicting only the rubber tappers.

Allegations of torture—fingernails pulled out, beatings with a wet towel, among other things—by some of the jailed rubber tappers accused of Nilão's death were only partially investigated. The judge, today the chief judge, Miracele Borges, ordered forensic examinations by the Forensic Institute.[4] These examinations found nothing on the bodies of the majority of the jailed rubber tappers. Those that did find something "disappeared" from the records. The marks are mentioned only in the Forensic Institute director's report to the judge, when he lists all the documents. Some are missing, but nobody looked into these lacunae.

Xapuri: Resistance Continued and Became More Effective

The plan of those who tried to destroy the union by killing Wilson Pinheiro and accusing the rubber tappers of involvement in Nilão's death was only partly successful. Although the rural workers' movement declined for about eight years in Brasiléia, the rubber tappers' resistance continued, moving its epicenter to Xapuri, where Chico Mendes was a city council member and the union was run (for a short time, it's true) by a woman, Derci Teles de Carvalho. This was a double victory.

Because the empates, which continued to take place, were not sufficient to keep the rubber tappers in their areas, a complementary form of resistance developed in Xapuri: the creation of better living conditions on the estates so the rubber tappers would feel motivated to organize to stay in the forest. Thus was born the Rubber Tapper Project to oversee the establishment of schools and cooperatives on the estates.

This was the work I helped evaluate six years later and led to everything I learned.

First planned for adults, the schools over time came to serve the rubber tappers' children. Even so, several rubber tappers were trained to read and write at these schools and became teachers. Some finished high school and are now studying at the university.

Another advantage of the schools was that as the rubber tappers began to read (98 percent were completely illiterate at the beginning) it was possible to send written invitations to the meetings, which facilitated organizing in general.

Because of the way they were set up at first and the cultural component of individualism and mistrust I've mentioned, the cooperatives were not successful. In fact, they failed. But their failure made it possible to continue discussing the idea of cooperatives, the work that occupied my time in 1987 and 1988.

Instead of decreasing, all this organizing and resistance increased, astonishing the ranchers: The more they cracked down, the greater the resistance. Bordon insisted on deforesting, managing to do so only a few times with police protection sent by the judiciary at the ranch's expense, and the rest of the time they were forestalled by empates. In addition, even when police were present, empates took place on the Nazaré estate. That's according to Antônio Edgar, whose homestead is still there today because of the final empate at Nazaré. Even with police protection, Bordon did not succeed in clearing the area it wanted, simply because at a hearing it was claimed that the area to be deforested included an old rubber tapper holding.

The judge, who had already ordered police protection for the clearing operation, decided that they must protect the old holding and required INCRA technicians to carry out an inspection of the area, since Bordon claimed no rubber tapper homestead would be touched.

The INCRA technician and I, as the union's agronomist, conducted the inspection. We walked about six hours to try to find the "rubber tapper" the ranch had named as its representative. When we found him and told him we had come to inspect the area to be deforested, to find out if Antônio Edgar's homestead would be affected, he immediately answered, "If you want to go, we'll go, but it's going to extend to three of his trails." The INCRA technicians asked us if it was necessary to inspect the area. We asked if they would put what we had just heard in their report. They said yes. We said the inspection wasn't necessary for us, since we knew the homestead would be affected. It was Bordon that was denying this.

With the technicians' findings, the judge decided that the Rio Branco homestead, which belonged to Antônio Edgar, should be left untouched. After this Bordon decided to sell the area and leave. Later a good part of the Nazaré estate was included in the Chico Mendes Extractive Reserve.

The rubber tappers' resistance during this whole period cost many precious lives. To recall a few besides Wilson Pinheiro and Chico Mendes: Ivair Higino, Raimundo Calado, Eliazinho. For us the struggle continues.

The School

As I've already mentioned, when I went to Xapuri for the first time, it was to help evaluate the cooperatives of the Rubber Tapper Project, created by a few advisers and accepted by the Xapuri Rural Workers' Union, which politically supported the experiment of placing cooperatives on the estates. At the time the rubber tappers' illiteracy made it impossible to carry out some basic tasks in the cooperatives, such as recording deliveries of the product and the purchases of each member. For this reason we thought of starting a school to teach them to read and write.

The school could not, however, take much time from the rubber tappers' lives; they had to keep working to support themselves and their families. So it was decided to build it in the most accessible place for the majority and to hold classes on weekends. This would allow the rubber tappers to keep working normally during the week, and when they went to school, they could eat and sleep there.

The dominant pedagogy in the schools set up on the Xapuri estates in the early 1980s was that of Paulo Freire,[5] inasmuch as the teaching materials were based on the words and experiences of the rubber tappers.

The first text the Rubber Tapper Project produced from the literacy experiment was *Poronga*, whose title was chosen because this is the term for the kerosene lamp the rubber tapper wears on his head to light his way when he goes out to work at dawn. The school was intended to "light the way."

The experiment developed in Xapuri, first in three schools, then in eight, and today in dozens, was very important, not only because it could be perfected and adapted anywhere in Amazonia, but also, principally, because it responded to a demand of the rubber tappers themselves and facilitated union organizing. Many union representatives were trained in the Rubber Tapper Project's schools, and others were teachers who, after learning how to read and write in one of the project's schools, would go to other areas where new schools were built, to teach other people.

Originally conceived as a means of politically instructing adults to join the union movement, the school went on to serve the rubber tappers' children in the mid-1980s. But this did not lessen its importance; on the contrary, since many children of rubber tappers went to primary school as part of the Rubber Tapper Project, when they grew up they could participate in organizing unions in their communities. Many of these young people stayed on the estates, learning to read, write, and do arithmetic. They're still there.

Today it is possible to disagree with the political direction of the schools, which were "adopted" by the state when the Xapuri mayor's office was under Workers' Party control, because they have traveled far from their original concept. But it must be pointed out that the first schools on the estates were very important, if not fundamental, for the organization of the rubber tappers in the 1980s and early 1990s.

The Cooperative

Another experiment I think it's important to describe is the one that took me to Xapuri, putting me in touch with the rubber tappers' reality—the cooperatives, set up as alternatives to the bosses and the small traders.

According to the original proposal, the rubber tappers would set up cooperatives on the estates, receiving initial financing to buy merchandise, collecting the product, marketing it together, buying more goods, and rotating personnel. These experiments failed everywhere they were tried, causing the complete breakdown of communities in some cases and creating internal problems that were only resolved more than a decade later.

In my opinion the mistake was in the methodology for spreading the idea. The cooperative arrived from outside, it was not created by the rubber tappers, and they themselves called it "the Rubber Tapper Project's cooperative," not "our cooperative."

Based on what I could see of the diagnostic work we did in February and March 1986, I proposed to Chico Mendes to start again from zero, with the creation of the idea of a cooperative, by discussing and building it collectively in the communities.

In 1986 we did not obtain financial resources to pay for my stay in Xapuri, so I stayed in Rio Branco, supported by friends in the Workers' Party and the Central Labor Federation,[6] who put together the minimum for me to feed myself and travel to Xapuri. This was the year I was closest to Chico Mendes and did the most work to help organize the union and the National Rubber Tappers' Council, which was in the process of development. Its treasurer was Big Raimundo of Xapuri, who needed a lot of help because the work was Herculean.

In April 1987 we finally got financing for a project from the Development and Peace agency of Canada to carry out the dream of creating the idea of a cooperative. We must have walked more than 1,000 kilometers in the Xapuri estates, attended hundreds of meetings in all the communities and general meetings in Xapuri—in short, we had a full discussion of cooperativism with the Xapuri rubber tappers.

Once again the cultural issue of mistrust and individualism greatly complicated the work. Even today these factors are very powerful among the rubber tappers, although lessened by decades of shared struggles.

There was considerable resistance from the workers, especially where experiments had already failed. Others feared that the people who had already had a negative experience would bring their negative attitudes with them to the new cooperative.

It was also common to hear questions as to how we—in this case the union people and I, who were talking up the cooperative—would solve problems of supplies, marketing, transportation, and so on. At that moment the questions were always answered with the statement that the cooperative would belong to the members, so whoever wanted to join it would have to present proposals to solve the problems.

I returned to each community at least once during the year of the project. We carried out several discussions in Xapuri. The initial work was to "build the idea." In all, perhaps some fifteen hundred rubber tappers participated in the meetings. At the union's general meeting at the end of 1987, it was decided to found the cooperative on June 30, 1988, and the discussions would continue to develop by-laws that would include everything we had discussed until that time. A committee of rubber tappers was set up, with me as an adviser, to make a draft to be discussed in the communities before the general founding meeting. Everything was done as we decided.

On June 30, 1988, the general meeting was held to found the Agro-extractive Cooperative of Xapuri, Ltd. (CAEX).[7] About ninety rubber tappers participated, but only thirty-three joined. It seemed as if the work had accomplished nothing. This was not true—mistrust meant that many would wait for the early results.

With the marketing of rubber for better prices than they were getting in the Xapuri market, the purchase of the first merchandise, and, later, better prices for Brazil nuts for the members, the cooperative slowly grew to include three hundred members, the number it has had for more than ten years.

The discussion and collective construction were very important, because in this period, CAEX faced many difficulties, serious crises, and some people suggested it be closed. The rubber tappers showed they would not agree to simply close a cooperative that belonged to them. Thus they obtained new support, and CAEX still exists today.

CAEX is a unique cooperative. Its by-laws are different from those of almost every other Brazilian cooperative because it is not necessary for members to own land. If this were a requirement, no rubber tappers could join since all are homesteaders.

CAEX is run by rubber tappers, although it has always had technical personnel to advise the group. But they do not have the last word. Some have proposed in bad times that it close, but the members—rubber tappers and farmworkers—have not accepted this.

Like every cooperative of small producers, CAEX has faced great obstacles maintaining itself, especially because it works with products like rubber and Brazil nuts, which are difficult to market. But it has survived. It is the fruit of a collective process, and this may be the most important factor in its success.

The UDR Appears: Conflicts Sharpen

In 1985, as a way to combat the National Land Reform Plan and prepare for the Constitutional Assembly elections, ranchers throughout Brazil organized a group that became famous nationally. Always in the headlines because of its involvement in land conflicts, the notorious UDR—Democratic Ruralist Union—is democratic in name only.

The UDR has acted on various fronts since its founding, seeking support among smallholders, defending the "sacred right" of private property and "free enterprise" (with government incentives), and promoting cattle auctions to raise funds for its activities, including buying weapons, especially during the 1980s and 1990s. To get an idea of the UDR's bellicosity, despite the organization's denials, funding private militias and weapons was one of its main expenditures during that period.

The president of UDR-Goiás and one of its national vice presidents, Salvador Farina, claimed in April 1987, "Today we can admit that we really are buying arms with the proceeds of the auctions. At the first one, in Goiânia, we bought 1,636 weapons. At the second, in President Prudente, we acquired 2,430 more, and then regional UDR groups proliferated. Currently we have more or less 70,000 arms, one for every UDR member, men who will not be left out of our nation's history" (quoted in a mimeographed IBASE document from 1988, *The Right-wing Offensive in the Countryside*).[8]

In Amazonia the UDR's presence has meant an increase in violence from the beginning, especially in a region that has long been tense, the "Parrot's Beak" of southeastern Pará, northern Tocantins, and southwestern Maranhão.

The tactic of selectively eliminating leaders and others linked to the rural workers' movement, especially priests, advisers, and lawyers, resulted in great setbacks and negatively affected the resistance of homesteaders and smallholders across the region. The worst is that in almost all cases the crimes remain unpunished, with a few honorable exceptions.

In Acre the UDR became active in 1986, when it ran a slate of candidates for the Constitutional Assembly as well as the state legislature. In 1987, already pursuing a strategy of confronting the rubber tappers because of their resistance to deforestation, the group sought reinforcements. They even brought lawyers from the interior of São Paulo state to Xapuri. They had great influence on the judiciary, especially because the judge of Xapuri district was none other than the new husband of Nilão's widow. He had a strong ideological hatred for the homesteaders because he had been a lawyer for the ranchers before becoming a judge.

In early 1988, the period when preparations for clear-cutting operations were beginning, any request in the Xapuri court from ranchers was quickly granted. For example, a rancher who was trying to deforest after losing an empate on the Equador estate was the one who got an injunction ordering fifty state police to the area to protect ten workers who were carrying out the clearing operation.

After much struggle in this final empate led by Chico Mendes, it was proven that the rancher was trying to deforest more than twice as much as IBAMA (then IBDF) had authorized. However, not content with protecting the ranchers, the judge ordered the indictment of Chico Mendes, "Duda," Big Raimundo, Targino, and me for "contempt," as a result of an empate carried out by the comrades of the Cachoeira estate, next to Equador. But Duda was the only one of the workers present because he lived there. The rest of us were in Xapuri and therefore had not disobeyed any judicial order.

The same judge gave a repossession order to Darli for a homestead, Brasilzinho, on the Cachoeira estate, although Darli had never owned it and three rubber tappers, only one of whom agreed to sell his share to the gunman, occupied it. So there was no claim to be repossessed or upheld for Darli, but this judge gave a preliminary order anyway. After several empates by the rubber tappers of Cachoeira and neighboring estates—Equador, São Miguel, Nova Esperança, São José—this action made the organization grow in the area. More than three hundred people joined with comrades from more distant areas, such as the São Pedro, Nazaré, Floresta, and Boa Vista estates, to name a few, on the other side of the river, five and a half hours from Xapuri, where rubber tappers gathered to reinforce the resistance at Cachoeira. It was fantastic.

The Empates

The empates were genuine creations of Acre's rubber tappers. There is no evidence that any other organization had developed them before. If anybody else had used such a tactic, the rubber tappers certainly knew nothing about it when they invented it.

At the beginning of the 1970s clear-cut operations were going ahead particularly in the Acre River valley, along the BR-317 highway, as far as Brasiléia and from there to Assis Brasil. Thousands of hectares of forest were cut down every year. It was during this period that thousands of rubber tapper families were evicted and migrated to the urban slums of Rio Branco or Bolivia.

Each year more rubber tappers lost their homesteads. They had no way to resist legally, since the paulistas had the land titles and the rubber tappers were squatters who never had the sympathy of the local judiciary. For the latter, it was the struggle of "progress" against "backwardness."

Abandoned to their fate, without many options, the rubber tappers decided they would fight for their homesteads. The expulsion of thousands of these families made some who still had not been affected by deforestation—those who remained on the closer-in homesteads—realize they could either organize to join those who would be affected that year or the next, or in two or three years it would be their turn to lose their homes.

Pressured by the devastation, they decided to fight. They would make their stand against the clearing operations. Brasiléia moved first on the Carmen estate, when dozens of rubber tappers got together to prevent an operation that used the herbicide Tordon (2,4D by Dow Chemical) as a defoliant.

How did an empate work? Normally the rubber tappers who would be affected by deforestation informed the Rural Workers' Union at the same time they called on their neighbors who had not yet been affected. They gathered dozens of workers, who often brought their wives and children, forming a large contingent that would arrive at the location of the clear-cut and talk with the workers who were doing the drilling,[9] convincing them to stop work. The action was always peaceful, although the rubber tappers often took their rifles, which they never used. Generally they could convince the workers right away, since the workers were mostly former rubber tappers supervised by a boss from outside the area.

Once the felling was stopped, the rancher would usually go to the judge, almost always getting his permission and the protection of the state police to deforest the area.

From the first empate in 1973 in Brasiléia until the final one in 1994 in Xapuri, hundreds were carried out. In 2003, in Rio Branco township next to the Chico Mendes Extractive Reserve, rubber tappers returned to carrying out empates in areas that IMAC had authorized for deforestation, even though they were occupied by traditional extractivists.

If not for the empates, there would certainly be no more forest where the Chico Mendes Extractive Reserve (almost 1 million hectares in Rio Branco, Capixaba, Xapuri, Brasiléia, Assis Brasil, and Sena Madureira townships) is today. In addition, the Cachoeira, Equador, Nova Esperança, Independência,

São Miguel, and São José estates in Xapuri would no longer exist. These areas, except for Cachoeira and Equador, where he participated, were defended after Chico Mendes's assassination.

I had to defend myself against an indictment as a result of the empate carried out by comrades from Xapuri on the Nova Esperança estate in 1994.

From 1989 to 1992 we conducted empates on the Independência estate at São José and São Miguel. We mobilized a large number of workers in that area, about four hours down the Acre River from Xapuri.

It was during the empate on the Independência estate that I paid back Raimundo Tatá for what he'd done to me, just to test me, when he made me walk so fast for two days when he was my guide in 1986.

One morning Daú, the director of the Xapuri union and a resident at Independência, Tatá, and I left Xapuri to mobilize people for the empate. We traveled for about an hour and a half by boat, landed, and started mobilizing everybody the next morning at dawn at Antônio Pinto's homestead, near the place where we would carry out the empate. We started walking at about nine in the morning. We walked the whole day from homestead to homestead. We walked fast. At about 6:00 P.M., Tatá gave up, saying one of his legs, which he had strained a while before, was hurting, and he would meet us the next morning at the meeting place. I took the opportunity to tell him he couldn't stand the strain, and that was my payback for what he'd done to me. He tried to excuse himself but couldn't. He really couldn't take the pace we had imposed, since we walked something like 60 kilometers that day. It really was a lot.

The next morning we had the empate. We had to go back to the area two more times, since the boss was a tough guy who stopped work when we were there but started up again after we left. The final time, after taking everything out of their huts, we destroyed the huts. The workers hired for the clear-cut decided not to go back to work anymore.

The final empate that I think should be recorded for the period of this story is the one on the Nova Esperança estate, where the comrades from Xapuri won a partial victory. They succeeded in preventing deforestation of part of this area, but several of them were prosecuted by a young but extremely reactionary district attorney who tried to indict several union leaders under the National Security Law. He used Decree 510, from the military dictatorship, a draconian law no longer in effect at the time.

In addition, the commander of the state police in Xapuri, who was as crazy as the prosecutor, tried to spread panic in town by saying the rubber tappers would invade it to free a comrade who was in police custody.

In 1994 I was in my third semester at law school in Rio Branco. I was hired by CNPT-IBAMA to inform the rubber tappers in the Chico Mendes Extractive Reserve about the reserve's legal status and how they should organize to obtain concessions from the government. This work had to be done during my vacation. I spent most of January and February that year on that project. I didn't manage to finish during my vacation so I set up several meetings on weekends during the month of March in Xapuri, the place I was most familiar with.

Right before one of these weekends the empate at Nova Esperança and the arrest of a comrade, Edson Paulista, took place.

I went out there the day before to get information and pass it to the lawyers who advised the movement, so they could decide what should be done. I arrived at Xapuri and discovered that the charge against him was for a bailable offense: They had found an unloaded firearm in his room in town. I tried to negotiate bail with the police chief, but on the prosecutor's advice he spent the whole day giving me a runaround.

I sent information to the lawyers in Rio Branco. They obtained a writ of habeas corpus and sent it by fax. I retyped it and we tried to finish work by 11:00 P.M. We were supposed to go to the judge's house right away. I questioned this because it was so late. They told me freeing him was a priority, and the hour was of no importance. With two comrades I went to the judge's house. We knocked and knocked. Nothing. A few minutes later the police arrived, asking me what we were doing. I answered that we wanted to petition for habeas corpus. They said it was late. I replied that a person was unjustly imprisoned, and this was more important. It didn't work. The judge wouldn't receive us. We went away. The next day I went to the estate to conduct the previously arranged meetings.

For this action, at the behest of the prosecutor, I was prosecuted for trying to invade(!) the judge's house, with a possible two-year prison sentence. The depositions of the witnesses, the judge's neighbor, the police, all said we were "on the sidewalk, knocking on the door." But the trial went to the end, and I was found not guilty but not before the judge had ordered several expressions used by the defense—exactly those showing that I was in front of the judge's house knocking, which would remove any possibility that I had committed the crime of "home invasion"—stricken from the record because the words were in boldface type, which he considered in "contempt of court," although this is not against any law.

I had the meetings on the estates as scheduled and returned to Xapuri on Sunday. When I arrived in town, the first comrade who saw me almost fainted, since the state police commander had spread the rumor that I had gone to gather two hundred rubber tappers to invade Xapuri, and the police would greet me at gunpoint. I arrived alone and knew nothing about this, which explains their fear, since they thought the police could take advantage of the situation to kill me and then claim I had provoked everything.

For the record, when I got back to Rio Branco, I worked with the lawyers and we succeeded in having the criminal charge thrown out against the jailed colleague I'd tried to free with the habeas corpus writ.

The Empates I'd Like to Remember

All the empates in which I participated were important, but three were special for me: the first, carried out on the Nazaré estate against Bordon; the second in Cachoeira against Darli; and the final one led by Chico Mendes on the Equador estate near Cachoeira.

Without a doubt my first empate was much more emotional than my first trip along the Acre River to the São Pedro estate, which I recounted earlier. It was June 6, 1986. The day before, World Environment Day, we conducted the first regional meeting of Acre River valley rubber tappers in Rio Branco, for rubber tappers from Assis Brasil to Rio Branco, Brasiléia and Xapuri, called by the National Rubber Tappers' Council.

The meeting was productive and advanced discussions held almost a year earlier at the first National Rubber Tappers' Meeting in Brasília. But we had urgent problems: Bordon was threatening to clear 700 hectares on the Nazaré estate, affecting Antônio Edgar's entire homestead.

One of the decisions of the meeting was that we would back the Xapuri rubber tappers who had already carried out an empate in the area. The next day we went straight to Xapuri. In addition to several rubber tappers from Brasiléia and Assis Brasil, several from Xapuri also went, plus some supporters and advisers. Among them was Marina Silva, then a director of the Central Union Federation and today the reelected senator from Acre who is now the environment minister; Mauro Almeida, an anthropology professor from Unicamp with a Ph.D. from Cambridge University and, as he authoritatively described himself, a man of Acre; Filomena, an agronomist sympathetic to the movement; and me, along with a photographer who took pictures of everything. If I have forgotten any of the "outsiders," it's my lapse.

After arriving at Xapuri, we went straight to the Cavalo Velho homestead, near the place where we would carry out the empate and where D. Maria Canção, a rubber tapper and local leader who took part in empates in Xapuri, lived. She was feisty and very experienced—thus her nickname, a type of stinging nettle. She died a few years ago.

We walked about four hours, arriving at Cavalo Velho in the late afternoon. For me it was a tiring trip, since I still was unaccustomed to walking, despite having done that research on the estates. When they arrived at Cavalo Velho, several Xapuri rubber tappers organized a soccer match on the grass in front of the house. I took a bath, put up a hammock, and went to sleep.

The next day, early, under the leadership of Big Raimundo, Chico's cousin and a nearby resident, and with D. Maria Cançāo in the lead with a Brazilian flag she had picked up at the union hall to commemorate the World Cup, we went to find the workers who were carrying out the clear-cut operation. There were several groups. Thanks to the persuasion of Big Raimundo and other comrades, we managed to convince them to stop work. It was a temporary victory.

We had another exhausting journey. We had to walk the whole day through places where the brush had been cleared, and this was very tiring. We met with all the clear-cut workers and gave them a deadline to leave their camps.

After this empate, Bordon went to court and succeeded in deforesting the area authorized for this, leaving out Antônio Edgar's homestead, as I've already recounted. In any case, we won—not totally, but at least partly. The empates were like that—sometimes we'd win, sometimes we'd lose, but we always were fighting. At the Nazaré empate more than ninety people participated, including many women like D. Maria, Marina Silva, Filomena, and several local rubber tappers, including Nande's daughters. Oh—before I forget, it was after this empate that Bordon decided to sell its land and abandon Xapuri, near where it had cleared about 3,700 hectares of forest while I was in the area.

Another empate I want to describe was not undertaken to stop a specific clearing operation, as on other occasions, but to stop Darli and his gunmen from entering the Cachoeira estate. This one took place in early March 1988, but I didn't participate from the beginning, since I was traveling on the other side of Xapuri, in the area of the Sāo José, Fronteira, and Sāo Pedro estates on the upper Xapuri River, and Nazaré, farther down, discussing the cooperative we intended to create. I learned about what was happening only about ten days later, when I arrived at the Rio Branco homestead on the Floresta estate. It was about noon.

Big Raimundo, the owner of the homestead, took me aside and asked if I already knew what was happening in Cachoeira. I said no. He told me everything, saying that José Brito, a rubber tapper from the Brasilzinho homestead, had sold his holding to Darli, who previously had bought or received the deed for about 6,000 hectares, or 25 percent of the Cachoeira estate, which he claimed to own. But Darli could not go in because the rubber tappers did not let him, since he had no claim inside, so he managed to convince José Brito to sell his holding. It happens that José Brito lived with his mother and brother, who also were homesteaders and would not agree to sell their holding. To defend the estate, since Darli's entry would pose a risk for everybody, the rubber tappers gathered the eighty families of Cachoeira, called the rubber tappers of Equador, São José, and Nova Esperança who were their neighbors, and set up camp at the entrance to Cachoeira, also guarding the side entrances.

When I found out the comrades had been camping there for ten days, I wanted to go to Cachoeira right away. It was the fastest journey I made from Rio Branco, Big Raimundo's homestead, to Xapuri. It takes about four hours, but having already walked five hours from Simplício's, which I had left early that morning, it took me about three hours to reach Xapuri.

I left the Rio Branco homestead at about two o'clock, after hearing Raimundo's whole story and eating lunch, and arrived in Xapuri at about five. I wanted to grab my motorbike and go directly to Cachoeira, but Chico Mendes, who was in Xapuri, asked me not to do that because the rubber tappers were prepared to confront gunmen and had set up guard posts. If I left in the late afternoon, I'd arrive at Cachoeira in the dark, and this would be very risky. OK. I slept in Xapuri. The next day I took the union's pickup with Chico Mendes and others to reinforce the encampment.

They spent almost a month camped out. When they let down their guard, a rumor soon spread that Darli and his gunmen would try to go in, so the rubber tappers quickly returned to hold a meeting, even though some homesteads inside the Cachoeira estate are up to six hours from Fazendinha, the homestead where we were camping. Everybody discussed everything. The leaders were the rubber tappers of Cachoeira, since Chico Mendes stayed in Xapuri, where he tried to gather support, get the word out, and obtain resources to feed the campers, who totaled some three hundred people. Every day Chico Mendes would come from Xapuri to bring information and coordinate with the comrades. The result was that the much-feared Darli and his gunmen did not have the courage to try to go into Cachoeira.

While we were camped at Cachoeira, deforestation began in Equador, a neighboring estate, about one hour (6 kilometers) away. We held two empates. The ranchers went to court, as I recounted when I spoke of the dubious judge who sent about fifty police to protect ten workers who were clearing Equador.

With the state police mobilized to protect the deforestation by judicial order, we decided in a meeting at Cachoeira that we would carry out an empate even if the police were there. The afternoon before, Marcolino, a rubber tapper friend, and I got two horses and went to check where and how the police were situated, so we wouldn't run any risks, especially because the rubber tappers' wives and children would participate, as in many other empates.

We went on horseback toward Equador. When we arrived at the ranch house where state police officers were staying, as if it had been planned (though it hadn't), the girth on my horse's saddle broke. I had to get down, obviously. The police quickly surrounded us to find out what we were doing. We answered that we were going to Baia, a creek about 6 kilometers farther along, toward town, to see if Chico Mendes had ordered victuals (food to be made into meals) for the people camped at Cachoeira. Since it had rained, perhaps the food could not be taken by truck to the camp site. In that case, it would have stayed at Baia.

The police wanted to know why we had stopped there. I showed them the broken girth and said it wouldn't be possible to leave without fixing it. Marcolino, who understood what to do because he had already worked as a mule driver, was trying at that moment to fix the girth so we could go on. In truth we took advantage of the situation to find out where the police were. We got all the information we wanted. With the girth repaired, we went another 3 kilometers, stopped for a little while, and went back, complaining that the victuals had not arrived.

With the information collected, at a meeting called that night by Chico Mendes, who had arrived in the late afternoon, we decided how the empate would proceed. Early the next day we set out. There were 159 people, including men, women, and children, at the site. We walked quickly. Less than an hour later we were already near the clearing site. We saw the police move in, in formation, and with their guns they took the characteristic "ready to fire" stance.

The women, led by the schoolteachers of Cachoeira, and the children started to sing the national anthem. It was an indescribable scene. Since the national anthem is one of the principal patriotic symbols, the soldiers must stand at attention and, if armed, present arms during the singing. That was how about fifty police stood—we singing the national anthem and the armed police standing at attention, presenting arms, with the lieutenant saluting.

When the national anthem ended, the commanding officer said he was there to carry out a judicial order and they would carry it out. Chico Mendes went forward and proposed that the deforestation be suspended that day so the officer and he, Chico, could go to Xapuri to see if the IBDF could call off the clear-cutting operation. The officer accepted the proposal, and the deforestation was stopped that day. Another victory—partial, but a victory.

We did not succeed in having the deforestation authorization withdrawn, but we did get an environmental agency technician to come and check if the area being drilled corresponded to the authorized total. I went along on this inspection. What we already knew was "discovered." The rancher was going to clear more than double the authorized area. Thus he was prevented from deforesting the entire other side of the branch that goes to Cachoeira, which is still there today. Again, everybody won: the forest, the rubber tappers, the planet.

It's the empates that I'd like to see remembered. The police lined up, presenting arms, while the rubber tappers' children and their teachers sang the national anthem in the middle of the Amazon forest certainly was a fantastic sight, even unimaginable. I admit that even now I get goose bumps when I remember this scene, especially because it wasn't planned or discussed at the meeting the night before, and the teachers of Cachoeira did it on their own, without asking anybody. I'm convinced that after this show of public spirit by the children and teachers, the police were well and truly disarmed, making dialogue possible, so that the officer accepted suspension of the deforestation for a day to see if the union could get the clear-cutting suspended for good.

The Extractive Reserve, Land Reform for Amazonia, a Model of Sustained Development, the Interest of Brazilian and Foreign Environmentalists

Whenever Chico Mendes's murder is mentioned, somebody asks: Why did his murder have such powerful repercussions? Why did the killing of a rubber tapper from Xapuri, Acre, produce articles in the most important media outlets around the world?

This question, certainly repeated dozens of times by those who planned Chico Mendes's death, thinking he would be just one more killed in the Amazon without creating bigger problems, was asked countless times, especially when I made presentations to students in Acre. Perhaps here it was most difficult to understand the magnitude the rubber tappers' struggle had acquired, in light of the old adage, "the local patron saint does no miracles."

In his final interview with Edilson Martins of the *Jornal do Brasil*, Chico Mendes himself said he didn't believe his death would accomplish anything for the rubber tappers' cause. He said if an angel came down from heaven and said his death would be important for Amazonia, he would die willingly. But that wouldn't happen because there had already been many deaths without any effect, and only the living could save Amazonia. These statements inspired the title of the documentary about Chico Mendes by London Central Television and the Catholic University of Goiás, as part of the *Decade of Destruction* series directed by Adrian Cowell: "I Want to Live!"[10]

But the repercussions of Chico Mendes's death do have an explanation: After the First National Meeting of Rubber Tappers, October 10–17, 1985, at the University of Brasília, the rubber tappers showed that they existed, they were occupying Amazonia, had demands to make and proposals to improve their lives.

Among the proposals that came out of that first meeting was one that was fundamental in giving visibility to the rubber tappers: the creation of the extractive reserves. This proposal evolved from the fact that the rubber tappers, especially those in Acre who called the First National Meeting of Rubber Tappers via the Rural Workers' Union of Xapuri, were constantly locked in battle with the ranchers and the clear-cutting operations in defense of their holdings and their way of life. The judiciary almost always stood behind the ranchers, leading to increasing devastation and expulsion of rubber tappers to urban slums.

At their meeting they therefore went on to say they wanted the forests demarcated, like the Indian reserves, so they could produce and live in the traditional way without the risk of expulsion by the ranchers. They proposed that within these areas the rules would be determined collectively by the communities and no one could destroy the forest. The advisers who were there thought of a name for the proposal. Based on the idea of Indian reserves, they proposed the creation of extractive reserves. In principle these would be public areas occupied by traditional populations that would exploit them in a self-sustained way. That is, they would use the Amazon forest without devastating it. The rubber tappers also had a land reform proposal for the Amazon. It was a model completely different from the one advanced by official policies for the region.

In addition to being an original idea of the rubber tappers, the proposal for the creation of extractive reserves contains several very important ideological elements: While the basis of the struggle for land reform in Brazil was to gain possession of the land for those who had none, the rubber tappers' proposal for creation of extractive reserves suggested that the land be public and that traditional populations have use rights over forest areas. It was ideologically different because it proposed combining official policies with support from landless workers, CONTAG, CUT, and the rural workers' unions in the Center-South.

But it wasn't only in regard to the issue of property in land that the extractive reserve proposal was different: It was in clear opposition to the official plan for the colonization of Amazonia, which put in motion the migration of thousands of unemployed or landless workers from the Center-South to Amazonia, where they would occupy 50- to 100-hectare lots in what we were then calling "squared-off rationality," defended by the entrenched technobureaucracy (of INCRA). In the form the rubber tappers proposed, the extractive reserves would be much larger areas than the INCRA lots and would follow the placement of the homesteads on the estates, which would continue to be the basic production units.

From the ecological point of view, the extractive reserve concept won hands down because it proposed utilizing the Amazon forest, developing the region via its traditional inhabitants. That is, now Brazilian and foreign environmentalists had an alternative to the Brazilian government's official, highly predatory model.

For several decades the environmentalists have worried about the conservation of Amazonia. They've been talking about this since the 1960s and 1970s, and each time they demanded conservation policies for the Amazon, especially during the military dictatorship but even after the political "opening," they got the response that it was "necessary to develop the Amazon, occupy it, since it was a 'demographic desert,' make it productive," and so on and so forth.

The environmentalists had no alternative to this development discourse for Amazonia. With the rubber tappers' presentation of the proposal for creation of extractive reserves as a rational and self-sustained way of using the forest, the environmentalists now had an argument. When the Brazilian government answered the demands for conservation of Amazonia with the developmentalist discourse, the environmentalists could reply: "We agree with what the rubber tappers are proposing: development that respects the forest and the people who traditionally live there."

The extractive reserves were a Gordian knot for Brazilian and international environmentalists, since they combined development with environmental conservation and sustainability. As a result of the rubber tappers' proposal, many intellectuals began studying the issue to scientifically back up the concept. Dozens of master's and doctoral theses were based on this new idea for Amazonia.

For the rubber tappers, all this was in fact simple: They wanted to keep living as they always had, and the extractive reserves would mean, in their view, the conservation of their way of life with an official guarantee that the land would be public property, so the ranchers could not destroy the areas where the rubber tappers were.

What was a great discovery for the world at large was for the rubber tappers only the expression of their way of life. They wanted to keep being rubber tappers without running the risk of being expelled from their homes. For the world this was a revolutionary proposal. For the rubber tappers and their leaders, it was a way of protecting their survival and their culture.

It's necessary to understand this to know why Chico Mendes's murder had such enormous and unexpected repercussions throughout the world.

It's because Chico Mendes became the principal, but not the only, spokesperson for the rubber tappers' ideas and for the Alliance of Forest Peoples[11] conceived by the National Rubber Tappers' Council and the Union of Indigenous Nations. This alliance suddenly transformed historic enemies into fierce allies in defending the forest and its inhabitants.

The fact that Chico Mendes became the main promoter of the extractive reserve concept, showing the whole world that the Amazon was populated and its traditional inhabitants—Indians, rubber tappers, river dwellers, among others—knew how to use the entire potential of the forest without destroying it, gave him ample space in the media, first internationally and then in Brazil.

Chico Mendes went to England, where he received the Global 500 Prize as the first Brazilian among the five hundred people in the world working on environmental issues who would be honored from 1987 to 1992, the date of the Earth Summit. He went to New York, where he received an award from the Better World Society.

Chico also participated in a meeting of the board of the Inter-American Development Bank, where he went to demand compliance with the conditions of the financial agreement for the paving of the BR-364 highway between Porto Velho and Rio Branco. On that occasion he was attacked in Acre as if he had asked that the funding be stopped, when actually he went to say that the money should be delivered. But in addition the Brazilian government must use its share to support the environment and the traditional populations that could be affected by the paving, to avoid the catastrophe that had happened in Rondônia when the Cuiabá–Porto Velho road was paved.

Finally, because he represented the rubber tappers and perhaps even the Alliance of Forest Peoples, Chico Mendes achieved visibility in the media for combining development with conservation—the use of the forest without destruction. The conservation of the forest, completely occupied by human populations, an unthinkable idea for more radical environmentalists, was the novelty that called attention to the rubber tappers and their strategies. Thus those who thought killing Chico Mendes would destroy his cause made a mistake. As I said in a poem I wrote soon after his death, "The shot missed."

Perhaps his death kept Chico Mendes alive. Those who thought destroying his physical body would destroy the ideas he put forth had no idea Chico Mendes represented not one but hundreds or thousands of rubber tappers, who had learned that with allies inside and outside the forest they could manage to defend it in increasingly bold and effective ways.

The rubber tappers' idea of the creation of extractive reserves got so much exposure that the concept could be applied to any environmental area occupied by the traditional populations that inhabit and exploit it, making it productive without destroying it. Thus an extractive reserve could be created in a forest, a marsh, a fishing area, and so on, in any part of the world—even, for example, among the Eskimos, if it were necessary, of course.

~~~~~~

Chapter 6

A LITTLE ABOUT MY FRIEND CHICO MENDES

[handwritten margin note: considered himself a worker. Did everything for worker"]

IAM NOT WRITING A BIOGRAPHY of Chico Mendes, first because I believe he himself would not like this to be done—especially by me or any friend—since it would prove we hadn't understood any of what he taught us. For him, the most important thing was the struggle, the organization, the union, the party, his comrades, and he always considered himself as one more worker. That's how it was when he received the two international awards—in his very brief remarks, he said he was receiving recognition in the name of the rubber tappers as their representative, because such prizes were for them, not him.

Furthermore, it won't do any good to ask; I'm not ready to look for biographical information. I remember my friend. I want to remember him as he was: a rubber tapper, a union man, a political activist, an environmentalist, a fantastic human being who succeeded in seeing and accomplishing a great deal ahead of his time. It was he who discovered he could combine union work, the empates, with environmentalism, and thus gain important allies in central-southern Brazil. It was he, the PT activist, who perceived that on environmental issues, it was important to ally with the Green Party,[1] where he found good and important friends.

To speak of Chico Mendes is first to speak of an ordinary man. He was a real rubber tapper, though some try to deny this. He was an environmentalist, although he did not internalize this concept at first but smoked cigarettes like a bandit. He knew he was wrong about this, he recognized it, but he said he couldn't manage to stop—even when the doctor in Brasília told him during a check-up if he didn't give it up immediately, he was running a great risk. Since he couldn't stop smoking, even when encouraged by colleagues who also smoked and stopped to encourage him, he said he was already involved in this business of risking his life, so he wouldn't stop smoking.

Many times I was after him to stop smoking, but he just couldn't do it. He had been hooked on cigarettes since he was seven years old. This unfortunately happens to the majority of the rubber tappers' sons who go out to "wait." That is, when the rubber tappers go out hunting, usually at night, they set up a blind in the trees until game appears. At night there are an enormous number of mosquitoes, so the rubber tappers light cigarettes to repel them. That's when they get addicted. Chico Mendes was one of these, and that's why in many photographs he is shown smoking. This might seem like a contradiction for an environmentalist, but he recognized that he wasn't perfect, as he said, although he admitted that this fact was no excuse.

As an ordinary man, Chico Mendes loved to play dominoes and cards, always wagering something, however little. He did not play for free, because, according to him, it was no fun. Although he bet, I saw him lose money he couldn't afford to lose—and God knows, he always had very little—but only on very rare occasions. I don't know if he was an excellent player or very modest. One time, I remember well, at Pedro Rocha's house, Chico spent the whole night playing cards with other comrades, losing very little and winning often. He always played with great confidence. Playing cards was, let us say, his favorite recreation, but usually he didn't have much time for it, especially during the short time I knew him—three years—because at that time he was always traveling to help organize the National Rubber Tappers' Council and spread the ideas and proposals of the First National Meeting of Rubber Tappers.

Recently somebody told me a recent arrival in Acre had said to several friends at their country place that he would like to see the Chico Mendes Park in Rio Branco and Chico Mendes's house in Xapuri. Immediately one of those present retorted that Chico Mendes was a "drunk" and was nothing like what the person had heard about him outside Acre.

First: I knew and spent time with Chico Mendes for three years. I know he was an ordinary man and never insisted on being different or passing as a superhero. But I also know he was certainly no drunk. He drank very rarely—and honestly, not even at the parties we attended did I ever see Chico drink until he got drunk. He was an extremely popular person; he would spend time with his friends, sip from a glass of one or another, but he was careful not to get drunk. Actually, I think his "tippling" from his buddies' glasses was to be sociable, since I never saw him the least bit tipsy.

Whoever said Chico Mendes was a drunk lied shamelessly, although this is not a problem if we're talking about an ordinary man. But if it isn't the truth, it's not because the claim has not been categorically denied.

Besides, as an ordinary man, they once told me—and I never tried to confirm it with Chico because I wasn't interested—that several years before I knew him (certainly well before 1986) he allegedly had an affair with a married woman on a rubber estate. But no one could prove the rumor because he was extremely discreet. If I'm repeating today what I heard, it's to show I'm speaking of my friend, a normal human being, ordinary, who made mistakes, but who had enormous dedication to a cause, a struggle, and, above all, a vision way ahead of his time.

I walked many times with Chico through the rubber estates, where I saw him coordinate meetings and speak at rallies, always in a clear and objective way in language accessible to the rubber tappers. When he spoke, everybody understood. He was a leader in the proper sense of the word.

When I recall Chico, I remember the good things—the assemblies, the meetings, the rallies—about a comrade in the struggle. That's how I will always remember him.

Another delightful thing to remember was the caring way Chico treated his children and how he'd stay with them every time he returned from his travels or as often as he could. There are countless photos in which he is with Elenira and Sandino. In 1988 he was thinking of bringing Angela, his daughter from his first marriage who was studying accounting in Rio Branco, to work the following year at the Rural Workers' Union of Xapuri with him. I think it was this love for his children that made him try to walk to their room, falling in the doorway, after the fatal shot hit him. I don't know what he thought at that moment—when he shouted only, "They got me!"—but I believe he was thinking of his children.

Speaking of his children, I think he left a message for them when he registered their births: He wanted his children to be revolutionaries, and that's why he gave the name of a guerrilla who died in the Araguaia war,[2] Elenira, to his daughter, and the name of a great Central American revolutionary, Sandino, to his son. I believe when he registered his children, Chico was already telling them what he hoped for them.

When Angela was born, Chico was not yet a full-fledged political activist with greater knowledge. Perhaps for this reason he did not give her the name of a revolutionary, as he did for the others, but he cared very much about her.

Fear of the Jaguar

I walked thousands of kilometers for many years in the forest, going from one rubber estate to another, and I admit I never saw a jaguar. The most I sensed of their presence where I walked was their roars and their paw prints. Once I passed a place where a jaguar of considerable size had recently passed; his paw print was more than half the size of my foot, and I wear a size nine, which is pretty big.

[handwritten marginal note:] Named children after revolutionarie/ *✦*

I am speaking of jaguars because during the many conversations I had with Chico Mendes, sometimes walking alone with him on the trail, I heard him confess that his greatest fear as a child in the forest was indeed the jaguars.

As has been said numerous times, Chico was a rubber tapper, although his enemies may try to deny this fact, which, however, is recorded in the testimony of hundreds of rubber tappers who knew him as such.

He was born at the Bom Futuro homestead on the Porto Rico rubber estate in Xapuri township, Acre, on December 15, 1944, son of a father from Ceará and a mother from Acre.

His early life was like that of any child in the estates, without many diversions. He had to work from a very early age, when he began to learn the secrets of the forest and its myths.

While still a child, Chico moved to the Equador estate, next to Porto Rico, where he spent a good part of his childhood and youth. It was on this estate, at the Pote Seco homestead, that Chico began his training as a rubber tapper. At age fifteen, he took charge of all the rubber tapping, replacing his father, who set about building a new house and then did only subsistence farming.

In the conversations I had with Chico, he told me many times that at the beginning of his work as a rubber tapper his greatest fear was of jaguars. He would walk on the rubber trails always on tiptoe. So he would feel safer, his father tried to teach him to shoot. But as an adolescent he could not learn, since he had difficulty aiming. He would shut both his eyes. His favorite companion in this period, he told me, was a dog that was sometimes more of a nuisance than a help, since he would startle when scenting a jaguar. This made both of them run in panic.

At fifteen, after having learned how to shoot and already knowing almost all the secrets of the forest—including which trees provided food, which provided water, and even which were medicinal for some conditions, such as nausea, headache, and so on—Chico not only mastered rubber tapping but also hunting for meat, even at night, during the "vigils."

When he stopped fearing jaguars, Chico began to fear the spirits of the forest, such as the Country Boy of the Woods, the Mother of the Rubber Tree, and others. After he had become a famous rubber tapper, whenever we asked if he really believed in these spirits, he would answer in a hesitating manner, with a half-smile, saying only, "I'm a rubber tapper."

Learning to Read: The Dream That Was Fulfilled

Chico Mendes's youth was like that of any young rubber tapper: work, a lot of work, recreation at parties, which his father allowed him to go to only with trusted friends such as Raimundo Monteiro and his cousins

Miguel and Zeca Mendes. His father was a "tough love" type and maintained rigid discipline that I never heard Chico complain about.

As he grew up, Chico felt an increasing desire to learn how to read and write, the rudiments of which he had learned from his father. He wanted to be able to understand the bills the bosses wrote, since his father, like other rubber tappers, was always in debt to the company store.

When he had already mastered rubber tapping on his homestead, around June 1960, a different kind of rubber tapper moved in not far away. This was Euclides Fernando Távora, known as "Euclides the Plank," who knew how to read and write and who spoke in a way the rubber tappers themselves sometimes had difficulty understanding.

Távora had been a member of the Prestes Column, the communist movement of the first quarter of the twentieth century.[3] Persecuted since that time, he had been imprisoned on Fernando de Noronha Island. He also participated in the "Communist Conspiracy," a movement of the second half of the 1930s. From an important family in Ceará, he succeeded in escaping from Fernando de Noronha, moving to Amazonia, where he hid out first in Bolivia, maintaining contact with the local Communists and being involved in revolutionary movements. When things got hot, he crossed the frontier and lived on the rubber estates of Xapuri township, especially Equador and Cachoeira, where he stayed for many years.

Euclides Távora was a rubber tapper the others enjoyed talking to, although sometimes they couldn't understand very clearly his way of speaking and the things he talked about.

Chico recounts his first contact with Euclides:

> In the month of June, I don't remember the day, I had arrived in the forest with the milk, and at that time a stranger arrives at our shack. We welcome this person and offer him coffee—the custom among the rubber tappers when they receive visitors. This gentleman was very lively, and it was easy to see—even though he was wearing rubber tapper clothes—his way of expressing himself made it obvious that his upbringing was very different. His way of speaking was very confident, and he impressed us. Finally he said he was also a rubber tapper and lived in the neighboring estate, called Cachoeira, only four hours' walk from our homestead along the trails. At first a little mistrustful, I became a bit confused, but little by little I started adapting to the speech of that man who was different from the others.

Euclides became friendly with Chico's father after asking permission to teach the boy to read and write, the young rubber tapper's great dream.

Chico's father gave permission for this instruction, since it would not hinder his work on the homestead.

To be able to work with Euclides Távora, Chico Mendes moved to his house on the weekends and spent Saturday and Sunday studying. In the tutoring sessions the teacher used newspaper clippings. Chico never found out how he got them from such a great distance away so that he could teach Chico to read. He also taught the young rubber tapper to write, using his own very personalized method of discussing all the newspaper clippings. In addition, Távora taught him important lessons about union organization and discipline. He even taught him to interpret the news broadcast in Portuguese from three international radio stations: the BBC in London, Radio Moscow, and the Voice of America in the United States.

Chico said Euclides Távora tuned in one of the radio stations, listened to the news, then tuned in the other and listened to that news. Then he tried to find out if the young rubber tapper could distinguish the political message of each station.

The newspaper clippings that Euclides used for the reading classes, according to Chico, always contained news linked to social and political problems, which he realized he had not understood very well when he was studying.

Only after several months of teaching and discussing the news did Euclides start revealing more about himself to his pupil, saying he belonged to the Communist movement and had known and worked with Luis Carlos Prestes, one of the historic Brazilian Communist leaders of the twentieth century. He also said he had been a lieutenant in the army and had fought alongside Prestes, perhaps as part of his participation in the revolutionary uprising of 1935.

An important fact in his apprenticeship, according to Chico, was that when the military coup happened in Brazil in 1964, the Voice of America newscasts spoke of "democratic revolution" as a way of "fighting Communism," while Radio Moscow spoke of a "military coup." Making this distinction, learning different turns of phrase depending on who spoke, was very important for Chico years later, when he maintained contact with the chairman of the U.S. Senate Budget Committee or participated in the meeting of the World Bank executive directors—or when, as a union leader, he would speak with his own comrades in a manner they could understand, since he had learned that this was of the greatest importance.

But why did Euclides Távora ask Chico's father's permission to teach his son to read and write? Perhaps because with his experience as a member of the revolutionary left, he had sensed in the conversations he had with the rubber tappers of the region that Chico was a potential leader who needed to be trained. His revolutionary spirit spoke aloud and he sought to indoctrinate this young leader.

With what he had learned from Euclides Távora, Chico managed several years later to become a literacy teacher in the Brazilian Literacy Movement, MOBRAL. This was a federal program during the dictatorship that sought to teach adults, since the rate of illiteracy in Brazil was very high, but the effort was not successful.

It was his work as a literacy teacher and employee of a rubber broker in Xapuri that served as the basis of his candidacy for city councilor. He was elected in 1977 and stayed on the council until 1982.

Also, what he learned from Távora made Chico one of the first to join the Rural Workers' Union of Brasiléia, founded in 1975, which he left to help found the union in Xapuri and run for city council there.

Chico always spoke of Távora with great affection and respect. Everybody who knew Távora has good memories of him. He was a good friend, a practical joker, but when he discussed things seriously he was the genuine article.

Chico spent time with Távora for several years but had to keep his distance after the 1964 military coup. This distancing has at least two explanations. The first, from Chico, says Távora received a message to go to Xapuri to take care of matters related to a bank account. Euclides found the message strange and did not go. A few days later he received another message, much more serious, which mentioned names of members of his family in Ceará and said his mother was very sick and needed his help. So Euclides went to Xapuri. The last time he was seen, two strangers were with him. The second version says Euclides was very sick because of an old ulcer and he went away for medical treatment and never returned to the region.

According to Chico, in his long conversations with Euclides after he learned how to read, his teacher tried to show him the great exploitation the rubber tappers were subjected to. Chico's father was very receptive to this, since he was one of the first to complain about the bosses' exploitation but without any larger idea of mobilizing people.

Only long after his teacher had disappeared did Chico begin to understand that it was necessary to struggle to organize the rubber tappers against exploitation. That was when he began to participate in the first discussions about founding the Brasiléia Rural Workers' Union, when he saw in practice the lesson the Communist militant, lost in the Amazon forests, had given him ten years before. Before this everything had been very theoretical.

The Beginning of Activism: From MOBRAL Teacher to Board Member of the Rural Workers' Union

After Chico's first, highly frustrating attempt at marriage—whose only good memento was his daughter Angela, as he always admitted—he left the estates a little more often and started dedicating himself to passing on his knowledge of reading and writing to his comrades, after a short stay in the city.

In his work as a MOBRAL monitor, Chico gained more knowledge of the extent of the rubber tappers' exploitation, which he had known about before only from his own experience. At the same time he began to witness the violence of the paulista ranchers who arrived in the area and used every means to expel the rubber tappers from their homesteads. They claimed they had bought the estates from their former owners and usually had records of these transactions.

At this time the first grassroots religious communities (CEBs)[4] of the Catholic Church started to spring up. Since he had a little more knowledge of reading, Chico helped read the biblical texts at the meetings.

In 1975 Chico heard about a union training course in Brasiléia and, remembering the teachings of his old tutor Euclides Távora, went to that town, participating in the founding of the first rural workers' union in Acre.

Chico was the secretary of the first board, a post he held until 1977, when he moved to Xapuri to help found the union in his home township.

His early days as a union leader coincided with the first empates and the increasingly tense confrontation with the ranchers. This ongoing acquaintance with conflict helped him to strengthen his character as an extremely consistent, even tough union leader who at the same time was capable of negotiating on an equal footing with his enemies. Not even his greatest political adversaries denied he had this talent.

During his work as a MOBRAL monitor and union leader came the opportunity to be a candidate for city council for the MDB, the only opposition party the military dictatorship allowed to operate, to present a facade of democracy in Brazil. He won in Xapuri.

Relevant Debates in the City Council

Elected MDB city councilor in Xapuri township, Chico tried, from the beginning of his term, to make sure that his activity as a small-town politician would serve to highlight the violence and exploitation his fellow rubber tappers confronted. Because of his way of acting, at first he was marginalized even inside his own party, threatened with expulsion and forced to tone down his behavior. As early as 1977 the first death threats against him occurred as a result of his work, according to his own reports.

During the first session of the 1979 legislative year, he succeeded in being elected vice president of the city council. The president belonged to ARENA.[5] The next day, in an attempt to drive out the mayor, the president took over the municipal government, remaining as acting mayor until the beginning of the next year, when the new mayor was sworn in.

When the president of the city council took over the mayor's office, Chico, who was vice president, became the president of the city council on March 2, 1979, staying in this office until November 29, when he was forced to quit the post in order not to lose his seat.

On April 7, 1979, Chico made a tough speech, summarized in the Xapuri City Council records, in which he emphasized that "the Acre politicians seem to have forgotten their promises to the people on the eve of the past election.[6] They promised to fight for a better land system that would benefit the farmer, and until now nothing has been done. There is no hope for the rubber tappers, and injustices against them are constantly noted." He continually wove in criticisms of the agencies responsible for that issue. "Gentlemen, we must not cry after acts of violence caused by the negligence of the responsible authorities who do not act promptly for justice."

At this point, in quoting from this speech, I must point out that aside from the denunciation of the situation of the rubber tappers and the invisibility to which the politicians relegated them, Chico takes an almost prophetic tone when he says, "Gentlemen, we must not cry after acts of violence caused by the negligence of the authorities who do not act promptly for justice." Nine years later Chico himself would become one of the victims of the acts of violence to which he had already alerted the authorities well before they happened. The negligence of the responsible authorities continued for years and years, and Chico's words reverberated only when he became a fatal victim.

As acting president of the city council, Chico announced a big meeting with rubber tappers and rural workers to discuss the issues of deforestation, violence, and exploitation in the region. The meeting Chico sponsored as the city council's acting president included participation of other city councilors, including one from his own party, the MDB, João Simão, who became a city councilor at the beginning of the year as a result of the resignation of Felix Pereira, who was elected state deputy. Simão allegedly was booed—or at least this was published in the *Gazeta do Acre* newspaper of Rio Branco.

Hurt by the incident, Simão didn't hold anything back. Although he was from the same party as Chico, during the next session, November 23, he introduced a motion for Chico's expulsion. The motion was presented in the plenary session to be sent to the president of the Constitution and Justice

Committee, another MDB councilor, Wagner Bacelar. The situation was unprecedented: The opposition party, the MDB, controlled the presidency of the chamber and the Constitution and Justice Committee, the most important, and saw one of its members proceed against another so that the other councilor could bring a case against him. The ARENA councilors watched from the sidelines and clearly added fuel to the fire of the MDB's internal dispute.

At the November 23, 1979, session, Chico had against him not only the motion of his party colleague but also condemnation by almost all the other councilors, who were criticizing him for having given the council's time to a meeting with rubber tappers.

Aware of the motion by his colleague, Chico presented his resignation from the vice presidency of the council under pressure and probably after much negotiation in a secret meeting on November 29, 1979. Thus the motion was shelved. On November 30, at an open session, the council elected its new vice president, councilor Eurico Filho of ARENA. That is, the MDB no longer controlled the presidency of the council because of the action of one of its own councilors.

It is interesting to note in this connection that although forced to resign from the vice presidency of the council in November 1979 and although his term lasted until early 1981, in the following election for the board, for the period of January 1981 to January 1983, Chico was again elected. Only now he had the post of secretary, counting on the complete support of the PDS[7] and, again, without the votes of his two former colleagues, Wagner Bacelar and João Simão.

Under pressure as a result of his work, Chico was subjected to tough interrogations by the Federal Police, already coordinated at this time by Mauro Sposito, a man who would reappear in a tragic way in his life—and death.

Chico never liked talking about the interrogations he underwent secretly in the Hotel Xapuri, which was owned by the township. According to him, the exhausting and grueling interrogations went on for hours on end.

Although he had quit the presidency of the city council, Chico continued as a councilor and as such always used his position to denounce the violence against rubber tappers and to reinforce the work of the Xapuri Rural Workers' Union.

During the period he was councilor and with the union's support, the advice given him by several progressive Catholic priests who were vicars at the time—Fr. Destro, Fr. Claudio, and Fr. Luciano—was fundamental.

All helped in Chico's political development, complementing what he had learned from Euclides and helping him to interpret things his former teacher had taught him that he had not yet managed to understand completely.

Chico always had great respect for these priests, although he was not a devout Catholic. Whenever I heard him talk about them, he spoke with great affection, especially for Fr. Claudio, whom I met in Italy after Chico's death. Fr. Claudio also spoke about his friend in a very emotional way on a television program in which we participated in May 1989.

Fr. Luciano, who also returned to Italy, where I met him at the same time, had a quieter but very goodhearted style. Fr. Claudio was more active, he joked with everybody and was a great walker, as well as being much thinner than Fr. Luciano. Until today in Xapuri, the rubber tappers of Chico's time, who are already nearing sixty, remember these priests and have great respect for them.

Chico Mendes the Councilor: A Politician Ahead of His Time

As a city councilor, Chico was, without a doubt, way ahead of his time, and this is recorded in the council records of 1977–1982.

As early as 1977, when the dictatorship was just starting to decline, Chico made several speeches supporting CONTAG and the creation of the Xapuri Rural Workers' Union. He did well in debates with Councilor Eurico Filho of ARENA about the participation of religions in supporting the union's founding.

Also during his entire term, Chico made countless speeches in which he denounced the humiliating situation and neglect of the rubber tappers, as well as their expulsion from their homesteads with police involvement. He also spoke out against the devastation of Amazonia, calling for policies to preserve the forest and more support for the rubber tappers.

Speaking about preserving Amazonia at the end of the 1970s and beginning of the 1980s was without a doubt very innovative, especially since this took place not in discussion with university students in the big cities but in a small town in Amazonia itself. On several occasions Chico also used the council podium to denounce deforestation, violence against rubber tappers, violation of human rights by state police, and so on.

I'll take this opportunity to transcribe some excerpts from many of the council's ordinary sessions that demonstrate what I've talked about above. The quotations are taken from the original as recorded.

> [Councilor Mendes] began by explaining that in the previous session he had made a statement defending a class that had contributed so much to the development of our homeland. But today, either through forgetfulness or the political interest of the government, they find themselves humiliated by the great pressure of economic

groups. Soon after my [Chico's] speech, the ARENA leader in this chamber asked that I [Chico] justify and prove my criticisms. And here I show what happened on May 30, 1977, to Mr. José Menezes of the Juaneri homestead. He had fenced fields with numerous crops, and the southerners bought the land and the misfortune began. Inhumanely, they did not allow him to mark off a small field to feed his family. A few days later his farm was destroyed by the workmen from the ranch with the authorization of the owner. Coerced by the secretary of public security, he accepted compensation of 2,000 cruzeiros. He then went to work on May 17 and on coming home was surprised by the former ranch manager, known as Neném, accompanied by two officers, and they took him before Capt. Hilário to explain. When he returned to his shack, everything he had was ransacked. Councilor Mendes continued that he was revolted to see that and at the same time to know the representatives of the people had ignored it. And he asked the MDB councilor why the government authorities had stopped enforcing the law in favor of the have-nots, to serve only their personal interests.

He continued, "The government that could do everything and had all the resources and powers to enforce the laws could have solved so many problems like those I have just related." He criticized the ignorance and lack of enforcement of the legislation and asked why Law 45048 and Decree 70430 had been passed. He said all this was to guarantee landownership, but to this day the laws are not implemented and are ignored by bad administrators who care only about personal benefit, forgetting hundreds of neglected workers, many of whom are subjugated and humiliated by big landowners. "When we seek to denounce such incidents, we are accused of being slanderers and then come demands for justifications that do not allow us to reveal what is obvious to everybody." (Session of June 3, 1977)

[Councilor Mendes] pointed out that since the collapse of the rubber monopoly, Acre had lost its only legitimate source of riches, and then came cattle ranching. Up till now we have seen nothing that leads to the development of our state. (September 30, 1977)

I stand at this podium at this opportune moment to introduce some comments about our current economic and financial situation, which has reached one of its lowest points. Our township is passing through one of its most difficult moments. Meanwhile, we receive constant complaints from various parts of the interior.[9] (June 30, 1978)

To conclude, it would be an injustice not to at least refer to the soldier who has such an important role in our state history, and who is not remembered or praised by the authorities: He is our "rubber soldier." The rubber tapper soldier came to develop our state lands and has received very little in recompense for the great work he has done. (Speech on the Day of the Soldier, August 25, 1978)

Look, gentlemen, the moment is critical on my side, but I am encouraged because I have a commitment to the people, for whom I am determined to sacrifice my own [life].[10] These people, who are always treated unjustly and marginalized, cannot be left unprotected. Your Excellency speaks of the law, but it seems you do not know that the land reform statute, Law 4504, says every occupant with more than a year and a day [on the land] cannot be expelled without being compensated first. Your Excellency received the votes of these people but you still abandon them. I'm not in love with my party, I'm not a coward to fear and fail to defend the people who trusted me with their vote. If I represent a class and don't have the courage to defend it, I will quit. If the MDB gains power in the same selfish way, I will no longer be part of it, I will always be in strong and determined opposition, since I owe the party nothing and have no commitment to it. (Replying to Councilor Wagner Bacelar about his party, the MDB, for having censured him for criticizing the behavior of the former councilor and state deputy Felix Pereira, of the same party, May 4, 1979.)

The frequent visits I made to several estates . . . had such effects that pressures and threats against me soon followed. Last Saturday I was warned by Mr. Rubiquinho of the Filipinas Ranch when he saw me at the Hotel Xapuri, and he threatened me with reprisals for the support I gave to those homesteaders. (May 18, 1979; Chico begins to record the threats he received with increasing intensity)

A few days ago, more than two thousand workers met in our neighboring township of Brasiléia, an event at which the state governor, Joaquim Falcão Macedo, was present. On that occasion I passed along the message to that crowd of workers, who were asking for a better agrarian structure and protesting against the entry of the big landholders who tried to disturb the rubber tappers' families by every means possible. On the other hand, it was strange that TV Acre broadcast only the government's message, while the voice of the union leaders was silenced. (June 22, 1979)

[Councilor Mendes] discussed the news in the *Rio Branco* newspaper that reported a rubber tapper had kidnapped a rancher and said he believed such a thing could happen because of the situation he has been confirming by talking to homesteaders and rubber tappers. He spoke again of the southerners who take over the homesteaders' lands in our state, thus hurting thousands of families who live there. And finally he appealed to the government to give more caring attention to these people, who are suffering a lot and need our support to improve their situation. (August 31, 1979. At this session Councilor Wagner Bacelar of the MDB, the party with which Chico was affiliated, who had tangled with him several sessions before, made a statement backing up what his colleague had said.)

The president, before concluding, said directly from the podium that he was ready to join the struggle against the big landowners and would fight for the workers' land rights no matter whom it hurt, but "my struggle continues in defense of the oppressed." (July 28, 1979)

Having once said he would continue in the PMDB, at the session of May 2, 1980, Chico announced he was leaving that party and affiliating with the Workers' Party. He was the first city councilor from Acre to join the PT.

Speaking about the recent events in our township, they leave much to be desired by those who know Xapuri as a respectable city where peace reigns. Those who came here to maintain and ensure public order caused the cruel death of the farm laborer Melquíades Gomes da Silva, disrespecting human rights in the process. Continuing in the name of the people of Xapuri and the Workers' Party, he appealed to the secretary of security and the governor of the state that incidents of this kind not happen again. Finally, he spoke in support of the rights of the homesteaders of our township. He spoke about the deforestation of the Brazilian Amazon. Finally, Councilor Mendes asked that necessary measures be taken about the exploitation of the Brazilian Amazon, since such exploitation is causing serious damage to our people. (May 2, 1980. I have combined excerpts from two speeches during that session because they complement this statement.)

[Councilor Mendes] defended the rural workers, who are being persecuted by the owners, then emphasized the dedicated work of our rubber tappers and concluded that he would continue struggling in favor of the working class. (June 13, 1980)

Councilor Mendes began by criticizing the federal government for not supporting the rural workers and appealed for the necessary measures to solve the land tenure problem. He spoke about the bloodshed[11] in the neighboring township of Brasiléia and pointed to the lack of responsible action by police authorities. Finally, he appealed to the authorities to ensure that such cases not be reported again in our state. (August 15, 1980)

[Councilor Mendes] spoke about the land tenure problem in our township and said this problem would be resolved only if the government showed interest in carrying out a real land policy that would help the small farmer. (August 8, 1980)

He denounced the conditions affecting the rights of the people of our state and said the workers are coerced and not attended to by security officials. He asked the councilors to show solidarity with them. (September 6, 1980)

Councilor Mendes, leader of the PT bloc,[12] spoke first about the political opening[13] proclaimed by General Figueiredo, which does not respond to the concerns of our people. He spoke of the expulsion of Fr. Vitor Miracapilo and characterized it as an arbitrary act. He spoke about the donation by Planning Minister Delfim Neto to the Japanese firm Suzuki of $200,000 and said he would never silence himself in the face of so many injustices. (October 31, 1980)

Councilor Mendes requested information from the agriculture minister, Angelo Amaury Stabile, about the Amazon forest, which is being cut down by the big southern businessmen, who are expelling the homesteaders who have been toiling here for many years. (November 7, 1980)

[Councilor Mendes] spoke about several conflicts here and said they come from the councilors of his former party. They have accused him even of being a subversive, and many times his own party misinterpreted him. He brought the auspicious news to these people that he had been indicted under the National Security Law[14] and said his attorney would accompany him. He had until Thursday to defend himself. He believed this had happened because he always says the truth and defends the rights of the people. Finally, he said that directly or indirectly, he would keep fighting. (November 14, 1980)

First speaking about the publication of the *Gazeta do Acre* newspaper, where it said members of the PT were indicted under the National Security Law,[15] [Councilor Mendes] stated his name and insisted this must be because he always spoke in support of the rural workers, who are persecuted by the big businessmen who arrive here and take over their earning power. He criticized the land-grabbers who attack the homesteaders, as well as all those who violate the laws of our country, and expressed solidarity with the rural workers and spoke about their miserable wages. (November 21, 1980)

[Councilor Mendes] said our township was the scene of great events, especially in the rural area. He spoke about the northeasterners who came to Acre without recompense, only to be expelled from their land. He also said the rural worker does not want violence, only possession of his land. He spoke about several ranchers who keep cutting down trees, thus hurting the homesteaders. He asked that INCRA and IBDF take measures. Finally he said in the next session he would ask permission to take a leave of absence to respond to the summons of the military prosecutors in Manaus. (March 20, 1981)

Councilor Mendes (Workers' Party leader)[16] spoke about Acre's history and compared the previous period with the present and said we had lived more quietly before; now we are going through a very difficult period. He spoke about the production of rubber, a source of wealth for our country. He described the businessmen who came here and seized the lands of our people who live here, stealing their land and expelling them. He spoke about the devaluation of rubber, especially by the government agency SUDHEVEA.[17] (May 29, 1981)

[Councilor Mendes] spoke about the programming of National Amazon Radio,[18] which broadcasts government demagoguery on its news programs and tries to deceive people who work the land. He then made harsh criticisms of serious Brazilian problems, the way the Brazilian government submits to them and then allows invasion of the Brazilian people's land by the big businessmen. Thus it does not allow for adequate working conditions for the rural people on their land. He criticized the devastation of the great Amazon forest, which is a source of natural wealth for Brazilians. (March 5, 1982)

[Councilor Mendes] criticized the federal government for installing an antidemocratic regime. He spoke about the destruction of our forests, which hurts our rubber tappers, and said actions of this kind are for electoral purposes, since the government should serve the people and not marginalize them as it is doing. (April 2, 1982)

[Councilor Mendes] spoke about human rights and criticized several state policemen in Xapuri. He said because he had denounced irregularities by the police, he had received threats. He said he would never back down in the face of such threats and would persist in defending the rights of our people and asked for the president of this chamber to take measures. (April 23, 1982)

[Councilor Mendes] said that class [rural workers] was the victim of capitalism. Then he criticized the government policy for its lack of support for rural people and its support for big business. He defended the rural working class in reference to the provocations currently going on in our country. He criticized the state government for having worked against the rural workers, favoring the deforestation of our rubber estates and failing to protect those who work and struggle for their survival. He said he would always be on the side of the poor, because with its actions the government is playing one class [rubber tappers] off against the other [big landowners]. He appealed for support from his colleagues to avoid bloodshed.[19] (April 30, 1982)

I don't know if readers like having so many fragments of Chico's statements transcribed. But they are not yet collected, and unfortunately it seems that his complete speeches cannot be recovered for what would doubtless be a beautiful book by Chico himself in a posthumous edition. The excerpts presented above show not only Chico's coherence in his positions and the firmness with which he defended them but also that he brought up issues, such as the devastation of the Amazon rainforest, that are still brewing on the national level.

In a determined way, Chico took on the role of councilor to put himself at the service of the rural workers. Although he made motions and criticized local problems, from the condition of the streets and electricity to the water supply in Xapuri, he focused on revealing the real situation of the rubber tappers. He denounced violence and received threats because of his work; but, as he repeated many times, he always stayed in the fight in defense of the poorest, the rural workers and the rubber tappers. Without a shadow of a doubt, he was a politician ahead of his time.

I should add that even when he wasn't part of the executive committee of the Xapuri City Council, during his entire mandate, almost always when the secretary was going to make a statement, Chico Mendes was asked about 70 percent of the time to fill in as secretary. This showed that the council members respected him as a legislator and trusted in his competence.

Chico could be considered an outstanding council member, just based on the initiatives he took, his insistence that measures be carried out, and his statements, as recorded in summary form (unfortunately!) in the minutes.

Communicating in Writing, a Habit of Chico Mendes

Although he had no regular schooling, Chico Mendes enjoyed writing very much and always tried to communicate in writing, whether to the union representatives on the estates or to the authorities.

Before his murder, Chico Mendes wrote several signed articles that were published in the newspapers *Folha do Acre* and *A Gazeta.*

He wrote countless letters to the authorities (the governor, the Federal Police superintendent, the Xapuri district judge, the state secretary of public security, among others), warning that he was marked for death and running a real risk of being assassinated. He was not taken seriously.

But it wasn't only to the authorities that Chico Mendes wrote. He also sent written messages to the union representatives and wrote to nongovernmental organizations asking for help for the rubber tappers' movement or denouncing the death threats he was receiving.

In *Ventania,* a mimeographed newsletter sporadically published by the city committee of the Workers' Party, he wrote many articles, especially the "briefs," little notes read and commented on by many people, in which he vociferously attacked the mayor of Xapuri.

The very text that later became the "testament" of Chico Mendes,[20] addressed to the "youth of the future," was written while he was trying to make a long-distance call on September 6, 1988. He wrote it and left it taped to my telephone. I found the utopian text and kept it. I made only one mistake—I didn't ask him to sign it. This is a pity, since I have the original without his signature, but his handwriting is unmistakable.

The man of the forest wrote as often as he could. He recorded his complaints in writing. It was a way of showing he was not afraid to take responsibility for his denunciations. It was also an act of citizenship.

Political Activism: The Daily Life of a Leader

After his death Chico Mendes became better known as an ecological martyr, in the almost pejorative and depoliticized sense of those words, than as a political activist. In my opinion, this confusion needs to be cleared up by taking another look at his daily life as a committed political activist.

For his first run as a candidate for city council, Chico sought out the only party in active opposition to the military dictatorship at the time.

In 1979 Chico Mendes could already be called a leftist militant, since his work as a councilor and a rubber tapper leader, whose first priority was the interests of the workers, put him in direct opposition to the interests of the big ranchers and the traditional politicians of the time.

In the early 1980s, as the Workers' Party emerged, Chico Mendes was a member from the beginning. As one of the founders of the party in Acre, he became one of the first PT city council members in the country.

During all his years of political activism, Chico Mendes was not only a political partisan but also, as the founder and first secretary of the Brasiléia Rural Workers' Union, a union leader. Later he was a founder of CUT and a substitute member of its national committee when he was killed. He was also president of the Xapuri Rural Workers' Union and a founder of the National Rubber Tappers' Council.

Chico Mendes often expressed his political militancy in discussions with rural workers themselves, at the STR assemblies in Xapuri, in the meetings before the empates, always speaking of a social project, interpreting class struggle as part of the regional situation. For this reason he was locally and nationally respected.

His engagement led to his prosecution under the National Security Law along with Lula and other unionists who were founders of the Workers' Party. He was found not guilty twice.

About two months before his death, in an interview, Chico Mendes made a statement that clearly expressed his position at the moment when he became known as an ecologist rather than as a union leader. The word "ecology" is not part of the rubber tappers' lexicon. It was something outside their struggle, which was and continues to be defending the Amazon to protect their means of subsistence. For the rubber tappers, defending the forest is much more than protecting the "green" because it's beautiful or the air one breathes; it means defending the place where one subsists and from which one gets one's daily bread.

If we look for the origin of the word "ecology," it comes from the Greek *oikos,* which means "house," and ecology means "the study of our house," etymologically speaking. Thus the rubber tappers of that time, although they didn't know the meaning of the word "ecology," were radical ecologists because they defended and still do defend their dwelling places, including the forest. In other words, they took ecology to its radical conclusions.

The rubber tappers' struggle, as waged by Wilson Pinheiro, Chico Mendes, and other leaders who are no longer alive to tell the story, includes a proposal for a new society where there is neither exploitation nor violence. This concept was very clear to Chico Mendes, and he expressed it countless times.

The confrontation with the ranchers was clearly understood as a confrontation between classes, where capital was represented by rich ranchers and large economic enterprises and labor was represented by the homesteaders, the rubber tappers—those who did and can rely only on their own labor to survive.

What I'm saying here seems very remote from the reality of the rubber tappers, and it was. These were concepts that were hard to absorb in the abstract; but translated into the daily confrontations, the empates, and the struggle each homesteader waged to stay in his home, it became easy to make them understood. And this Chico Mendes knew how to do better than anybody.

It wasn't hard to discuss with the rubber tappers the reasons for the violence, the way the judiciary was always on the side of the powerful, the ranchers, to the extent of sending state police to protect the clearing operations, of always expelling the homesteader and upholding the claim of the "owner," even when no analysis was done of the documentation of the claim.

Chico Mendes was not an opportunist. He was a political activist twenty-four hours a day, seven days a week, and he showed this wherever he was, whether at a meeting with rubber tappers on the estate or at the general assemblies of the Xapuri STR or afterward at the regional meetings of rubber tappers or in the speeches he gave in São Paulo or Rio de Janeiro.

I've made this record to tell Chico Mendes's true story, which has been told in so many ways, depending on who's talking. As a witness, I'm telling it from my point of view, recovering what I think it's necessary to recover, without any pretense of knowing everything. I tell it as I understood and learned it.

But if I didn't tell it, it would be recorded in the rubber tappers' struggle, in the legacy of the organization Chico left in Xapuri and through the way he lived and died.

"He Knew It Would Come, Death without Warning"

A Nicaraguan song, which Chico Mendes knew as an admirer of the Sandinista revolution in Nicaragua, recounts the death of one of its leaders: "He knew it would come, death without warning."

For Chico Mendes it was no different. Since 1977 he had been receiving continual death threats from the ranchers, the main ones hurt by the organization of the rubber tappers in Brasiléia and Xapuri, whose basic activity was the empate.

On July 21, 1980, paid gunmen murdered Wilson Pinheiro, president of the Brasiléia STR and the first great union leader in the region, with whom Chico Mendes had worked since 1975. According to information gathered later, Chico Mendes should have been killed that day, but he wasn't found by those who were supposed to kill him.

After Wilson Pinheiro's burial in Brasiléia and especially after the death of Nilão, the ranchers' main enforcer in the region, Chico had to spend about two months in hiding, sleeping in a different place every night, followed by gunmen who were waiting for a chance to kill him with impunity. Those were very tense days, according to Chico's own account.

Every year the threats continued, especially during the burning season,[21] as a result of the workers' organized resistance.

Up to the time of his death, to Chico Mendes's knowledge, he was close to being killed six times, managing to escape on several occasions by chance, by changing his travel plans or simply, for other reasons, by delaying trips he had already planned. At other times, warned that an armed ambush would take place, Chico changed his route.

In a log he made in 1987, Chico Mendes noted on August 10: "Two A.M., threats, break-in attempt in the kitchen at the union hall." That morning, when by chance Chico was not alone at Xapuri STR headquarters, someone tried to break into the building by jumping through the window near the kitchen sink. He failed only because the wood was rotten and collapsed under the gunman's weight. The gunman fled, leaving his footprints in the mud outside, under the window.

A few weeks before his murder Chico Mendes left a note to a friend in the office of the Amazon Workers' Center in Rio Branco, saying gunmen had been following him all day.

Chico Mendes knew he was marked to die and denounced this situation throughout 1988, sending many communications to the authorities at both state and federal levels. The press and politicians in Acre said he was claiming to be threatened just to get his name in the papers.

Knowing that he didn't have much longer to live, each time he gave a speech in 1988, before returning to Acre he would say good-bye to his friends as if it were the last time he'd see them. This became very obvious in the speeches he gave in Piracicaba, São Paulo (December 7), and Rio de Janeiro (December 9), when he said he was threatened with death and perhaps he was returning home to be killed.

As the Nicaraguan song honoring the Sandinista revolutionary (and priest) Commander Gaspar says, "He knew it would come, death without warning, but death has to be faced when a people is behind you."

From Xapuri to the World: The Same Simple and Humble Man

After the First National Rubber Tappers Meeting in 1985, the rubber tappers' struggle spread beyond Amazonia to gain national and international importance as a result of the proposal to create extractive reserves.

The recently founded CNS began receiving invitations to put forward and explain the extractive reserve concept in diverse places in many parts of the world.

The then-president, Jaime Araújo, a rubber tapper–poet from Novo Aripuanã, Amazonas state, was invited to be a visiting professor for several months at the respected University of Brasília, while many people came from other countries to get to know the forest defense work of the rubber tappers firsthand.

As a result of the dangers to the environment caused by paving the BR–364 highway between Porto Velho and Rio Branco and especially in light of the devastation caused by paving the stretch between Cuiabá and Porto Velho, with the help of international environmentalists the rubber tappers found an opportunity to participate in discussions with the Inter-American Development Bank (IDB), responsible for funding a third of the cost of the paving.

Representing the CNS, Chico Mendes went to the United States—

specifically, Miami—to participate in an IDB annual board meeting, in which representatives of each member country participate. On arrival at customs in Miami, the first problem arose: Chico didn't know a single word of English, which made communication difficult until they sent an agent who spoke Spanish.

The conversation began: "How much money are you bringing?" the agent asked. "None," Chico answered. The agent was puzzled: "How is it you're coming into the United States and not bringing any money? What have you come to do?" Chico's answer was simple: "I've come to participate in a meeting of the IDB." "Are you a banker?" asked the agent. "Not even a bank clerk," answered Chico.

The situation was beginning to get sticky. Worse yet, Chico thought the person who should have been waiting for him, the anthropologist Steve Schwartzman,[22] might have gone away, since Chico had already been held up for more than one and a half hours in customs. This was very worrying for Chico because in that case he would have to take the next plane back to Brazil. Remembering Steve, Chico recalled he had an invitation in English, sent by environmental organizations, with the schedule of the meeting. He showed the invitation to the agent and finally was allowed to enter the United States.

At the IDB meeting, always introduced by representatives of environmental organizations, Chico Mendes spoke with representatives of several member governments of the Bank. This was after getting press credentials from Central TV in London to enter the meeting, since he had no way of attending as a representative of the rubber tappers.

After participating in the IDB meeting and as a result of a visit to Xapuri by Robert Lamb of the UN Environment Program, Chico Mendes was awarded the Global 500 prize, becoming part of the first group of people from around the world who had distinguished themselves in environmental advocacy. Among about ninety winners, there was only one Brazilian: Chico Mendes.

To protest the fact that the Global 500 award had not been given to governmental officials, the Brazilian government insisted on ignoring the prize and was one of a few countries absent when the certificate was presented on July 6, 1987, in London. Praised outside Brazil, the prize got almost no coverage in our country.

In his very brief acceptance speech, Chico Mendes dedicated the prize to all the rubber tappers of Amazonia.

On his first trip to the United States in March 1987, in a meeting with staff members of the U.S. Senate Budget Committee, Chico took the opportunity to denounce the fact that the multilateral banks were financing the devastation of the Amazon, giving as an example the case of Rondônia and the paving of the BR-364 between Porto Velho and Rio Branco.

On September 21, 1987, when he received his second international award from the Better World Society, Chico again dedicated the prize to all the rubber tappers of Amazonia and the Forest Peoples Alliance, on which he had already started working with Indians from UNI.

Taking advantage of this second visit, Chico made new contacts, including one with Senator Robert Kasten,[23] chairman of the very powerful Budget Committee, personally making the denunciations he had already sent before.

On his return to Brazil Chico was attacked by Acre politicians, who accused him of being a false leader and playing the game of the Americans by damaging Acre's development, among other things.

In an attempt to pressure Chico one of the deputies called him to appear before the state legislature to clarify the reasons for his trips. When he went before the legislature, with the same tranquillity that he had when conducting general assemblies of the Xapuri STR, Chico educated the deputies about Acre's situation, to prove to the public that the deputies were completely misinformed about documents of the greatest importance to Acre, such as the agreement between the Brazilian government and the IDB for paving the BR-364 between Porto Velho and Rio Branco.

From the podium of the legislature, Chico showed the deputies a copy of the agreement and asked if they knew of its contents, which included an appropriation of U.S. $10 million for protection of the environment and traditional populations, to prevent what had happened in Rondônia from being repeated in Acre. The legislators didn't even know the agreement existed, much less that money was to be invested in initiatives in Acre, part of Rondônia, and part of Amazonas in the BR-364's so-called sphere of influence. The legislators went in search of wool and ended up sheared.

All the publicity given Chico Mendes, especially the prizes and international trips, made the local traditional politicians uncomfortable and worried that a rubber tapper might even manage to win the 1990 elections, competing on equal terms with the Acre state government and other politicians representing the interests of the ranchers and the big economic enterprises.

It's certainly true that until his death Chico Mendes was much better known internationally than in Brazil.

In 1987 two British journalists visiting Brazil told us that when they were in Rio de Janeiro they had contacted journalists from the *Jornal do Brasil*, from whom they sought information about the rubber tappers' struggle in Amazonia and the extractive reserve idea. The journalists responded that they had never heard of this.

The national visibility of Chico Mendes and the rubber tappers' movement really began in 1988, thanks fundamentally to the work of the Support Committee of the Peoples of the Forest, which was created soon after Chico's visit to Rio de Janeiro in September 1987.

Despite all the publicity and the international prizes, as well as his having given dozens of speeches throughout Brazil, Chico Mendes never lost his humility and always lived under very difficult conditions. For example, with help from friends in the Center-South of Brazil, he bought the simple wooden house where he lived until he was killed. The second of two installments was paid only a month before his death, because on other occasions Chico Mendes spent the money his friends had sent for the house to pay the salaries of the Xapuri STR's employees.

All the financial support he received for his work, Chico Mendes passed directly to the union and its activities. He led a very simple, almost poverty-stricken life.

~~~~~~~~~~~~~~~~~~~~~~~~~~~~~~~~~~~~~

Chapter 7

AN INTERVIEW WITH
CHICO MENDES

CHICO MENDES GAVE MANY INTERVIEWS to national
and international journalists, environmentalists, university professors and
graduate students. Much of what he said is recorded. In December 1987 I
carried out an interview with him that was never published.

So long after, publishing an interview like this one might seem strange,
but I think it is a way of recovering what Chico Mendes originally thought
about the rubber tapper organization, when the extractive reserves were only
a faraway dream.

The following is the entire interview.

Guma: Chico, you've been in the news lately because of a recent trip to the
United States, where you talked about the issue of the BR–364 highway.
What's the situation right now?

Chico Mendes: This issue has led to a lot of debate, first because after my
return the press and the politicians who support the big ranching interests
were worried about the denunciation I made in the United States. They
started saying on radio, television, and in the papers that I had gone to the
U.S. to ask for suspension of the paving of 364. So therefore I was against
progress in Acre and was branded as a false leader, representing nothing, and
an obstructionist. What happened was completely different. What I said there,
what I denounced was the neglect, the lack of commitment by Brazilian
government authorities to the agreement they themselves had made with the
IDB. We have information that when the Brazilian government got this loan
from the IDB, it had to make a commitment to environmental protection,
protecting the forests, the rubber tappers, the Indian areas. This commitment
was not carried out. To this day it's only a scrap of paper. That includes the
PMACI[1] plan to consult with the rubber tapper and union leaders about

environmental policy. This has never happened. It's only on paper, and in practice nothing has been done. So it was this that led the authorities, the IDB representative himself, and the environmental groups to mobilize and send a denunciation to the Bank. It suggested the suspension of the Bank's remaining disbursement to Brazil as long as this issue was not discussed seriously or examined and the Brazilian government didn't carry out the part of the bargain it made when it signed onto the Bank's loan for paving the 364.

Guma: About this issue of progress, how do you see this? What does progress mean to you? What is progress with or without the rubber tapper?

Chico Mendes: They say this paving project will bring progress to Acre. The way it's being done, progress means rewarding the big ranchers. For the rubber tapper, the small farmer, and Acre's workers, there is no progress. The proof is that the worker has not been heard. What one sees is the interest of the big rancher to take control of the land along this highway. We believe the progress they're talking about is what happened in Rondônia with the creation of the Polonoroeste project, which resulted in paving the road from Cuiabá to Rondônia. They talked a lot about progress and now Rondônia is being transformed into a desert. Today you don't see any of the rubber tappers who used to live near the highway. Rondônia has been turned into a desert, and as far as we can see, they have the same objective in Acre: Progress means cattle, devastation, expulsion of the rubber tappers, genocide of the rubber tappers in Amazonia.

Guma: Since the National Rubber Tappers' Meeting in Brasília in 1985, a plan for extractive reserves was proposed as a way to protect the rubber tappers. Do you think this is viable? Can the extractive reserve improve living conditions and ensure the rubber tappers' survival?

Chico Mendes: Not only that. In my opinion it's the only proposal to defend the economic interests of Amazonia, the only way to protect the forest, the rubber trees, the Brazil nuts. Furthermore, we have another idea in addition to this extractive reserve concept supported by the National Rubber Tappers' Council and several unions in Xapuri and Plácido and other opposition union movements. This is not only to protect the forest, it's another economic proposal, still in the early stage. In general the extractive reserve project is the only way to guarantee the rubber tapper's future and the future of Brazil, because Amazonia can be developed in a rational way. In the future it could be a great economic area not only for the people in the region—Indians, rubber tappers, and urban workers—but for all of Brazil. So what we see as an alternative proposal is not a short-term idea, it's a project—a political project of Amazon workers that could ensure the development of the region and the Brazilian people.

Guma: For defending the forest, you recently won two awards, one from the UN Environment Program and the other from the Better World Society. How do you feel about these two prizes?

Chico Mendes: Well, it all still seems like a dream. Now we can't sit back. From my vantage point, I think the reason we received these prizes is because of the struggle we've been waging over the years. So despite the prize being given to me, it's also an award to the rubber tappers of the Amazon, of Acre. I don't consider it a prize to Chico Mendes, I think it's a prize that will help advance the rubber tappers' resistance movement as a whole. The most positive result I see is this: Through these awards we gain much greater international recognition and more possibility for us to gain allies in the battle we're waging to protect the Amazon.

Guma: You've received two international prizes, but in our state you've been severely criticized by politicians and business leaders and different sectors of Acre society. How do you explain this? What is the difference in positions?

Chico Mendes: Well, we have to be very mature to confront this reaction. I know the attacks have been fierce, and they've even tried to convince the workers that I'm using this, perhaps even for personal advantage, and so on. They are capable of anything. Now the only thing I see is that it's clear, when you start hurting the interests of capital, the big landowners, they get desperate and look for ways to denigrate the workers. In a sense I consider this a victory of the workers, but also a big preoccupation of Acre's big landowners and politicians—especially those elected with support from the big landowners. To me it's clear that they are against us and are worried by the situation because they defend the landowners. So it's obvious they feel bad because their interests are being threatened. It won't end there. We know that in the process of this struggle and the growth of our movement, the more we start limiting their actions and the consciousness of the rubber tappers increases, they're going to get much more worried. These criticisms exist and will continue to exist because the only way they have to fight us today is to try to set the workers' principal leaders against the workers through slander and libel. They have control of the media, and it's very easy for them to spread disinformation to the workers. Sometimes the workers are not prepared, and they often believe these falsehoods. But I believe that little by little, the level of the workers' consciousness is rising. It will reach the point where even these slanders and libels will be worthless because the workers will become aware.

Guma: You've been in the headlines a lot recently, but what's your life like, the life of an ordinary man? How does this guy live?

Chico Mendes: That's a very good question. I insist on giving a thorough answer. The problem is, when I got involved with the union movement in

Acre in 1974 and 1975, that's exactly when the early union movement emerged. It was exactly at that moment that the biggest confrontation, the biggest attack by the ranchers, happened. With the arrival of the big landowners here in Acre, the rubber tappers were being expelled with no way of defending themselves. They saw their huts burned, and gunmen forced them to leave their homesteads. Often they were forced to sign documents at gunpoint by the big landowners. From that moment I decided to get into the union movement to raise the banner on behalf of the rubber tappers and defend the homesteaders. When I got involved in this movement I was already aware I'd have to give up my own interests, including economic interests. I was going to take on a tough struggle, the struggle of the little guy against the millionaires, of the rubber tapper against the landowners. I had to be serious and take a coherent stand on behalf of the workers.

During this whole period I've been fighting, from 1977 to 1987, my stance hasn't changed. It's been a struggle alongside other comrades in the resistance. Many comrades who started out with me during the 1970s quit because they couldn't take it. They didn't manage to mature politically as regards idealism. When they saw their financial situation deteriorate, they had no way of resisting and dropped out. Others, unfortunately, have sold themselves to the highest bidder and are living quite well today. And there are those who did resist. I'm proud of being among comrades who took on the struggle. To this day I don't have my own house. My family lives in houses owned by our parents, thanks to the support I still receive from my relatives, who put us up. If not for them, I don't know how it would be, but the important thing is the ideal that we stay true to, confronting the tough circumstances. Unfortunately, there are still workers today who believe I use the union's money. But one thing I'm proud of is that any comrade, worker, rubber tapper—or even our opponents or those who have doubts—can come to the union, which is open, to see if there's any document proving Chico Mendes has a salary from the union or if any comrade who works in the union earns a salary. Nobody makes any money. We, I at least, receive funds to resist, I still get help from comrades who support our struggle. With this I keep going, supporting myself through this ideal we have. I have to keep holding onto this craziness, this belief, this idealism as long as I can resist. This is the commitment we've made to the movement, to the workers' struggle. If you think only about your private issues, about finances, about personal advantage, you won't succeed in holding onto this idealism or in fighting for the workers.

Guma: One of the charges raised when you came back from the United States is that you returned with your pockets full of dollars. How do you respond to this? Did you really come back with your pockets full of dollars?

Chico Mendes: The people who accuse me of coming back with pockets full of dollars are precisely the enemies of the workers, those who want to destabilize the workers' movement. To give you an idea, I had problems on arrival in the United States because I didn't take money with me. I had problems at customs because when the customs agent asked me how much money I had, I said I hadn't brought any dollars because I wasn't going to do any sightseeing, I wasn't on a tourist trip. I was going at the invitation of environmental groups to represent the rubber tappers of Acre and Amazonia. This caused a bit of a dispute because I said I had no dollars. All of a sudden I began to be a suspect. The way I defended myself was by showing the invitation from environmental groups that I had in my hands. That's what made the customs agent give me back my ticket. On my return the only help I had was that the organizations collected $30 for meals, since I had no money and had to pay some fees on the trip out of Miami and from the U.S. back to Brazil. I didn't have any money because I went there to discuss the interests of the workers of Acre. I didn't go to help myself financially. What I really went to do was to take a proposal from the workers of Acre, defend their way of life, and denounce the injustices these workers have suffered for many years. Those who make accusations must present proof, but this evidence will never materialize because I didn't bring any money from there to here. What I got was the meal allowance, because I had to eat something until I got back to my comrades in Brazil.

Guma: Another big question that was raised in the legislature of Acre was about what "an ignorant rubber tapper" went to do in the United States. Why should an "ignorant rubber tapper" suddenly be receiving prizes? How do you respond to these claims, Chico, especially the "ignorance" of the rubber tapper?

Chico Mendes: It isn't so surprising to me that the legislators we have here in the State Assembly are still saying this. I'd be surprised if they were actually praising me. It's no surprise. What workers have to expect from these legislators are these statements because their interests don't correspond to those of the workers. It proves once again when they make accusations, when they don't credit the capacity of the rubber tapper to represent himself, this proves exactly where their interest lies. Despite having been elected with the rubber tappers' votes, they don't have any commitment. Their interest is in defending the capitalists and the big landowners. For them, this business of the rubber tappers is only valid on election day. I consider these charges against me an accusation against the rubber tappers, because I belong to the class of rubber tappers. Even though I'm not tapping rubber trees at the moment, I've been part of the group since I was ten years old, and I worked as a rubber tapper for twenty-five years without a break. So I consider myself a rubber tapper because I'm with them. Today I have the privilege of defending the rubber tappers' interests because I was chosen by the rubber tappers themselves to defend their interests. So I'm not surprised. Who are the legislators we have in the Assembly? They're the ones who defend the interests of Bordon, of the UDR, of capital, and their own interests. They earn more than 100,000 cruzados a month to do nothing on behalf of the workers, who have no one representing them. To this day no rubber tapper has ever seen one of those legislators in the Assembly or a federal deputy from Acre support an alternative project on behalf of the workers of Acre. Nobody ever will, because they don't represent the workers' interests.

Guma: Is the "New Republic"[2] for the workers, Chico?

Chico Mendes: We believe we exchanged a uniformed dictatorship for a dictatorship of the guys in suits. The workers are still being repressed in the same way, exploited even more, by the hyped-up New Republic. I believe that this stands for the new interests of capitalism, the big landowners, and that's why they gave it the name New Republic, because it's a new populist system to protect the interests of the "haves." The proof is there, and it's very clear: The workers keep suffering more and more, the rubber tappers are increasingly threatened, surrounded. Their crop has no value because the government, together with the big landowners, has an interest in trying to discourage the rubber tappers so they'll leave their holdings, abandon their homesteads, so they'll be delivered to the big ranchers. This is the philosophy of the New Republic: They kill the workers, exploit the workers, as the documents show is happening in the north and south of the country. Hundreds of workers have been killed during this New Republic. That's what the New Republic is about. That's how we see this kind of New Republic.

Guma: And the New Republic's land reform?

Chico Mendes: The land reform of the New Republic is exactly what I was talking about before: It's the land reform that benefits the big landowner. The proof is there: When the workers and some others joined this Republic intending to carry out land reform, they left because the New Republic's interest is not in carrying out land reform for the workers. The New Republic wants to create a new discourse to fool the workers and find a more strategic, more intelligent, craftier way to protect the big landowners. That's what one sees: more strategic, more attractive discourses to fool the workers. And many workers still believe the New Republic can carry out land reform. No way! There is no land reform. What exists is precisely a plan to protect the interests of the big landowners. It's no coincidence that in this period of the New Republic the UDR was created. You see, the workers' movement (I'm speaking in political, partisan terms now) has been resisting for a long time—the landless movement, some union movements, the CUT, the most combative resistance sector defending land reform in the country. Last year they didn't elect even twenty deputies to the Constitutional Assembly, while the UDR, created during the New Republic with the support of the New Republic, managed to elect almost seventy and succeeded in a short time in silencing more than one hundred union leaders in the country.

Guma: What do you think has to be done to change all this—right now?

Chico Mendes: First, I think that when you think about a change of this nature, you have to consider the political situation, policy questions in general, from the president of the republic to city council members. First, what has to happen immediately to change the situation is that the workers have to organize through their class organizations, right away, and fight for direct elections. We believe that while the Brazilian workers don't organize and push—because we can't expect anything of this Constituent Assembly, these deputies who are there right now—we have to expect the workers' movement, through CUT and the militant union movements, to push ahead on the national level, involving the rural and urban workers, in the effort to campaign for direct elections[3] for the presidency of the republic. From there, if the organized workers succeed in electing a president committed to the workers' interests, land reform, and social change in the countryside and the city, this person will have the backing of the workers themselves to change the situation. And if, by chance, this elected person becomes a victim . . . because without a doubt, the minute a president is elected who's committed to the workers, the capitalists, landowners, and multinational corporations will not hesitate to bring down this person. But then if this person is elected by the workers, it's clear the workers will be organized to keep this person in power.

I think that for change to start, there has to be a struggle for immediate elections, against payment of the foreign debt. Whatever president is elected in Brazil, if he commits himself to pay the foreign debt, the situation will stay the same or get worse. We have to elect committed people who pledge to the workers' movement that we are not responsible for the foreign debt. The workers did not contract the debt, and therefore we should not have to pay it. A government elected by the workers must maintain this position. If not, there will be no change because he won't have the will to carry out land reform, which will only be done if we break with the IMF and have a government committed to the workers' movement.

CHICO'S DREAM

BY LINDA RABBEN

Even if you kill the cock, the dawn will come.
—BRAZILIAN PROVERB

CHICO MENDES LIKED TO PLAY DOMINOES, tell ghost stories, and play practical jokes. I should know; he played one on me in July 1988. As we walked the forest near the Cachoeira estate, he pulled a strip of bark from a tree next to the rubber trail. Sucking on it in delight, he told me how sweet it was, but when I put the bark in my mouth it tasted horribly bitter. I couldn't stop grimacing. Chico laughed uproariously. "It's good for stomach ache," he said.

As the coordinator of a small NGO based in Washington, D.C., the Brazil Network, I went to Acre with the award-winning filmmaker Miranda Smith[1] and the Brazilian anthropologist Mary Allegretti to meet him. We walked from the shabby Xapuri bus station along dusty, brick-paved streets to Chico's wooden shack, where he lived with his wife and two small children. After a big lunch, we rested. Chico sprawled asleep on the living room floor while Mary lay in a nearby hammock, chatting with Gomercindo, an intensely serious young man who was near the top of the local landowners' hit list. As the head of the Rural Workers' Union, Chico was at the top of that list.

The next morning at seven o'clock we ate breakfast at a small food stand on one of Xapuri's main streets. I noticed a pickup parked about two blocks away. Leaning against it in a leisurely but somehow ominous way were five or six men, wearing the straw Stetsons landowners use in the Brazilian West. I asked Mary who they were. "Those are the men who are threatening Chico," she replied. Clearly, they wanted everybody to know about their intentions. A few weeks before they had sent a gunman to kill the young union activist Ivair Higino as he walked along a lonely road early one morning.

Almost two years later I returned to Xapuri and paid a visit to Chico's tomb, a large cement structure covered with white tiles in the municipal cemetery. Next to him, in a smaller grave, lay Higino. It seems a shame that the two must lie there instead of in the rubber tappers' graveyard we passed in 1988 when we walked on the rubber trails with Chico. It was twilight then, and the fading orange sun tinged the wooden crosses and the forest behind them. He would have been more at home there, I thought. For Chico was a country boy, whom Gomercindo remembers as an "ordinary man."

Like thousands of others, Chico's father had gone out to the Amazon frontier from the crowded, destitute, drought-ridden northeastern countryside during World War II to extract latex from wild rubber trees for the Allied war effort. The newcomers were called rubber soldiers. As Gomercindo recounts, their working and living conditions were terrible—few managed to escape the same debt peonage they had fled from.

As a boy, Chico had little time to play or study. He was out in the rubber groves, tapping the trees, from an early age. Like his father he would rise before dawn, grab a glass of coffee and a bite to eat, put on the *poronga* and set off for many hours of walking and tapping, walking and tapping. Chico learned the lore of the forest on these treks, which provided his only schooling. It was likely he would spend the rest of his life on the estate, earning a pittance, struggling to support a growing family as his father had done.

When he was a teenager, in 1960, Chico met Euclides Fernando Távora, the man who would change his life. Nobody was sure where Távora had come from to follow the reclusive ways of the tappers in the remote forests of Acre. He told Chico stories of the Prestes Column, an army of peasants, renegade soldiers, and intellectuals that had crossed Brazil's interior during the 1920s under the leadership of Luis Carlos Prestes, who later became the longtime chief of Brazil's Communist Party. During the Vargas dictatorship in the 1930s, Távora said, he had participated in a quixotic Communist uprising that led to his imprisonment in a fortress on an island off Brazil's northeast coast. He finally arrived in Acre, where he hid out in the rainforest, tapping rubber like his poor, unlettered neighbors.

Távora asked Chico's father if he could teach the boy to read and write. The old man agreed, as long as the "classes" wouldn't keep the boy from fulfilling his responsibilities to the family. Távora taught Chico using newspaper clippings and short-wave radio broadcasts as pedagogical materials. The two would discuss the news they heard on the BBC World Service, Radio Moscow, and the Voice of America. Távora also explained the principles of grassroots organizing to Chico. Then one day after the military coup of 1964 Távora went away and never came back. Chico had learned enough from him by that time to become a literacy teacher for a federal government program.

Years later Chico founded the rubber tappers' union in his hometown of Xapuri. In 1977 he was elected to the Xapuri City Council, on which he served until 1982. That year he was indicted—along with Luiz Inácio "Lula" da Silva and other Workers' Party leaders—for "subversion" under the dictatorship's National Security Law. Chico, Lula, and the other defendants were acquitted after a long trial. Lula was already famous as one of the founders of the Workers' Party, but Chico continued as a rather obscure local unionist in Acre, despite his involvement in the national movement for democratization. It was Chico who successfully lobbied the Workers' Party to include an environmental protection plank in its national electoral platform.

Chico spent the final decade of his life leading the rubber tappers and other rural workers in their struggle to protect the rubber groves, the rainforest, and their traditional way of life against the assaults of would-be landowners, political mafias, and others who wanted to cut down the forests and expel their traditional inhabitants. He led dozens of nonviolent empates to prevent deforestation. Rubber tappers and their families would go to rubber estates where land-grabbers were clearing the area for cattle pasture and try to persuade the workers to put down their chainsaws. The tactic often worked, inspiring traditional forest dwellers in other regions to do the same.

Chico also organized rubber tappers for the union and represented their interests locally, regionally, nationally, and internationally. He was elected the first president of the National Council of Rubber Tappers in 1985. In 1987, wearing a rumpled, ill-fitting suit, he came to the United States to receive two international prizes for his work as a grassroots environmentalist. But to his comrades in Acre he was first and foremost a union leader, protecting the rubber tappers and advancing their cause. Chico, they said, was a "pure" person, governed by unselfish motives no matter how much recognition he received. He lived and died in poverty.

Even before he became known as a rubber tapper leader, Chico recognized his work would be risky. His comrade Wilson Pinheiro, leader of the Rural Workers' Union in Brasiléia, was assassinated in 1980. Other comrades were attacked, killed, or threatened into silence. Grassroots rural leaders had—and have—a short life span in Brazil. Because Amnesty International, Human Rights Watch, and other international human rights organizations publicize and support their efforts, they are often better known outside than inside the country. Perhaps Chico survived as long as he did because of the international attention he got during the mid- to late 1980s. But the sixth assassination attempt succeeded.

Chico was shot to death on the evening of December 22, 1988, as he stepped off his back porch on the way to a backyard shower stall. He had celebrated his forty-fourth birthday a week before. His bodyguards, grudgingly supplied by the state police, ran away in terror when he fell. Two of his killers were caught and convicted, but the intellectual authors of the crime remain at large. Gomercindo speculates that the state political elite wanted Chico dead because they feared he would run for governor in 1990. A decade later a Workers' Party candidate was elected governor of Acre for the first time.

The Aftermath

Chico left a brief political testament, written in September 1988. "Attention, youth of the future," his scrawl reads:

> September 6, 2120, centenary of the world socialist revolution that unified all the peoples of the planet in one ideal and one conception of socialist unity, and put an end to all the enemies of the new society.
>
> Here remains only the memory of a sad past of pain, suffering, and death.
>
> Excuse me—I was dreaming when I wrote of these events, which I myself will not see. But I have the pleasure of having dreamed.

A month after Chico's murder, in Washington, D.C., more than three hundred environmentalists, social justice activists, human rights advocates, Democratic and Republican politicians, church people, reporters, and others attended a memorial service for Chico in a Catholic church on Capitol Hill. Having met Chico and walked along the rubber trails with him only six months before, I felt his loss personally. So I volunteered to help organize the service, along with others who had worked with him. The environmentalists brought his cousin, Raimundo, from Acre to give the eulogy. Chico was richly grieved. But his testament was not mentioned; it came to light only later.

Another memorial observance for him took place a year later in a smaller church in Washington. I read Chico's testament aloud at that service.

"Some people have tried to whitewash Chico into an apolitical environmentalist," I said, as right-wing Senator Robert Kasten sat listening in the second row. (Kasten, an isolationist opponent of the "New World Order," pushed hard for American withdrawal from the World Bank. He had temporarily allied with Chico during the last few years of his life to pressure the Bank to stop funding projects that devastated the Amazon rainforest.) But Chico was proud to call himself a socialist, and he wanted to be remembered as a socialist. In that spirit, he named two of his children for Latin American revolutionaries.

An exemplary activist, leader, and martyr, Chico was formed in the crucible of a dangerous grassroots struggle, far from the halls of power but close to its victims and heroes. His testament weaves classic socialist values, illusions, and hopes into a shining fabric. It combines sentimental simplicity with visionary purity. A close reading of the testament yields important understandings. It is not Chico's monument. The trees that still stand, the tappers who live in the forest, the extractive reserves he promoted, the progressive reformers who now hold office in Acre, are that. But the testament does show what socialism means on the ground, in its essence, for millions of people who still believe "another world is possible."

Chico may have been a utopian at heart, but he found and built on a larger, practical truth in the forest. The immediate reality and his experience of injustice, "pain, suffering, and death," informed whatever he did. His vision was not a rhapsody but a report from the front lines.

The Revolution

As the Cold War approached its end, Chico still believed that what his testament called a "world socialist revolution" could happen within a generation. Because he so carefully avoided violence in his own work with the rubber tappers, he may have believed that a nonviolent revolution was possible.

He had lived through and participated in the peaceful, grassroots movement for democracy that swept in waves across Brazil in the late 1970s to early 1980s, as the military dictatorship slowly receded. Thousands of political exiles returned to the country in 1979 under an amnesty (which also made it impossible for torturers, killers, and backers of the military regime to be prosecuted). Workers went on strike and the government failed to convict them of subversion under the antiquated labor laws. Brash new publications, usually critical of the military regime, appeared. In 1984 millions of Brazilians marched in favor of direct presidential elections. Although they did not achieve their objective that year, the movement for democracy exerted strong pressure on the government and established the right of the people to assemble freely and express opinions publicly. By 1985, just three years after Chico's trial for subversion, the military officially returned to the barracks and left governance to a transitional, indirectly elected civilian regime.

Rule of Law

The year before Chico's death a national directly elected assembly convened to write a new constitution. Members of the public, unions, religious groups, and other civil society organizations submitted more than ten thousand "popular amendments" for the convention's consideration. A belief crackled in the air that real change, bottled up for two decades, finally could break out. The constitution mandated such change: direct presidential elections, almost universal suffrage, guaranteed press freedom, lowered voting age, expanded workers' rights, government land distribution, indigenous reserve demarcation, and a host of progressive provisions. Many still have not been put into force, although civil society organizations continue to work for their implementation. And Chico's codefendant in that long-ago subversion trial, Luiz Inácio Lula da Silva, eventually became president of Brazil.

In the 1980s Brazilians could read, hear, and see evidence that grassroots movements were spearheading massive changes in other countries. The new Workers' Party largely abandoned rigid adherence to old-fashioned state socialism and took flexible positions as part of the Socialist International. Brazilian democratic socialists, who constituted one of several strong factions in the Workers Party, saw the decline of ossified, post-Stalinist regimes and the rise of grassroots reform movements in Poland, Russia, and other Eastern European countries as positive harbingers or models. They often compared Lula to Lech Walesa. Many Brazilians also saw Nicaragua and Cuba as positive examples of socialist experimentation, especially in their redistribution of wealth and their provision of social and medical services to all their citizens.

Chico's efforts partook of this effervescence. If he could just stay alive, he could be in the vanguard of a grassroots movement for social, economic, and political change on a grand scale. Brazilians working for change chose not to see the impending end of the Cold War as the death of socialism; yes, it was a dangerous moment, but it was full of opportunity. In the midst of an international ferment of mobilization, organization, and debate and the great changes Chico himself was fostering in Acre, his vision of a "world socialist revolution" within thirty years might have seemed to him and others not only possible but likely.

The Memory of a Sad Past

Great obstacles to change remained entrenched, however, like giant boulders blocking an uphill road. Getting killed was still a real possibility for union leaders, their supporters, and members. During a big strike at the national steel works at Volta Redonda, near Rio de Janeiro, in November 1988, army troops and state police sent to break the strike killed three unarmed workers. A statue erected in their memory was later bombed. If such violence could happen in the highly industrialized and urbanized part of the country three years into a civilian regime, it was much more likely to break out in the backwoods of Acre and other frontier states, where traditional oligarchies still wielded almost absolute power. The enemies of change would stop at nothing, it seemed.

In photos taken during the last months of his life, Chico seems increasingly bowed under the weight of exhaustion. Dark circles appear under his eyes. He has to sleep in a different place every week, then every night, to keep one step ahead of his pursuers. He pleads for state police protection and goes to Brasília, the national capital, to ask for federal protection, which he does not get. He makes an application to carry a firearm; it is denied. He fails to convince the state director of the Federal Police to arrest, on an outstanding murder warrant, one of the men who will later kill him. He talks of his own end as a quickly approaching certainty. He has seen too many "deaths foretold" to believe he will escape the fate of his predecessors in the Rural Workers' Union. His allies outside Brazil, increasingly worried, arrange for him to receive international awards, as much to protect as to honor him.

Under these grim circumstances, the dark color of the words "put an end to all the enemies of the new society" in his testament seems all too apt. Such words might remind liberals in the Global North of Stalinist tendentiousness. But for Chico, among the enemies of the new society were the figures shrouded in black rain capes that skulked at the bottom of his backyard, waiting for him with triggers cocked. They were not figments of an overheated imagination—they were real, and they were there, waiting for their opportunity. His last words were, "They got me!"

Socialist Hero

Because Chico was an "ordinary man," a common man who gave his life for his friends and beliefs, he made a splendid hero. Indeed, Lula's government declared him a national hero in 2004. But in an interview given shortly before his death, he said he didn't want to be a martyr: "I want to live!" He kept trying to get help from every possible source to stay alive. At the same time, he could not stop taking the actions that put him in the assassins' sights. He continued denouncing Acre's corrupt political and economic elite, responsible for allowing outside investors and entrepreneurs to steal and depredate public land. He was one of the most determined opponents of what Brazilians call "savage capitalism," the unchecked concentration of wealth and power in the hands of a few unscrupulous operators and their corrupt political allies.

Chico's vision of socialism as expressed in the testament might seem simplistic or one-dimensional. But his words, quoted extensively in chapters 6 and 7, reflect the stark situation Chico confronted. Tremendously powerful men with private armies, political influence, and economic clout were trying to drive the defenseless poor from their homes, using any and all means at their disposal with the tacit support of the government. What Chico called socialism was embodied in his determined work for justice, the poor, the powerless, and the voiceless.

The Workers' Party contained plenty of doctrinaire or demagogic "Shiites," as they were called. But Chico was too far away, too involved in serious business to get involved in the ideological battles raging in the party. Those were for professors in well-tailored suits and self-styled intellectuals whose opiate was ideology. His first priorities were defending the rubber tappers and ensuring that their traditional way of life and the forest that supported them would not be destroyed. His conception of socialism was bound up in that struggle.

In a Religious Spirit

C hico had a broader vision of life and socialism than many of his immediate comrades. He addressed his testament to "youth of the future" and used a fairly sophisticated literary device—the flashback—to express his vision. He was not completely immersed in the demands, terrors, and crises of the moment. Instead he could step out of the rushing current of his life to imagine a distant future when "pain, suffering, and death" would no longer prevail. This expression of a utopian vision has clear religious overtones. And Chico worked closely with priests, nuns, and pastoral agents whose mission was to build the kingdom of God on earth by making liberation theology's "preferential option for the poor."

Religious language and ideals permeated the discourse of the Brazilian democratization movement, and the socialism Chico and other grassroots leaders talked about was religious in spirit. For Gomercindo, he may have been an ordinary man, but for many who followed him, he had the lineaments of a saint. His martyrdom burnished this aura, which still lingers.

Chico's socialist environmentalism seems to have been an offshoot or alternative to a Catholic ethos that had lost much of its elemental power but not all its influence on Brazilians' beliefs and behavior. Protecting the forest, as well as its inhabitants, was a sacred task. It implied a moral imperative, a commitment to the common good that meant nothing to those who sought to destroy Brazil's natural patrimony for their own aggrandizement. Socialism, for Chico, stood for doing the right thing: defending the defenseless, be they humans, animals, or plants, and thereby upholding the natural order, rooted in the land.

As the grassroots activists saw it, this order was not the unchanging hierarchy glorified in the official teachings of the church. It was the paradoxical order of Jesus' teachings, where the last shall be first and the meek inherit the earth. How the great transformation from present injustice to perfect equality would take place was unclear. But the Brazilian grassroots social movements had access to a long tradition of visionary belief and action that buttressed their hopes.

A Utopian Tradition

In the northeastern homeland of Chico's father, millenarian movements under the leadership of prophetic, charismatic figures periodically swept across the drought-stricken region. The rubber soldiers of the 1940s took the lore of these movements, some within living memory, to the rainforests of the western frontier. Even the 1920s Prestes Column, which Euclides Távora described to Chico, could be seen as a revisionist crusade, in imitation of earlier treks through the Brazilian backlands led by politicoreligious visionaries in search of a promised land for the downtrodden.

The most famous of these backwoods prophets was Antônio Conselheiro, who roamed the arid hills and valleys of the northeastern state of Bahia during the last quarter of the nineteenth century. In the 1890s he gathered thousands of recently freed slaves, peasants, and indigenous people and founded Canudos, a daub-and-wattle city in the backlands that became a focal point for resistance to the national government. Its very existence challenged the political hegemony of the big landowners and their semifeudal economic dominance. In his *History of Brazil*, Bradford Burns described Canudos as

> far from hostile landowners, repressive government officials and disruptive "civilization." There the folk adapted—or reverted—to a communal life. Probably their negative reaction to experience with the individualism of expanding capitalism revived their faith in the community. They felt uninhibited in adopting a type of folk Roman Catholicism which provided further structuring of life in the *sertão* [backlands]. They recognized the easily visible figure of Antônio Conselheiro as their patriarch. They unquestioningly followed him as their folk leader. The people and the patriarch identified with each other. In that folk society, the land belonged to the community.
> . . . The name, reputation and cause of Antônio Conselheiro raced like a wind through the interior of the Northeast. (1993: 250–251)

As Euclides da Cunha recounted in Brazil's national epic, *Os Sertões*, it took four heavily armed military expeditions almost two years, in 1896–1897, to wipe out Canudos. To this day, *Os Sertões* is an assigned text in Brazilian schools. Popular singers and artists, especially in the Northeast, continue to portray Antônio Conselheiro as a tragic hero, a victim of an unjust government controlled by the greedy and unscrupulous, and an icon of resistance by the weak against the strong.

Clearly, Chico was not a modern-day Antônio Conselheiro, but his vision of socialism owed something to the millenarian example of Canudos that Brazilians keep in their hearts. It is bittersweet, tinged with blood and the poignancy of failure.

After the Dream

In the testament Chico wakes from his dream, acknowledging not only its unreality but also the pleasure it gave him. His statement is affirming, poignant, but not melancholic. Steeped in "the sad past of pain, suffering, and death," Brazilians still seek joy. Laughter and tears are juxtaposed in the national culture. A northeastern poet wrote of Carnival celebrants, "They laugh but their eyes are sad." People proverbially say, "You laugh so as not to cry." A few months after Chico's death, Lula's first presidential campaign featured the slogan, "Unafraid of Being Happy." But happiness cannot be carefree; it must be struggled for. In the face of systematic injustice, soul-destroying poverty, and the killing of children, it takes courage—and work—to hope.

In the years after Chico's death, it became clear that nobody could replace him as a charismatic grassroots leader of international standing. Activists in Acre did set up independent extractive reserves with federal assistance and protection. In these reserves rubber tappers continue to live and gather latex and other forest products, which they sell to a marketing cooperative and traditional buyers in Xapuri. Gomercindo became a lawyer and has made a career representing rural workers in Acre's capital. He also became president of the Chico Mendes Committee and received the Chico Mendes medal of resistance from the Brazilian human rights group, Tortura Nunca Mais (Torture Never Again).

Marina Silva, who wrote the preface to this book, grew up as a rubber tapper and followed in Chico's footsteps; she has had the most remarkable career of Chico's comrades. Raised on a homestead in the rubber groves of Acre, she helped her father tap trees until age sixteen, when she learned to read and write in a government-sponsored literacy course. After passing a high school equivalency examination, she went to university—an extraordinary accomplishment in Acre or, indeed, anywhere in Brazil—and received a history degree. Later she was elected to the Brazilian Congress. Lula appointed her federal environment minister in 2003. The last I heard, she was working on a master's degree.

Will the Forest Survive?

After returning to Xapuri in 1990 to find out what had happened to the movement Chico led to preserve the rainforest, I published an article in which I asked, "Will the memory of his life and death be strong enough to help turn the racing tide of destruction?"

The answer to this question remains to be seen. Deforestation in the Amazon region has continued at a high rate. Multinational corporations based in North America, Europe, and Asia are cutting down trees on an industrial scale. Brazilian agribusinesses clear-cut the forest to set up cattle ranches and soybean plantations for export production. Old hydroelectric and road-building projects that would destroy vast areas of forest and drive out the traditional inhabitants are being revived. Every battle to preserve the forest and protect the people who live there must be refought numerous times. Chico's heirs cannot rest in their struggle.

While they were making their mark in Brazil, a worldwide movement was growing to fight the excesses of capitalist globalization. Between 2001 and 2005 the World Social Forum met four times in Porto Alegre, Brazil, to offer alternatives to the policies promulgated at the World Economic Forum of elite decision makers in Davos, Switzerland. Each time, the number of participants in Porto Alegre more than doubled. The slogan of the forums was "Another World Is Possible." Its undertones are rich and deep, very much in tune with Chico's testament. But to go beyond the static, perfect beauty of a dream, people have to make change happen. That is the messy, exhilarating process millions of activists plunge into every day.

The "world socialist revolution" Chico dreamed of will not magically come about on September 6, 2020, as he hoped. But it does exist as something more than an artifact of his imagination. In hundreds of thousands of places around the world, grassroots groups are working to reform the local economy, defend civil and human rights, help the poor, and do works of justice. They are moving along the paths Chico traveled, struggling to protect their communities, their livelihoods, their environment, and, perhaps, in spite of everything, the world. Chico lives in their actions, as he lives in the hearts and memories of those who knew him.

AUTHOR'S AND EDITOR'S NOTES

Foreword

1. Wilson Pinheiro was a comrade of Chico Mendes and the head of the Brasiléia, Acre, Rural Workers' Union; he was assassinated in 1980. Ivair Higino was a twenty-five-year-old union activist when he was killed in June 1988; he is buried next to Chico Mendes in Xapuri. [LR]

2. The Rubber Tapper Project, sponsored by the National Council of Rubber Tappers with support from Oxfam, Brazilian NGOs, and the Brazilian education ministry, assisted Acre's rubber tappers in establishing sustainable development initiatives such as marketing cooperatives and schools. [LR]

3. The *poronga*, for which the bulletin is named, is a tin hat with a candle or other light that rubber tappers wear when they work in the rubber groves in the hours before dawn. [LR]

4. *Empate*: a nonviolent demonstration during which rubber tappers and their families try to prevent hired workers from cutting down trees in the rainforest on rubber estates. [LR]

5. Cachoeira: a rubber estate outside Xapuri. Chico Mendes's killer, Darli Alves da Silva, claimed the estate in 1988 and tried to deforest it and drive out its rubber tapper inhabitants in the months before Mendes's death. It is now part of the Chico Mendes Extractive Reserve. [LR]

6. Bordon: A large Brazilian meat packing company that tried to deforest rubber estates in Acre in the 1980s. [LR]

7. Bishop Moacyr Grechi was Catholic bishop of Rio Branco, Acre, from 1986 to 1998; he is now archbishop of Porto Velho, Rondônia. [LR]

8. CONTAG, or the National Confederation of Agricultural Workers, founded in 1963, represents thousands of union locals and six regional labor federations throughout Brazil. [LR]

Chapter 1

1. Amazon Workers' Center (CTA): A small nongovernmental organization founded in 1980; collaborated with the Rubber Tapper Project on literacy and other projects. [GR]

2. Darli Alves da Silva and his son Darci were convicted and sentenced to long prison terms for the murder of Chico Mendes. They escaped from prison in Rio

Branco, fled to Bolivia, and were eventually captured and imprisoned in Brasília, Brazil's capital. [LR]

In 2006 Darli was on parole and living in Rio Branco and Xapuri; Darci was living near Brasília, also on parole but still under indictment for crimes committed in 1988. [GR]

3. In an attempt to stop the widespread use of firearms by criminals, the Brazilian Congress passed a strict gun control law in 2003. A national referendum to ban sale of firearms to civilians failed in 2005. [LR]

4. Amazon winter: the rainy season from November or December to April or May. In this region there are only two seasons: dry (summer) and wet (winter). It has nothing to do with lower temperatures common in the winter in other parts of the country or the world. On the contrary, the "frosts," short periods when the temperature drops the most in the region, occur in the Amazon summer, between June and September. [GR]

5. Construction of a highway linking Brazil to the Pacific Ocean is a long-term development priority of the Brazilian government. During the military regime, in the mid-1980s, the government borrowed funds from the Inter-American Development Bank to pave the road between Cuiabá and Rio Branco, triggering a land rush in the state of Rondônia that led to widespread deforestation, human rights violations against traditional inhabitants, and environmental devastation. [LR]

6. Reintegration of possession: a judicial order permitting a land claimant to expel squatters from his or her property with police assistance. [LR]

7. Delta Group: a construction company that purchased and sought to deforest the Ecuador rubber estate in May 1988. [GR]

8. IBDF, the Brazilian Institute of Reforestation, became the Brazilian Institute for the Environment and Renewable Natural Resources (IBAMA) in 1989. A federal agency under the secretary of the environment, it has regulatory and police powers. [LR]

9. National Rubber Tappers' Council: a nonprofit organization representing rubber tappers in the Amazon region, founded in 1985; Chico Mendes was its first president. [LR]

10. Institute of Amazon Studies: a nongovernmental organization founded by Mary Allegretti. [LR]

11. While researching her master's thesis on the traditional rubber estates in the mid-1980s, Mary Allegretti taught for some time at the project's primary school on the Nazaré estate. Since her first involvement in the early 1980s, she has never completely left the movement. Later she founded the Institute of Amazon and Environmental Studies with its headquarters in Curitiba, Paraná. She was the Amazon secretary in the environment ministry during the Cardoso administration (1994–2002). [GR]

12. The First National Meeting of Rubber Tappers took place in Brasília in October 1985. [LR]

13. Pastoral Land Commission (CPT): a Catholic Church agency that promotes land reform and assists rural workers throughout Brazil. [LR]

14. Action for Citizenship: a coalition of thousands of local groups, founded in 1993 by the well-known and influential activist Herbert de Souza (Betinho), who coordinated the national Campaign against Hunger in the mid-1990s. [LR]

15. Before Chico Mendes was indicted for subversion during the military regime, he was investigated by the Federal Police, who apparently suspected him of being a Communist. Union leaders were frequent targets of the military regime's repressive apparatus. [LR]

16. Calha Norte: a federal project to protect and populate Brazil's frontiers by stationing troops and encouraging colonization along its international borders; initiated in secret under the military regime and continued during the civilian regime that followed. [LR]

17. My emphasis. This testimony is in Folio 603 of the fifth volume of trial record No. 5929/89 of the Xapuri district, under "Chico Mendes Case." [GR]

18. DEIC-SP is the criminal investigation division of the São Paulo state police; Unicamp, the State University of Campinas (São Paulo state), has a respected Department of Forensic Science. Investigators from both agencies were sent to Acre to work on the Chico Mendes murder case. [LR]

19. Workers' Party (PT): socialist political party founded by trade unionists, intellectuals, theologians, and others, ca. 1980. Chico Mendes was one of the first PT city council members in Brazil. In 2002 Lula won the presidency of Brazil as the PT candidate, and in 2006 he was reelected. [LR]

Chapter 2

1. Nazaré: an estate claimed for a long time by the Bordon Group; thanks to union organization, several empates took place there. These made the powerful processing firm stop deforesting and sell the property to other ranchers. The estate is completely occupied by rubber tappers today. [GR]

2. Floresta: the estate where Raimundo Barros, Chico Mendes's cousin, lived for about ten years; he began participating in the Rubber Tapper Project as a monitor (teacher) at the Rio Branco homestead, about four hours' walk from Xapuri.

São Pedro: an estate located on the banks of the Xapuri River, where an experimental school and cooperative were later started. [GR]

3. The bosses or rubber barons claimed ownership of immense areas of forest, although they usually had no documents to prove it. They had economic and political power in the entire Amazon region and were the only authorities on the estates, thereby assuming the right to punish the rubber tappers. These punishments were often cruel; for example, they would burn a rubber tapper alive by setting alight a rubber ball tied to his body if he tried to sell the product to another buyer. [GR]

4. *Paxiuba*: a common palm tree in the region whose wood is used for flooring and rustic benches in the rubber tappers' houses. [GR]

5. Pedro Teles: general secretary of the Xapuri Rural Workers' Union at the time of the meeting and one of the monitors of the Rubber Tapper Project at the Pimenteira homestead on the Boa Vista estate. [GR]

6. Nonato: one of the coordinators of the associations—or cooperatives, as they were called—on the estates, as part of the Rubber Tapper Project. [GR]

7. The motor: Purchased by the cooperative, it was for processing manioc to make flour or, in the areas where a boat could dock, to unload the boat. [GR]

8. According to Brazilian land law, property owners must leave half their landholding in its original state when it is located in a protected or an endangered area such as a rainforest. [LR]

9. *Marreteiro*: a petty trader who brings goods from town to trade with the rubber tappers for their products. He might have a store, as was the case with Jaci, or a boat (called a *batelão* in the region) with which he travels along the rivers, selling goods and articles the rubber tappers find indispensable and buying their products. [GR]

10. Line: a trail that passes through several rubber tapper homesteads, sometimes with landings (*varadouros*) and fords (*varações*). [GR]

11. Rubber trail: a small trail in the forest linking one rubber tree to another, with an average of 130 to 250 "trunks," which is what the rubber tappers normally call the rubber trees (*Hevea brasiliensis*). There are an average of 150 rubber trees per trail. Each trail has a "mouth," where the rubber tapper begins and ends cutting; that is, the trail begins and ends at the same place, which facilitates the rubber tapper's work. At the tree where he finishes cutting he can begin collecting the latex. [GR]

12. The novel *White Rain*, by the Amazonas writer Paulo Jacob, tells the story of a rubber tapper who went out to hunt a tapir and got lost in the forest for more than three weeks. This writer, who, as far as I know, was a circuit judge in small towns in Amazonas, has an unusual style and the content of his books is always very dense. [GR]

13. *Igarapés*: the name given throughout Amazonia to creeks, streams, and small rivers. [GR]

14. This was an example of a *mutirão*, a cooperative work crew in which rubber tappers trade workdays as a way of getting urgent tasks done efficiently. They also clear landings and construct public buildings such as schools, health posts, and community warehouses. [GR]

15. Knife: a large knife used to "hoe" the rubber trails, crack nuts, clear landings and fords, and so on; the rubber tapper's inseparable companion when he walks the forest. [GR]

16. INCRA: National Institute of Colonization and Agrarian Reform, a federal agency, responsible during the military dictatorship for the resettlement of thousands of workers from central-south Brazil to Amazonia, in accordance with the dictatorship's slogan, to "integrate, not surrender," and to "send men without land from the Center-South and the Northeast to the lands without men in the Amazon." The so-called Integrated Colonization Projects or Directed Settlement Projects, generally with no infrastructure, were presented as veritable paradises, causing an extremely predatory migration to the entire Amazon; worse yet, they expelled rubber tappers from their homes and caused the deaths of thousands of workers caught up in the dream of Eldorado. INCRA was responsible for resolving land and ownership claims, which almost always meant giving possession to the ranchers. [GR]

17. Assis Brasil: a Brazilian town located on the border with Bolivia (at Bolpedra) and Peru (at Inapari) on the Acre River, about 350 kilometers (210 miles) from Rio Branco. [GR]

18. Line: part of the structure of the house that connects one joist to another. [GR]

19. SUCAM: now called the National Health Foundation, a government agency responsible for fighting endemic diseases (malaria, leishmaniosis, dengue, and others). [GR]

20. FUNRURAL: pension paid by the National Institute of Social Security to rural workers when they reach retirement age. [GR]

21. Rubber soldier: a rubber tapper born in Amazonia before 1933 or brought from the Northeast between 1940 and 1945, granted a pension under a provision of the Constitution of 1988. [GR]

22. Paca: a rodent the size of a suckling pig yielding about 10 kilograms (22 pounds) of meat. [GR]

Chapter 3

1. Serra Pelada: a huge open-pit gold mine in the state of Pará; at its peak during the 1980s it attracted thousands of miners. [LR]

2. *Aviamento*: a financing and labor contracting system at its height during the Amazon "rubber boom," 1880s–ca. 1912. [LR]

3. Paraguayan War: 1865–1870 war involving Brazil, Paraguay, and Argentina. Half the adult male population of Paraguay is said to have died in the war. [LR]

4. Dispatch houses: large commercial houses, usually located in Belém and Manaus, that provided all the merchandise to the rubber barons in exchange for delivery of the annual rubber crop from the estates. [GR]

5. Trading post: almost nonexistent today in Amazonia, it was the headquarters of the traditional estate, where the main warehouse was always located. (Some very extensive estates had depots between the headquarters and the more distant homesteads.) It was where the rubber baron or at least the estate manager usually lived. Also, the bookkeeper who oversaw the estate accounts and the employees, including the manager, clerks, oxcart drivers, inspectors, and guards, lived there. Normally the latter were responsible for catching the rubber tappers who tried to flee from the estate or were caught selling rubber to "peddlers" or small traders. [GR]

6. *Regatão*: a merchant who traveled the rivers of Amazonia in midsized boats, carrying goods to be traded for extracted products. Until recently, with the passing of the bosses, they dominated business with the rubber tappers along the rivers. Today, with the opening of roads in many areas and the low price of rubber, they have almost disappeared. [GR]

7. *Péla*: a ball of coagulated latex, produced by smoking for several days, a week, or a month. This is the form in which natural rubber is bought, transported, and sold. [GR]

8. In Portuguese, *correria*. [LR]

9. Markham: a British diplomat who alerted the British government to the exis-

tence of rubber trees in the Amazon. At Kew Gardens in London the smuggled seeds were grown into trees. British planters in Malaya cultivated the trees on plantations, eventually making Brazilian rubber uncompetitive on the international market. [LR]

10. *Uti possidetis*: "As you possess now." This legal principle favors the effective occupier of a disputed territorial space. [GR]

11. Acre River: According to a widely repeated but unconfirmed story, a clerk in a commercial house in Belém wrote "Acre" instead of "Aquiri" on boxes of goods sent to a rubber baron on that river. Thus the river acquired a new name. [GR]

12. Constitution of 1988: Brazil's current constitution, drafted after the end of the military regime by a directly elected constituent assembly in 1987–1988. [LR]

13. *Forró*: a northeastern country dance now popular throughout Brazil. [LR]

14. Duty visit: annual pastoral visits by Catholic priests. Given the enormous distances and the difficulties of travel, often a priest takes several years to return to a remote area. On these visits the priest conducts masses, baptisms, and marriages. [GR]

Chapter 4

1. General Golbery do Couto e Silva: chief geopolitical theoretician and eminence grise of the military regime of 1964–1985. [LR]

2. Center-South: the richest of Brazil's five geographic regions, comprising the states of São Paulo, Rio de Janeiro, Espírito Santo, and Minas Gerais. [LR]

3. Rubber Bank/Bank of the Amazon: established soon after World War II to finance rubber trading; today its headquarters are in Belém, and it operates throughout the Amazon region. [GR]

4. SUDAM: Superintendency for the Development of the Amazon, a federal agency recently closed after a spate of accusations about the theft of public funds from innumerable projects. [GR]

5. Polamazônia: a program set up in 1974 as part of the military government's Second National Development Plan, "based on large-scale, intensive economic activities such as mining, timber extraction, cattle ranching and hydroelectric energy production. Colonization was expected to occur on its own . . . but there were no explicit plans for frontier development or controlling the environmental and social processes brought on by the projects" (Carvalho et al. 2002: 36).

Polonoroeste: a disastrous development project for the Amazonian state of Rondônia, including construction of the BR-364 highway, financed by the Inter-American Development Bank and the World Bank in the 1980s and 1990s; documented in Adrian Cowell's *Decade of Destruction* film series. [LR]

6. Planafloro: "designed [in 1992] by the state government of Rondônia in part to offset some of the social development problems not addressed by the Polonoroeste project. . . . One of the principal features . . . was land-use zoning which represented an innovative attempt to bring some measure of order to the state's chaotic agrarian patterns and consolidate conservation areas" (Garrison and Aparicio 1999: 2). Local and international NGOs challenged the plan in 1995 and eventually persuaded the World Bank, the principal funder, and the Rondônia government to reform it. [LR]

7. Rio Doce Valley Company: a public-private mining company formed to extract minerals including iron and manganese from a vast area in the Amazon; linked to northern ports via a 500-mile rail line. [LR]

8. Jari project: an unsuccessful development project in the northern Amazon, owned by the American tycoon Daniel Ludwig. [LR]

9. SIVAM: a controversial Amazon radar surveillance project managed by the American firm Raytheon for the Brazilian government. [LR]

10. Cachimbo Mountains: the area where the Brazilian military secretly installed a nuclear project in the mid- to late 1980s. President Collor ordered its closure in 1990. [LR]

11. Eletrobrás: a public-private electric power company that has developed hydroelectric and other projects in the Amazon and other regions. [LR]

12. Yanomami: an indigenous group living in northern Brazil and southern Venezuela, endangered by wildcat gold miners, development projects, and epidemic diseases since the 1980s. [LR]

13. *Paulistas:* "the men from São Paulo" was what the rubber tappers called all the ranchers who moved to Acre in the late 1960s and early 1970s, no matter where they came from. [GR]

Chapter 5

1. MDB: Brazilian Democratic Movement, the only opposition political party permitted to exist during most of the military regime. [LR]

2. The author's account of the killing of Nilão conflicts with Chico Mendes's version in *Fight for the Forest*, a compilation of interviews published after his death. [LR]

3. National Security Law: promulgated to prevent dissenters from challenging the military regime, used to indict Chico Mendes, Luiz Inácio Lula da Silva, and other prominent trade unionists in the early 1980s. [LR]

4. Forensic Institute: police crime lab. [LR]

5. Paulo Freire: Brazilian educator who became internationally famous for developing a "pedagogy of the oppressed"; he was one of the first people to be arrested (and exiled) after the Brazilian military came to power in 1964. [LR]

6. Central Labor Federation (CUT): an independent left-wing union federation linked to the PT. [LR]

7. CAEX: a cooperative for processing rubber and Brazil nuts in Xapuri, funded by international NGOs and foundations. [LR]

8. IBASE: one of the first Brazilian nongovernmental organizations, founded by Herbert de Souza and other political exiles who returned to Brazil under an amnesty law in 1979. [LR]

9. Drilling: removal of the brush before cutting down the big trees, when small trees and vines, which could obstruct the felling of the larger trees and cause accidents, are cut. [GR]

10. *Decade of Destruction:* a documentary film series by the British filmmaker Adrian Cowell about the devastation of the Amazon. One of the films focuses on

Chico Mendes, whom Cowell knew through his then-partner, Mary Allegretti. [LR]

11. Alliance of Forest Peoples: a coalition started by members of the Union of Indigenous Nations, a small group of indigenous activists prominent in Brasília during the 1980s. [LR]

Chapter 6

1. Green Party: a small political party that often has made coalitions with the PT. [LR]

2. Araguaia war: an armed conflict in rural Pará in the late 1960s and early 1970s between left-wing guerrillas and the Brazilian military, which "undertook a massive counter-insurgency operation. . . . The rural guerrillas were defeated before they had even got started and most were summarily executed, but the anti-communist hysteria that had taken hold of the military made a far-reaching programme of agrarian reform inconceivable" (Branford and Rocha 2002: 5). [LR]

3. According to scholarly sources, there is no evidence that Távora participated in the Prestes Column, and no record has been found of his imprisonment at Fernando de Noronha or his participation in the 1935 Communist uprising known as the *Intentona*. See Maxwell 1991. [LR]

4. CEBs: grassroots groups of Catholic activists who meet to discuss the relevance of the gospels to political, economic, and social issues. More than 100,000 of these groups were said to exist in the 1980s, and many political and union leaders got their start in them. [LR]

5. ARENA: a right-wing political party that supported the military government during most of the twenty-one-year dictatorship. (See note 7 below.) [LR]

6. The past election: In 1978 elections for state legislators, federal deputies, and senators took place. [GR]

7. PDS: successor to ARENA, this right-wing party backed the unelected governors and the government in the last years of the military regime. [GR]

8. Law 4504: the land reform law, mandating ownership rights and procedures to recognize ownership, property, and expropriation for the social good. [GR]

9. Parts of the interior: the interior of the township, that is, the homesteads on the estates where the rural workers lived and still live. [GR]

10. Sacrifice my own [life]: This sentence doesn't make sense. Apparently it's unfinished. The full phrase may have been, "I am determined to sacrifice my own life." Note, once again, the almost prophetic tone. [GR]

11. Bloodshed: the murder of STR President Wilson Pinheiro, assassinated July 21, 1980. Seven days later the farm manager Nilo Sergio de Oliveira (Nilão) was killed. See chapter 5. [LR]

12. PT bloc: All the minutes up to 1980 refer to the "parliamentary bloc" instead of "party," although the Workers' Party wasn't part of any bloc, and Chico was the only PT member on the Xapuri City Council. [GR]

13. Opening (*abertura*): a policy of gradual political liberalization during the final years of the military regime, spearheaded by the last military president, General João Figueiredo. [LR]

14. Indicted under the National Security Law: as a result of Chico's participation in a public demonstration honoring Wilson Pinheiro and the launch of the PT in Brasiléia on July 27, 1980. Several PT founders, including Luiz Inácio Lula da Silva, president of Brazil, also participated and were subsequently indicted and acquitted. [GR]

15. Chico's lawyers at the subversion trial in the Manaus military tribunal were Arquilau de Castro Melo, now chief judge of the Acre State Court, and Luiz Eduardo Greenhalg, now a PT federal deputy from São Paulo. Other defense lawyers included current federal Supreme Court Justice Sepúlveda Pertence. [GR]

16. This is the first time Chico appears in the minutes as the "leader of the Workers' Party" instead of the "PT parliamentary bloc." [GR]

17. SUDHEVEA: a federal agency that made and implemented policies related to natural rubber production in Brazil. It was abolished and incorporated into IBAMA when that agency was created. [GR]

18. National Amazon Radio: a government radio station based in Brasília, from where it broadcasts to the Amazon region. [GR]

19. Again, Chico's tone is prophetic. I'm insisting on pointing this out because I understood the meaning of Chico's statements as a city council member only in the final phase of writing this book, about fourteen years after his death. [GR]

20. See the afterword for the full text and editor's comments. [LR]

21. Burning season: August–November, when farmers slash and burn trees and undergrowth before planting. The smoke is so extensive that local airports throughout the Amazon region must be closed for days at a time. [LR]

22. American anthropologist on the staff of the Environmental Defense Fund (now Environmental Defense), who worked with Brazilian and international colleagues to help Chico Mendes and the rubber tappers gain international attention and support for their sustainable development initiatives. [LR]

23. Republican U.S. senator from Wisconsin; an isolationist who made an alliance with Chico Mendes in the mid-1980s to campaign against World Bank loans to Brazil. See afterword. [LR]

Chapter 7

1. PMACI: Project for the Protection of the Environment and Indigenous Communities (1985–1995), a federal initiative established in conjunction with the IDB to remediate damage done by the BR-364 highway and the Rondônia land rush. "The PMACI project was launched . . . at the local, regional, national and international levels, marked by the transition from a development model with a geopolitical and military orientation towards occupation of 'empty' frontiers to a new model based on community participation and organization, defense of alternative uses of the land compatible with cultural and historical traditions, and activities sponsored by local NGO[s], an innovative experience in Brazil" (Allegretti, Ramirez, and Deruyttere 1998: 6). [LR]

2. New Republic: first civilian government after the military returned to the bar-

racks in 1985, headed by indirectly elected President Sarney, who continued military development policies and projects in the Amazon, with disastrous results for the environment and the traditional inhabitants. [LR]

3. Campaign for direct elections: a massive public campaign for direct presidential elections in 1984–1985. It was not successful—the first civilian president was elected by Congress in 1985—but President Collor de Mello was directly elected (running against Lula) in 1989. [LR]

Afterword

1. Miranda Smith: winner of the CINE Golden Eagle and other awards for her documentary film *Chico Mendes: Voice of the Amazon* (1989). [LR]

EDITOR'S BIBLIOGRAPHY

Allegretti, Mary, Carlos Ramirez, and Anne Deruyttere, eds. 1998. "Public Participation and Sustainable Development in the Amazon: The Case of PMACI." Report. Inter-American Development Bank.

Amnesty International. 1988. *Brazil: Authorized Violence in Rural Areas.* London: Amnesty International. September.

Branford, Sue, and Jan Rocha. 2002. *Cutting the Wire: The Story of the Landless Movement in Brazil.* London: Latin America Bureau.

Burns, E. Bradford. 1993. *A History of Brazil.* 3rd ed. New York: Columbia University Press.

Campanha Nacional pela Reforma Agrária. 1985. *Violência no Campo.* Petrópolis, RJ: Vozes, 1985.

Carvalho, Georgia O., et al. 2002. "Frontier Expansion in the Amazon: Balancing Development and Sustainability." *Environment,* April, 34–41.

Cockburn, Alexander, and Susanna Hecht. 1989. *The Fate of the Forest: Developers, Destroyers, and Defenders of the Amazon.* London: Verso.

Dean, Warren. 1987. *Brazil and the Struggle for Rubber: A Study in Environmental History.* Cambridge: Cambridge University Press.

Dwyer, Augusta. 1991. "Was Tavora There?" *New York Review of Books,* November 7, 61–62.

Fajardo, Elias. 1988. *Em julgamento: A violência no campo (Relato das mortes analisados pelo Tribunal Nacional dos Crimes do Latifúndio.* Petrópolis, RJ: Vozes/FASE/Instituto de Apóio Jurídico Popular.

Garrison, John, and Teresa Aparicio. 1999. "The Challenges of Promoting Participatory Development in the Amazon." Memorandum. World Bank.

Gross, Tony, org. 1992. *Fight for the Forest: Chico Mendes in His Own Words.* 2nd ed. London: Latin America Bureau.

Martins, Edilson. 1998. *Chico Mendes: Um povo da floresta.* Rio de Janeiro: Editora Garamond.

Maxwell, Kenneth. 1991. "The Mystery of Chico Mendes." *New York Review of Books,* March 28, 39–48.

———. 2003. "Chico Mendes." In *Naked Tropics: Essays on Empires and Other Rogues.* New York: Routledge.

Maybury-Lewis, Biorn. 1990. "The Agrarian Reform Debate in Brazil."

Working Paper No. 14. New York: Columbia University Institute for Latin American and Iberian Studies.

———. 1994. *The Politics of the Possible: The Brazilian Rural Workers' Union Movement, 1964–1985*. Philadelphia: Temple University Press.

Mendes, Chico. 1989. *Fight for the Forest*. London: Latin America Bureau.

Rabben, Linda. 1989. "When a Man Is Felled in Brazil, Who Will Hear?" *National Catholic Reporter*, January 27, 1, 17.

———. 1990a. "Chico Mendes' Memory Haunts Amazon Forest." *National Catholic Reporter*, October 12, 13–14.

———. 1990b. "Scorched Earth, Barren Lives." *TDC The Discovery Channel*, April.

Revkin, Andrew. 2004. *The Burning Season: The Murder of Chico Mendes and the Fight for the Amazon Rain Forest*. 3rd ed. Washington, D.C.: Island/Shearwater.

Rodrigues, Gomercindo. 2003. *Caminhando na Floresta*. Rio Branco: Grafica Editora Floresta.

Shoumatoff, Alex. 1991. *Murder in the Rain Forest: The Chico Mendes Story*. London: Fourth Estate.

Souza, Márcio. 1990. *O empate contra Chico Mendes*. 2nd ed. São Paulo: Marco Zero.

Ventura, Zuenir. 2003. *Chico Mendes crime e castigo*. São Paulo: Companhia das Letras.

Yungjohann, John C. 1989. *White Gold: The Diary of a Rubber Cutter in the Amazon, 1906–1916*. Oracle, Ariz.: Synergistic Press.

INDEX

developmentalism in Brazil, 11, 15, 143–145, 147–148, 157, 173n23; environmentalism in, 18n2; memorial observances honoring Mendes in, 157; Mendes in, 143–145, 150–151, 156; nineteenth-century westward migration in, 90; and Voice of America, 127, 155
urbanization, 6, 92, 95
Urizzi, Acir, 23, 26–27
utopianism, 162–163

Vargas dictatorship, 155
Veio, Cabo, 76
Venezuela, 171n12
Ventania newsletter, 140
Vicente, Valderi, 55–56
Vietnam War, 18n4
violence: assassination of grassroots rural leaders generally, 100, 106, 156; Calado's murder, 106; Eliazinho's murder, 106; against farm laborer, 135; and gunmen, 8, 20, 23, 25–27, 34–39, 45, 99–101, 110, 116, 142–143, 154; Higino's murder, xii, 22, 26, 106, 154, 165n1; Mendes's murder, xii, 1, 2, 3, 7–8, 15, 21–23, 31–34, 40–43, 92, 101, 156–157, 160, 165–166n2, 165n5, 167n18; Nilão's murder, 103, 104, 142, 171n2, 172n11; Pinheiro's murder, xii, 10, 16, 101, 102–104, 142, 156, 165n1, 172n11; against rubber tappers, 23, 25, 26, 35, 36–39, 45, 99–102, 129; and rubber tappers' response to murders of Pinheiro and Higino, 10, 16, 22; at strike, 159; threats of, against

Mendes, 130, 134, 138, 142–143, 154, 160; threats of, against Rodrigues, 36–40; and UDR, 109–110; Urizzi's murder, 23, 26–27

Walesa, Lech, 159
water pollution, 98
weddings. *See* rubber tappers, marriages of
White Rain (Jacob), 19, 168n12
Wickham, Henry, 70–71
women: and *empates* (nonviolent demonstrations), 114–118; lack of, for rubber tappers, 67, 68, 80; and marriage of rubber tappers, 79, 81–82, 170n14; and prostitution, 98–99; as rubber tappers, 114–115, 163
Workers' Party (PT): and Acre governorship, 157; and democratic socialists, 159; founding of, 156; and Higino, 25–26; ideological battles in, 161; and Mendes, 14–15, 16, 43, 135–137, 140, 156, 167n19, 172n12, 173n16; and Mendes's murder, 28; and Rodrigues, 36–37, 60–61; *Ventania* newsletter of, 140
World Bank, 11, 41, 42, 94, 95, 127, 157, 170nn5–6, 173n23
World Economic Forum, 164
World Social Forum, 164
World War II, 8, 74–78, 155

Xapuri rubber estate, 1, 57–58

Yanomami, 98, 171n12